Microeconomics:
Theory, Applications,
Innovations

Microeconomics: Theory, Applications, Innovations

Gerald Garb

Lehigh University

Macmillan Publishing Co., Inc.
New York
Collier Macmillan Publishers
London

Macmillan Publishing Co., Inc.
866 Third Avenue, New York, New York 10022

Collier Macmillan Canada, Ltd.

Library of Congress Cataloging in Publication Data

Garb, Gerald.
  Microeconomics: theory, applications, innovations.

  Includes bibliographies and index.
  1. Microeconomics. I. Title.
HB171.5.G218   338.5   80-16049
ISBN 0-02-340400-0

Printing: 1 2 3 4 5 6 7 8   Year: 1 2 3 4 5 6 7 8

Preface

This is an intermediate microeconomic theory textbook. It is intermediate in the sense that it is primarily designed for the undergraduate microeconomics course following the principles of economics course. But it would also be suitable for an MBA microeconomics course in which students have had only the principles course or an intermediate course. Having said this, I hasten to add that this book is virtually self-contained in that it presents all the basic definitions, concepts, principles, and theories generally associated with traditional microeconomics. This is the orthodox part of the book, and the guiding idea here is to present in a clear and relatively concise way that which most economists would regard as standard microeconomic theory. As part of an effort to make the concepts and theories clear and meaningful, each chapter contains one or more applications of the theory to the real world. For example, the New York City restaurant industry is used to illustrate the application and problems of the theory of monopolistic competition. In some cases, the applications serve to broaden the basic theory. For example, the Edgeworth box diagram is first employed in Chapter 3 as a means of showing how indifference curve theory can be applied to the analysis of exchange between two individuals.

There are many features designed to explain and to extend standard microeconomic theory further. The appendix to this book contains a brief introduction to the nature, method, and purpose of science, especially in relation to the economist and his objectives. Economics is indeed a science, and it is my belief that the student of economic theory can benefit from an explanation of the meaning of science. However, the material contained in the appendix can be covered either before or after Chapter 1, or it can be omitted altogether, depending on the approach to microeconomic theory taken by the instructor. Almost every chapter includes a section entitled *Innovations*. The purpose of the innovations sections is to present significant contributions to microeconomics that are usually not considered part of the basic theory. Some of these contributions, such as linear programming, have by now found their way into most intermediate microeconomics textbooks. Other important theoretical innovations, such as Kelvin Lancaster's technology of consumption, Harvey Leibenstein's concept of X-efficiency, Armen Alchian's ideas on cost, and W. Leontief's input–output model of the world economy are usually neglected at the intermediate level. By now these developments should be included in books on intermediate microeconomic theory. Therefore these as well as other significant contributions are presented throughout this book.

Chapter 13, on general equilibrium theory, is somewhat different in that it develops the concept of general equilibrium at three levels of aggregation. The chapter starts at the micro level of Walras, goes on to the intermediate aggregation of Leontief, and then concludes with the substantial aggregation of Keynes. This treatment not only permits a brief introduction to some fundamentals of macroeconomics but also helps to bridge the gap between micro and macroeconomics. Chapter 14 presents a comprehensive introduction to the theory and problems of modern welfare economics, including a discussion of the role of property rights.

Every chapter ends with a summary of the material presented in the chapter, and in each summary the major ideas of the chapter are brought together. Every chapter also includes a list of problems and questions designed to test the reader's understanding of the major topics covered in the chapter. Throughout this book all important definitional and conceptual words and phrases appear in boldface type when first used. Finally, the mathematics employed is elementary and consists of the kind of algebra and geometry that should be accessible to every college student.

I would like to thank the editors and staff of Macmillan Publishing Company, as well as the excellent outside reviewers secured by Macmillan, for their help. Of course, I am responsible for any errors that may remain in this book.

G. G.

Contents

1

Fundamental Concepts
of Microeconomics

The purpose of this chapter is to present some of the basic ideas of microeconomic theory. We consider the basic functions that must be performed by all economies and explain how the price system performs these functions in a private enterprise economy. In addition, several fundamental concepts of economic theory are introduced, and the meaning of "microeconomics" is explained. Finally, this chapter provides an initial insight into the basic process of price formation—demand and supply.

THE ECONOMIC SYSTEM

Scarcity

Goods and services as well as the resources employed to produce them are scarce. In fact, one of the functions of the price system is to ration the available goods and services. So when we say that there is not enough of a good or service to go around, we mean that there are people who would like to have the good or service but cannot pay the price.

1

To appreciate the problem of scarcity better let us consider its opposite, which we will define as a world of completely free goods and services, that is, a world in which there is a total absence of scarcity. All people would then be able to acquire everything they desire merely by asking for it. In such a fantasy world work would be unnecessary and money would be superfluous, for everything would be abundant and free. However, in the real world, goods and services must be produced, and production involves cost. If goods and services are produced at a cost, they cannot be free, and if they are not free they are by definition scarce. Therefore, scarcity involves cost.

If economic scarcity is determined by cost, then what do we mean by cost? We may push our argument back another step by saying that goods and services are costly because in their production resources must be used and resources are not free.

We can classify productive resources into three groups: human, natural, and produced. **Human resources** are the workers and managers of the economy. **Natural resources** include all nonhuman and nonproduced resources found beneath or upon the surface of the earth, such as petroleum, coal, forests, rivers, and fertile land. **Produced resources** are those that are fabricated to produce other goods and services. Produced resources are therefore what economists and others also call **capital goods**, and include factories, machines, tools, trucks, and so on. The production of goods and services usually requires the cooperation of all three types of resources. But resources themselves are costly, because costs must be incurred before they can be used; coal must be mined, oil drilled, wheat harvested, workers trained, and machines constructed. Hence most resources cannot be free. In a competitive economy the cost of the resources used in the production of a product will in the long run determine the price of the product.

Thus, the **economic problem** reduces to the existence of scarce resources relative to the virtually unlimited desires of people for the goods and services capable of being produced by these resources. This statement is a generalization and as such omits all the detail. To pursue these matters further we turn to the concept of an economic system or an economy.

Basic Functions of an Economy

In broad terms we can think of an **economy** as any number of people, generally a large number, involved in the production, exchange, and consumption of goods and services. These are indeed broad terms, but this very generality makes it possible for us to talk about the international economy, or the economy of a nation, state, or region. It all depends on which people are included, or, what is nearly the same thing, the geographical limitations of the economy. Large numbers of people are not necessary to the concept of an economic system, nor is it required that the people be governed by a specified political system. There are certain basic functions that all economies, large or small, must perform, and these functions can be performed under a variety of social and political conditions.

First, since the scarcity of resources prohibits the production of all conceivable goods and services at the same time, or even of some in unlimited amounts, all economies must somehow determine what should actually be produced and in what amounts. Consider the many thousands of different products available in the United States economy, and suppose that these products were put on a list along with their quantities. This list would be so long that it would be impossible for any individual to duplicate it; yet the economic system makes sure that each item is available. But what an economy should produce is far from obvious. We cannot say that an economy should produce what the people want, for most people would want large quantities of practically all known goods and services. Yet every economic system, whether small or composed of hundreds of millions of people with diverse and frequently conflicting wants, must solve this basic problem.

Second, every economy must determine how to go about producing those goods and services it decides to produce. This is a question of how the productive resources will be organized. Most products can be produced in a variety of ways, depending on the technology available. The production process can be highly mechanized, using much machinery and little labor, or the reverse. The solution to this problem is not simply a matter of using the most efficient method as determined by the engineer, because some of the resources necessary to conform to the engineer's specifications may not be available to the economy, or they may be very expensive relative to other resources. In China, earth-moving equipment is scarce and expensive relative to human labor, so men move gravel and stone on their backs; this is a method rarely used in the United States, where the reverse relationship between capital and labor exists. Many products can be made using either one material or another, and the economy must decide which to use, for example, whether to substitute plastic for glass.

Third, every economy must decide how its total output will be distributed among its members: How much of the total goods and services will each individual receive? Should the output be divided equally between every man, woman, and child, regardless of the quantity or quality of work performed? No economy has ever adopted this practice, even though many people seem to think that this is fair. The division of the economy's annual output is a difficult practical problem that always seems to leave many people unhappy no matter which approach is used or proposed. A major avowed purpose of labor unions is to see to it that the working man gets his fair share. But what is "fair" is itself a subject of perennial discussion.

Finally, there is the matter of economic growth. This can be a formidable problem if the population is growing and the productive resources, especially capital and trained labor, are not. Countries like India and China have found that an expanding population leads to impoverishment. Since the population of the world has been increasing steadily since earliest times, it becomes imperative that economies somehow provide for the expansion of their productive resources and hence of the output of goods. Contrary to popular belief, usable natural resources are not static and can be increased: New oil fields can be discovered; natural gas can be put to new basic uses (e.g., as a raw material in producing plastics); land can be reclaimed; forests can be grown; and sewage may yet be turned into palatable food. Capital goods can be expanded by making fewer consumer goods and using the released resources to produce capital goods. Another important way of increasing output is to replace worn-out capital with more efficient capital; this depends on inventions, better engineering, better management, and so forth. Not only capital but labor can be made more productive. Better-educated, more skillful labor is more productive labor.

The Price System

We have examined the four functions that all economies must somehow perform regardless of the political system. In predominantly private enterprise economies, like that of the United States, these functions are performed in large measure by the price system. It is mainly the price system that guides producers in their determination of what to produce and in what amounts. According to the **doctrine of consumer sovereignty** consumers spend their incomes on those products yielding the most satisfaction; and if they want any commodity enough to pay a price that will cover all the costs of its production, including profit, then it will continue in production. The greater the profit, the more attractive will be the production of this commodity to producers, and so more of it will be made. On the other hand, if profits cease to be earned by it, firms will eventually stop producing it. In this fashion consumers, in the expenditure of their incomes according to their tastes and preferences, determine through the price system the nature and size of the output of goods and services.

The price system also determines how the output of each product will be produced. The choice and organization of resources in the productive process of the firm will be such as to produce the output decided upon by the firm at the lowest total cost. The lower the total cost of producing any given output, the higher will be the profit to the firm. We are here making the plausible assumption that a firm prefers a large profit to a small one, if everything else is unaffected. In short, the relative prices of all the productive resources, together with the technological alternatives, determine how the output is produced.

The distribution of the output, that is, the amount of the total output obtained by each individual, also depends on the price system. Although wage payments are costs to the firm, they are income to the workers, and the more income a worker receives, the more goods and services he can buy. The same applies to all the other human productive resources. If an individual is able to sell any productive service for a relatively high price, then he will be able to command a larger proportion of the total output. Usually, productive resources are divided into four groups—labor, land, capital, and entrepreneurship—and their prices are called wages, rent, interest, and profit, respectively.

The problem of economic growth is also solved, at least in part, by the price system. If prices are high enough to yield large profits for a businessman, that businessman will want to expand his productive capacity in order to make even more profits. At least part of his profits will be employed to finance this expansion, and perhaps additional funds will be borrowed. If a businessman perceives an opportunity for profitable investment in a related field, he will again borrow or use his profits and savings to expand his productive capacity and hence that of the economy. In the process of expanding production, producers seek out and encourage improvements in the efficiency of both capital and labor. Consumers play a part in this process of economic growth too, for by saving part of their income they help to provide the funds and resources for expansion. Consumers also indicate to the producer the kinds and amounts of products that they desire.

A Simple Abstract Model

The four economic functions discussed above are performed by the price system interdependently. This is illustrated by means of Figure 1-1, which shows an abstract model of a very simple economic system consisting of only consumers and firms. In return for supplying the firm with labor and any other productive services they own, consumers receive income payments (wages), which may then be used either for the purchase of goods and services or for accumulation in the form of savings. As we have seen, the purchase of goods and services calls forth their production and also makes it possible for the firm to make income payments. Although consumer (and business) savings take income away from the purchase of goods and services and hence reduce future income payments, business investment at the same time augments the amount available for income payments.

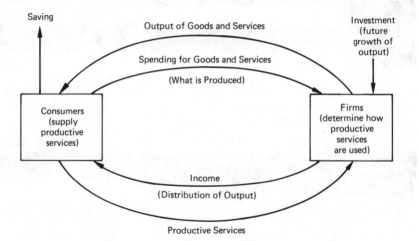

Figure 1-1. The circular flow of economic activity.

Figure 1-1 is really a simple representation of some macroeconomic relationships, since we are considering not individual consumers and firms but aggregate consumption, savings, investment, and income. Later in this chapter we distinguish between microeconomics and macroeconomics. The diagram indicates that if all of the economy's productive services are employed in the production of consumer goods and therefore all of the resulting income is used to purchase consumer goods, then no resources will be available to produce additional capital goods. Therefore, consumers must abstain from spending all their income on consumer goods, that is, they must save, in order to free resources from consumer goods production so that investment in capital goods can occur. This is the beneficial aspect of saving, but there can be a negative side to saving. If consumers save and businessmen for some reason do not want to invest an equal amount, then total spending declines, our circular flow shrinks, and total income falls. Figure 1-1 is usually called a **circular flow diagram**, since it depicts the flow of payments for goods and for productive services.

The Government

We have ignored the government's role in the economy; but, as we all know, government plays a large and important role in all economies, not least in that of the United States. To the extent that the government spends on ships, planes, highways, and similar products, it is the government that determines what is produced in the economy. If the government engages in the actual process of production, it determines how the goods will be produced; even without direct participation in the productive process the government may specify to firms how certain government products are to be produced. This is the case in much space and defense production. The government also affects the distribution of income, not only through its own payroll but also through various programs on behalf of veterans, the unemployed, the aged, and so on. The government affects economic growth by means of legislation favorable to business, such as investment credits, patent protection, and depreciation allowances, and also by means of various fiscal policies that influence interest rates, credit availability, and the course of the business cycle. As a consequence of these government activities, the United States represents a mixture of private and public enterprise.

SOME ANALYTICAL CONCEPTS OF ECONOMIC THEORY

Economists have originated or have borrowed from other disciplines many concepts that facilitate the development of economic theory. Some of the more important of these concepts are considered below.

Positive and Normative Economics

Positive economics is the study of how the economic system actually functions. By applying the scientific method the economist attempts to develop laws and theories that aid ~~in the explanation and prediction of~~ economic events in the real world.

Normative economics, also called **welfare economics**, compares the real-world economy with some ideal economy. The ideal economy represents the best way to achieve certain desirable goals or objectives, such as the satisfaction of consumer wants or preferences. The actual performance of the economy (the subject of positive economics) may then be compared with what would be the ideal performance (normative economics) and differences between the two may lead to economic policy proposals for improving the performance of the economy. In short, normative economics provides the standards against which we can evaluate the operation of the actual economic system.

Microeconomics and Macroeconomics

The study of economic theory is usually divided into two major parts. One part is called **microeconomics** (or price theory), which is the subject of this book. As the prefix *micro* implies, it is concerned with the study of the small elements of the economic system, of the basic building blocks of the economy. These include individual consumers, business firms, individual productive resources, single prices, separate industries, and so forth. In microeconomics the major concern is how a specific price is established by the economy. Earlier in this chapter, we discussed the functions performed by the price system in a free enterprise economy. Much of the remainder of this book is devoted to the development of a body of theory that provides a general explanation of how the price system determines what is produced, how it is produced, and how individuals share in this output of goods and services.

The other part of economic theory is called **macroeconomics** (or income and employment theory); this focuses on the behavior of, and relationships among, the large aggregates of the economy, such as total consumption, total investment, national income, the price level, and total employment. Here economists are concerned with explaining why there are such economic problems as recessions, inflation, foreign trade imbalances, and lack of economic growth.

In both microeconomics and macroeconomics much effort is devoted to developing policies designed to counter the adverse effects of undesirable economic developments, such as recessions and industrial monopolies. There is no particular reason to give precedence to microeconomics or to macroecomics, for both are useful. Depending on the problem to be analyzed, one may be preferable to the other, but to a large extent they supplement each other.

The Concept of Equilibrium

The dictionary defines *equilibrium* as a "state of rest caused by the action of forces that counteract each other." Similarly, in economic analysis **equilibrium** is said to exist when the set of variables under analysis shows no tendency to change. If one of the variables is changed this produces a state of **disequilibrium**. If the original equilibrium position was a **stable** one, then all of the variables will return to their original positions. But if the system was in a state of **unstable** equilibrium, then any disturbance will not be followed by a return to the original equilibrium position. We should always be aware of the differences between economic theory and the real-world economic system. Although equilibrium is a useful analytical concept that may reveal much about the behavior of our models and about the real world, we should not actually expect to observe a state of equilibrium in a real economy, where a state of flux is normal.

In our theories we can include many or few variables, depending on what we seek to examine. If we wish to analyze the equilibrium conditions of an entire economy, we are engaged in what is called **general equilibrium** analysis. This type of analysis can be conducted at different levels of aggregation, from the micro level to the macro level. On the other hand, **partial equilibrium** analysis isolates only certain key variables; during the analysis of these variables all other variables and conditions are assumed to remain unchanged.

Statics and Dynamics

Much of economic theory is **static** in the sense that the element of time is ignored: If an equilibrium position is disturbed by some change, it is assumed that all adjustments take place without a time lapse. The economist can then compare the new equilibrium position with the old one in order to evaluate the effects on the system of the initial change. This approach is called **comparative statics**. By contrast, **dynamic analysis** includes a time element and seeks to trace relationships among variables that are dated and that therefore can occur at different points in time. The emphasis is generally placed on the nature of the time path from one equilibrium position to another, or perhaps to no equilibrium position if the system happens to be unstable or represents a continuing process.

Economic Efficiency

An **economically efficient firm** is one that produces any given dollar amount of output at the lowest possible cost. There is usually more than one way of producing any particular good. Some production techniques employ much labor and little capital; others use just the reverse. The economically efficient firm seeks out that combination of inputs costing the least, relative to the dollar value of its output.

But note that it is not always to the firm's advantage to use the most efficient machine in the mechanical sense—the one capable of producing the most output per hour.

Suppose that a firm can choose between two different machines to produce a good. Assume that machine *Super* produces 10 units per hour and machine *Super-Duper* produces 20 units per hour; in this case *Super-Duper* is mechanically more efficient than *Super*. But suppose that the full cost of operating *Super* is $100 per hour, so that the 10 units produced per hour will cost $10 each. Now suppose that the total cost is $400 per hour to run *Super-Duper*, giving a unit cost of $20 for the 20 units produced per hour. If all other costs are the same, the economically efficient firm will choose two *Supers* instead of one *Super-Duper*, assuming that it wishes to produce 20 units per hour. The two *Supers* can produce 20 units per hour at a full cost of $200, as compared with a $400 full cost for the mechanically more efficient *Super-Duper*.

The Concept of a Market

Consumers and firms interact in the various markets of the economic system. Since goods and services are exchanged and prices are established in markets, these therefore play a key role in the allocation of resources in a private-enterprise economy. We have seen in this chapter that the price system is the main determinant of what is produced, of how it is produced, of how the total output is shared, and to a large extent of the economy's rate of growth. As we shall see, prices are formed in markets through the interaction of the demand by consumers for goods and services and the supply of goods and services offered by firms. But first it is essential to get a firmer idea of what is meant by the term *market*.

When they hear the word *market*, people often visualize an old-time market place where cabbages and fish are heaped up. They are right, but they have a very narrow concept of a market if this is all they visualize. For the economist, a **market** is any configuration in space and time wherein goods and services are exchanged and prices are set. By this definition, a market may consist of a residential neighborhood in which a small store sells its goods, or it may cover much of the world, as is the case for many basic raw materials such as copper and wheat. The buyers and sellers may see each other every day at a shopping center or they may never meet, all transactions taking place by mail, telephone, or telegraph. The price may be so sensitive to the behavior of buyers and sellers that it changes from minute to minute, as in the case of many stock prices on the New York Stock Exchange; or the price may stay at a certain level for weeks or even years. The price may be fixed in a very impersonal manner, as in the stock exchange, where the buyer and the seller transact their business through brokers, or the price may be subject to face-to-face negotiation, as happens when a homeowner decides to sell his house without the services of a realtor. Clearly, the term *market* as employed by economists is very broad and includes a large variety of specific kinds of markets. However, in all markets, the economist seeks to explain how the market price is determined, and this explanation generally runs in terms of demand and supply. Before looking at the concepts of demand and supply, we shall review the various market structures usually distinguished by economists.

MARKET STRUCTURES

Markets are classified according to the structure, or nature and characteristics, of the industry serving the market, that is, the group of firms supplying the goods or services for the market. Two main criteria are usually used in the classification of industries: the number of sellers in the industry and the extent to which the product of one seller can be substituted for that of another by the buyer. Largely by applying these criteria, economists have delineated four major kinds of industries and markets: pure and perfect competition, pure monopoly, monopolistic competition, and oligopoly.

Pure and Perfect Competition

There are three major characteristics of a **purely competitive market**. First, sellers must be so numerous and small that no individual seller can influence the market price by his behavior with respect to output or price. By the same token, we must stipulate that the buyers be so numerous and small that no individual buyer can exert any influence on the market price. Second, the products of all sellers are interchangeable or homogeneous, so that buyers have no reason to prefer the products of one firm to that of another. Third, firms and resources must have complete mobility, which implies that there are no barriers preventing them from entering or leaving the industry. This last condition pertains to long-run adjustments, when all productive inputs are considered to be variable, and assures that the allocation of resources is responsive to the operation of the price system. These are the main conditions for pure competition, and a competitive market structure exists when these exist.

For the purposes of theoretical analysis, it is often preferable to use the more rigorous concept of **perfect competition**. The first two requirements for pure competition hold for perfect competition, but the third is made more exacting, and a fourth requirement is added. In a perfectly competitive market there is perfect mobility, meaning that resources and firms possess the necessary skill or technology to enable them to move from industry to industry without any qualms, costs, or hindrances. The new requirement of perfect competition is perfect knowledge. The latter requires that all participants in the economic process must be fully aware of all costs and prices in which they have an economic interest, and they must know the outcome of all economic events which pertain to them.

Pure Monopoly

In terms of our two main criteria for classifying market structures, number of sellers and product substitution, we can define a pure monopoly as a market in which there is only one seller, who produces a product for which there are no satisfactory substitutes. In other words, the single monopolistic seller is also the industry, and he is able to set the price of the product at whatever level happens to be consistent with his objectives. For a monopoly to survive in the long run it must not be possible for new firms to enter the industry. Pure monopoly is the exact opposite of pure competition, in which many producers produce the same product. Both of these industrial structures are theoretical abstractions; real-world examples of either one are rare.

Monopolistic Competition

Monopolistic competition is characterized by a large number of small sellers, as in competition, but the product of each seller is differentiated in some way from the product of every other seller. This product differentiation is not so great that buyers do not consider all the available products as good substitutes, but it is great enough to appeal to the differences in tastes and preferences to be found among consumers. Therefore, the various products may be distinguished by such variable features as color, style, packaging, brand names, quality, and design—singly or in any combination. There is also the possibility that two products need not be different at all, as long as consumers believe that they are different, that is, the difference may exist only in the minds of consumers. Think of the endless variety of candy bars and milk chocolate bars, many of which are distinguished merely by a different wrapper or an unusual name or a claim of superior flavor.

In monopolistic competition, each seller supplies such a small part of the total market that he does not find it necessary to give any consideration to how his actions will be interpreted by his competitors; for example, he is not concerned about the possibility of any kind of retaliation, such as price wars, by these competitors. Each seller therefore formulates his price, product, and selling campaigns without regard for any of the other sellers. Finally, in the long run, when all productive inputs are considered to be variable, there is generally easy entry into and exit from the industry.

Oligopoly

In an **oligopolistic industry** the number of sellers is more than two, but few enough so that each seller is aware that his market actions will not go unnoticed by any of the other sellers. Before changing his price or his product, an oligopolistic seller must consider how the others in the industry are likely to react. The main distinguishing element of oligopoly is this awareness by every seller of interdependence or interaction. Two sellers in the industry constitute a limiting case of oligopoly, to which the term **duopoly** is applied. The products produced by the oligopolists may be homogeneous, in which case we have a **pure oligopoly**; or they may be differentiated, and then it is called a **differentiated oligopoly**. In the long run, if the oligopoly is to persist, there must be barriers to entry that serve to limit the number of sellers; otherwise the industry would tend toward competition or monopolistic competition.

DEMAND AND SUPPLY ANALYSIS

The Market Demand Curve

In this chapter, we shall merely introduce the concepts of market demand and market supply for the purpose of providing an initial insight into the basic process of price formation. A comprehensive treatment of the derivation of demand curves and supply curves is furnished in Chapters 4 and 7. Figure 1-2(a) shows a **market demand curve** D_1, which reflects the relationship between two variables; the price of the good and the total quantity of the good purchased. More accurately, the **market demand curve** gives the total quantity of a specific good purchased by consumers at every possible price during a specified time period. The curve indicates that more of the good is purchased as its price declines; that it to say, an inverse or negative relationship exists between price and quantity. At price P_1 in the graph a total of X_1 units of good X are purchased, and at the lower price P_2 consumers buy X_2 units. In Chapter 2 a theoretical explanation of this price-quantity relationship is developed. In this chapter we take this relationship as given, and we recognize that movements along the demand curve are a result of price changes only.

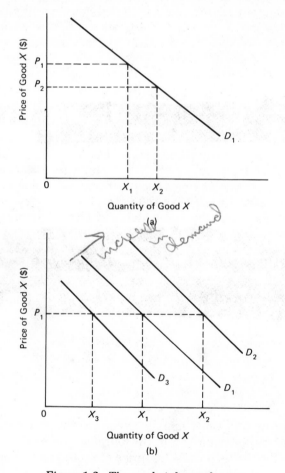

Figure 1-2. The market demand curve.

There remains the possibility of a shift of the demand curve to the left or right, as in Figure 1-2(b), which shows a rightward shift from D_1 to D_2, as well as a shift to the left from D_1 to D_3. A shift of the demand curve reflects a change in the quantity purchased as a consequence of a variation in anything affecting demand, other than price. For example, the shift from D_1 to D_2 in Figure 1-2(b) may represent an increase in the income of consumers, so that they can now purchase more of the good, X_2 rather than X_1, at the same price, P_1. Similarly, the shift from D_1 to D_3 in the graph shows that even though the price remains at P_1, consumers prefer less of the good: they want X_3 rather than X_1. The various determinants of consumer demand are discussed in Chapter 2.

The Market Supply Curve

The **market supply curve**, like the market demand curve, shows a relationship between two variables, price and quantity. The supply curve indicates the quantity of a good that would be offered for sale by sellers at each of various prices during a specific time period. To simplify this initial presentation of market supply, we assume that the supply is that of a purely competitive industry in the short run. Figure 1-3(a) shows a typical market supply curve, which unlike the market demand curve, has a positive slope, indicating that more of the good is offered for sale as the price rises. Why firms should offer more for sale when the price increases is explained in Chapter 7. We must emphasize that the supply curve shows the relationship between two, and only two, variables, price and quantity. All other factors that may affect the seller are held fixed. Changes in other factors that may influence seller behavior, such as input prices, are reflected in the graph by shifting the supply curve as in Figure 1-3(b). A shift from S_1 to S_2 is called an increase in supply, meaning that more of the good will be offered for sale at the same price, P_1. The shift from S_1 to S_3, a decrease in supply, indicates that less of the good will be available at P_1.

Demand and Supply

We have yet to see how prices are established in competitive markets. We know that buyers and sellers interact in a market and that the demand curve shows the quantity of a good that buyers will purchase at various prices; the supply curve shows the quantity that sellers will offer for sale at these prices.

By putting the market demand curve and market supply curve on the same graph we can compare the market behavior of both buyers

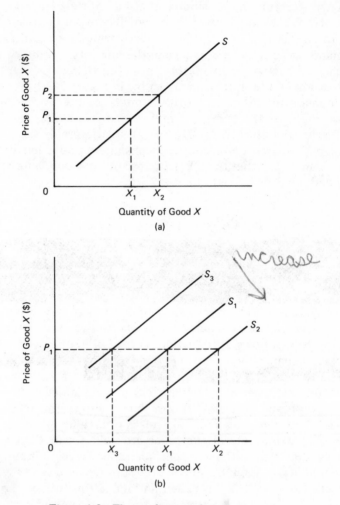

Figure 1-3. The market supply curve.

and sellers with respect to both quantity and price. This we do in Figure 1-4. Suppose that sellers initially offer for sale an amount X_2 at price P_1 as shown by the supply curve. At P_1 we see from the demand curve that buyers desire only X_1, so that an amount equal to $X_2 - X_1$ will go unsold. Under these circumstances, sellers are disappointed, since they expected to sell X_2 but find that only X_1 has been sold. In terms of individual sellers, this means that the average seller will be willing to sell his good at a lower price in order to move the unsold goods. In other words, sellers now offer their goods at

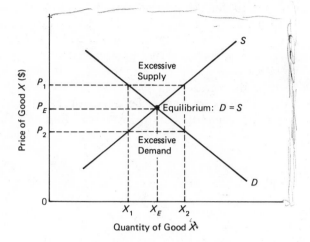

Figure 1-4. Market equilibrium.

lower prices and continue to reduce prices until supplies are no longer excessive relative to demand. Therefore, reductions in price and output continue until supply and demand are equal, which occurs at the intersection of the demand curve and the supply curve, at P_E and X_E. This is an **equilibrium point,** meaning that there is no further tendency for quantity or price to change.

If the price is P_2, the amount supplied would be X_1 and the amount demanded would be X_2, indicating excessive demand equal to $X_2 - X_1$. In this event, buyers will tend to offer higher prices, since they are not able to satisfy their requirements at P_2. Again, the situation will not be in equilibrium until demand and supply are equal at P_E and X_E. These, then, are the forces that drive the price of the good to P_E, which is the equilibrium market price.

The equilibrium position, where $D = S$, may be stable or unstable. A stable equilibrium will be restored by market forces if there is any deviation from the $D = S$ equilibrium position. The equilibrium position in Figure 1-4 is stable. An equilibrium position that is unstable is not reestablished if the equality between demand and supply is disturbed. Unstable equilibrium positions are illustrated in Figure 1-5. If the slope of the supply curve is negative (an inverse relationship between price and quantity) and less steep than that of the demand curve, as in graph (a), any slight movement away from the intersection will not produce forces to restore the equilibrium. For example, if price moves from P_U to P_1, the amount demanded is X_2, which exceeds the amount X_1 offered for sale. Buyers try to outbid each other to get the limited supply, sending the price even higher and aggravating the situation. The same reasoning can be applied to graph (b) if the price rises from P_U to P_1, except that here the supply curve has its characteristic positive slope (a direct relationship between price and quantity) but the demand curve now has a positive instead of its normal negative slope. In both graphs a decline in price from P_U to P_2 results in excessive supply; sellers then tend to reduce the price even further in order to eliminate the excess.

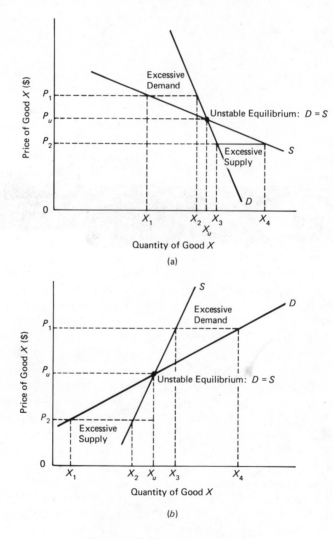

Figure 1-5. Unstable equilibrium.

But this makes matters worse and leads to more price reductions. As in all economic theory, we could develop additional interesting propositions on stability conditions and market behavior by simply altering our assumptions or introducting new ones.

SOME APPLICATIONS OF SUPPLY AND DEMAND ANALYSIS

The Price of Lead

Lead is a metal that has an international market. Changes in demand and supply are reflected on the London Metal Exchange, where the international price of lead is established. In the early months of 1977, the price shot up from $0.24 per pound to around $0.34 per pound, an increase of more than 40%. The rise was attributed largely to an increase in demand, shown as a shift to the right of the demand curve in Figure 1-6. The graph also shows a very steep supply curve, which indicates that the industry was unable to supply much more lead even at very high prices. Why this kind of a supply situation should exist is explored in Chapter 7. Here we may note that there was not enough time for lead smelters to increase production to meet the surge in demand. Under such circumstances there is usually a sharp price increase, as illustrated by the increase from P_1 to P_2 in the graph.

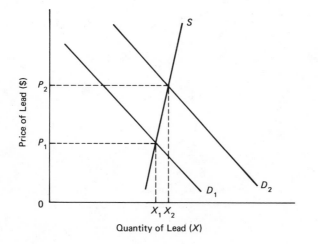

Figure 1-6. The price of lead.

What caused the sudden shift in the demand curve for lead? The demand curve shifted mainly because of increased purchases by the Soviet Union in the world market. Demand for lead advanced also in the United States because the abnormally cold winter of 1976–1977 was hard on car batteries, which absorb almost half of the lead consumed in this country. The increased demand by these two major world buyers forced the price upward.

The Price of Asbestos

In 1975 the price of asbestos jumped about 40%. In this case the problem was not an increase in demand, but a decrease in supply. This is represented by a shift of the supply curve to the left and a corresponding price increase from P_1 to P_2, as shown in Figure 1-7.

Asbestos is used in numerous goods, from boiler gaskets and brake linings to floor tiles and insulating cloth tape. About 95% of the asbestos used in the United States is supplied by Canada, and 1975 was a disastrous year for Canadian asbestos producers. First of all, there was a very destructive fire at one of Canada's biggest mines. On top of this, there was a rash of strikes, including one that lasted for seven months. Consequently, Canadian asbestos production skidded from an annual average of about 1.8 million tons to 1.1 million tons in 1975, and the price shot up.

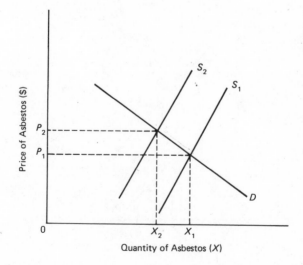

Figure 1-7. The price of asbestos.

Governmental Price Controls Analyzed in Terms of Demand and Supply

Rent controls represent a good example of governmental interference with the pricing mechanism. During and after World War II, New York City and other cities in the United States enacted laws designed to keep the price of housing (rent) down in the face of generally rising prices. More recently, a booming housing market in southern California led to demands by angry tenants in various cities and towns that the spiralling rise in rents be stopped by law. Senior citizens were especially agitated, since they found that a larger and larger proportion of their relatively fixed monthly incomes had to be used for rent. Are rent control laws the answer to this problem?

Suppose that the housing market is in equilibrium in Utopia, California. Figure 1-8 shows the demand curve D and the supply curve S for housing in Utopia, the equilibrium price (rent) and quantity being P_1 and X_1, respectively. Imagine that the demand for housing increases to D_2. As the rent rises to $\bar{P}$, the supply of housing advances to X_2, and equilibrium is once again restored. But suppose that the rise in rent to $\bar{P}$ leads to an outcry for rent controls, which are then promptly imposed at $\bar{P}$. Rent controls cannot stop demand from increasing, and suppose that demand soon moves to D_3. With rent at $\bar{P}$ the quantity of housing demanded is X_3; but the quantity supplied remains at X_2, thereby producing a shortage of housing equal to $X_3 - X_2$. This is the universal consequence of rent controls, whether in Utopia, California or in New York City. The pricing

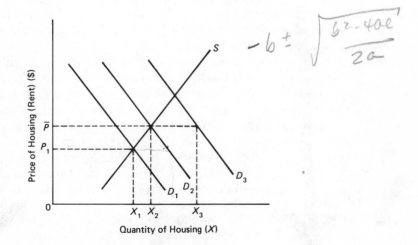

Figure 1-8. Rent controls.

mechanism has been prevented by the controls from calling forth greater supplies. In general, governmental efforts to put a so-called **price ceiling** (or maximum price) on any good, whether it be housing or natural gas, inevitably leads to shortages. Government interference with the pricing mechanism is considered further in Chapter 7.

SUMMARY

The economic problem arises from the existence of resources that are scarce relative to virtually unlimited wants by people for the goods and services capable of being produced by these resources. Productive resources or inputs can be classified into three groups: human, natural, and produced. Human resources are the workers and managers, natural resources include all nonhuman and nonproduced resources, and produced resources are fabricated inputs used in the production of other goods and services.

The economy consists of a large number of people involved in the production, exchange, and consumption of goods and services. All economies must perform certain basic functions. First, all economies must determine what should be produced and in what amounts. Second, they all must decide how to go about producing these goods and services. Third, every economy must allocate the total output of goods and services among its members. Fourth, an economy must produce increased quantites of goods and services at a rate exceeding that of its population growth in order to have more output per person. This is economic growth. In a private enterprise system all of these functions are performed by the price system. Because of the role of government, the United States represents a mixture of private and public enterprise.

A number of analytical concepts are introduced in this chapter. Positive economics is the study of how the economic system actually functions, whereas normative economics compares the real-world economy with some ideal economy. Microeconomics is the study of how the price system performs the basic economic functions. Macroeconomics is concerned with the behavior of large economic aggregates, such as national income, total employment, and the overall level of prices. In economic analysis, equilibrium is said to exist when the set of variables under consideration shows no tendency to change. In partial equilibrium analysis, the focus is on the behavior of a limited number of key variables; in general equilibrium analysis, we are concerned with equilibrium conditions for the entire economy. In static analysis the element of time is ignored, but in dynamic analysis a time dimension is taken into account. A firm is economically efficient if it produces any given dollar value of output at the lowest possible cost.

A market is any configuration in space and time wherein goods and services are exchanged and prices are set. Markets are classified according to the structure of the industry serving the market. There are four major types of industries and markets: pure and perfect competition, monopoly, monopolistic competition, oligopoly. There are three major characteristics of a purely competitive market: (1) there must be a large number of small sellers and buyers so that any individual seller or buyer cannot influence the price; (2) all sellers must produce an identical or homogeneous good; (3) firms and resources must be completely mobile. In the case of perfect competition, we further assume perfect knowledge. A pure monopoly is a market in which there is only one seller, who produces a good for which there are no satisfactory substitutes and who faces no threat of entry by new firms. Monopolistic competition has the same characteristics as pure competition, with the exception that the good of each seller is slightly different from that of every other seller. Oligopoly is distinguished by a small number of sellers, with each seller observing, and possibly reacting to, the actions of every other seller. The goods produced by the oligopolists may be identical or differentiated. In the long run there are obstacles to entry, varying in degree, in an oligopoly.

A market demand curve gives the total quantity of a good purchased by consumers at every possible price during a specified time period. A market supply curve indicates the quantity of a good that would be offered for sale by sellers at each of various prices during a specified time period. By putting the market demand curve and the market supply curve on the same graph, we can compare the market behavior of both buyers and sellers with respect to the price and quantity of some specific good. Market equilibrium occurs when the quantity supplied equals the quantity demanded at the same price, or where the supply curve and the demand curve intersect. This equilibrium may be stable or unstable. A stable equilibrium will be restored by market forces if there is any deviation from the equilibrium position, but an unstable equilibrium will not be reestablished if there is a disturbance.

This chapter concludes with some applications of supply and demand analysis. The prices of lead and asbestos are used as examples of how shifts in demand and supply affect the price of a good. Supply and demand analysis is then employed to show the consequences of governmental interference with the pricing mechanism, with rent controls in the housing market providing a good example of the distortions caused by this policy.

Problems and Questions

1. Explain how the price system in a private enterprise economy performs all of the basic economic functions.
2. Can you explain why economists find it necessary to distinguish between positive economics and normative economics?
3. What is the difference between technical efficiency and economic efficiency?
4. a. What is the difference between pure competition and monopolistic competition?
   b. What is the difference between monopolistic competition and oligopoly?
   c. What is the purpose of making these distinctions?
5. What is the purpose of demand and supply analysis?
6. What happens when the government tries to help people by keeping prices lower than they would be without such intervention by the government?
7. What is the problem of scarcity in economics?
8. What are capital goods?
9. What is the doctrine of consumer sovereignty?
10. Draw a circular flow diagram and explain the significance of this diagram.

Recommended Reading

Hutchison, T. W. *The Significance and Basic Postulates of Economic Science.* London: Macmillan & Company Ltd., 1938.

Machlup, Fritz. *Essays in Economic Semantics.* Englewood Cliffs, N.J.: Prentice-Hall, Inc., 1963.

Robbins, Lionel. *An Essay on the Nature and Significance of Economic Science.* London: Macmillan & Company Ltd., 1935.

Schumpeter, Joseph. "The Nature and Necessity of a Price System," in R. V. Clemence, ed., *Readings in Economic Analysis*, Vol. II. Reading, Mass.: Addison-Wesley Publishing Co., Inc., 1950.

Zeuthen, F. *Economic Theory and Method.* Cambridge, Mass.: Harvard University Press, 1955.

2

The Basic Theory of Consumer Demand

In this chapter and in the two chapters that follow, we focus on the consumer. Primarily, we wish to use economic theory to demonstrate that for a representative consumer an inverse relationship between price and quantity demanded exists for the typical good. If we can show that this is the case for a representative consumer, then we can conclude that the market demand curve also has a negative slope. Remember, the market demand curve, along with the market supply curve, determines the price of a good; and prices serve to allocate resources in a free enterprise economy.

THE DETERMINANTS OF CONSUMER DEMAND

In a democracy the major purpose of the economic system is to satisfy the needs and desires of consumers for goods and services. By spending his income on the goods and services he prefers, the consumer stimulates and makes possible further production of these goods and services. If consumers significantly reduce their purchases of a particular good, the producer will find his sales and profits declining and may eventually go out of business. In brief, this is the doctrine of consumer sovereignty, as defined in Chapter 1. Actually, this doctrine is a half-truth. The consumer is not all-powerful. He is the target of grandiose advertising and selling campaigns, of government regulations, and of various kinds of institutional influences, to mention but a few of the forces that help shape the direction of consumer spending. In any explanation of a consumer's behavior with respect to his purchases of goods and services, the following must be considered: the consumer's tastes and preferences, the price of the good, the prices of other goods, the income of the consumer, socioeconomic factors, financial factors, and the expectations of the consumer. We shall briefly consider each of these determinants of consumer demand.

Tastes and Preferences

The formation of consumer tastes and preferences is a complex matter, and to understand it fully requires an interdisciplinary approach through such areas as psychology, sociology, history, marketing, and advertising. Consumer tastes are molded by many influences, not the least being the selling efforts of producers. The seller does not usually regard the demand for his good as something beyond his control. He puts much ingenuity and effort into making his good preferable to that of other producers. The complexity and importance of consumer preferences make it mandatory for economists to define and delimit this factor for the purpose of theoretical analysis. The usual method of dealing with this problem is to set it aside, that is, to assume that tastes and preferences are given or determinate and that they do not vary during the course of a theoretical analysis.

Price

So much emphasis has been placed on prices by economists and others that it is important to remember that the price of a good is only one of the many determinants of a consumer's demand. When a consumer is considering whether or not to purchase a good, the price is usually not all-important, as we can see with a glance at our list of factors influencing consumer behavior. Some consumers would not want eggs at any price; others would gladly pay a dollar per dozen. Actually, for any particular purchase most consumers take the price as given and usually regard their income and preferences as the main determinants of their demand. But the key variable for the economist is the price, and the other factors are generally held constant during the analysis. This emphasis reflects the broad functions of the price system in a free enterprise economy, as described in Chapter 1.

Price of Other Goods

A consumer's demand for a specific good will usually be influenced by the prices of other goods which are substitutes or complements for the good under consideration. A **substitute** good is one that will serve the same purpose as another good. Often the degree of substitution depends on the tastes of the individual. For example, the different major brands of gasoline are fairly close substitutes for the average motorist; coffee and tea are close substitutes for some people but not for others; and golf and swimming as forms of recreation may not be substitutes at all for many people. If a consumer feels that there is no difference between coffee and tea, then for him they serve the same purpose; and if he wants to maximize his satisfaction per dollar spent he will buy tea when the price per cup is less than that of coffee, and vice versa. Even if the consumer prefers coffee to tea, if the price of tea gets low enough relative to that of coffee, he will switch to tea or at least consume more tea. In this manner, the demand for any particular product will vary as a result of variations in the price of substitute goods. There is a direct relationship between the price of the substitute and the demand for the desired good: Less of the desired good will be purchased as the price of its substitute goes down.

The demand for a good is influenced not only by the prices of substitutes but also by the prices of complements. A **complement** is a good that is used in conjunction with another good. There are **discretionary complements** and **nondiscretionary complements**. The former are those goods, such as bacon and eggs, that may or may not go together, depending on preferences; the latter are goods always consumed together, as in the case of cars and tires. There is an inverse relationship between the price of the complement and the demand for the good, that is to say, when the price of the complement goes down, more of the good will be consumed; when the price of bacon goes down, people tend to consume more eggs. These concepts are treated with greater precision in the discussion of cross-elasticity of demand in Chapter 4.

Income of the Consumer

The total amount of goods and services purchased by most consumers is restricted by their income. Except for the wealthy, people cannot for long allow their purchases to exceed their income. Economists have studied the relationship between consumption and income intensively, and out of this study have come three rival hypotheses concerning the consumption-income relationship: the absolute income hypothesis, the relative income hypothesis, and the permanent income hypothesis. These hypotheses have been used to explain the behavior of the individual consumer as well as the aggregate behavior of all consumers. We shall merely distinguish these hypotheses here. The **absolute income hypothesis** holds that, as a consumer's income increases, his consumption will also increase but by a smaller amount, and the proportion of income consumed will decline. The **relative income hypothesis** states that an individual's consumption expenditures depend on his income in relation to the income of the community, and the proportion of income consumed will be constant. The **permanent income hypothesis** asserts that consumption depends on what the consumer expects his flow of income to be when he looks into the future (e.g., what his annual income is expected to be over the next several years) and that there will be no change in the proportion consumed. Economic research continues to test and develop these competing hypotheses.

Socioeconomic Factors

No attempt will be made here to present a complete coverage of socioeconomic determinants of consumer behavior. But these factors have been receiving increased attention from economists in recent years, and some of them should be mentioned. The consumer's age is an important factor in spending patterns, and so are the size and age of his family. More education generally leads to higher spending because greater education generally makes for an optimistic job outlook, and the prospect of larger earnings in the future. Occupation, whether blue-collar, professional, or managerial, influences asset accumulation and ownership patterns, and hence consumption. Spending habits of city dwellers and their country cousins are different.

Financial Factors

The overall financial situation of the consumer can be important in his consumption behavior. Economists have long been interested in the relationship between the consumer's wealth and his spending habits. The English economist A. C. Pigou advanced the hypothesis more than a quarter of a century ago that declining prices increase the real value or purchasing power of some forms of consumer wealth and that consumers will therefore spend more, largely because they are relatively richer at lower prices. This hypothesis is called the **Pigou effect** and has been the object of considerable controversy in economics.

Consumer Expectations

Finally, the consumer's psychological outlook will condition his spending. His expectations may involve some of the factors already discussed, such as price, income, wealth, and family size. Or they may be shaped by political events, international developments, or general business conditions. Undoubtedly, the consumer's view of the future is important in his spending decisions, but not of overriding weight, for certain types of spending will usually occur regardless of most expectations, such as spending for food, clothing, shelter, transportation, medicine, and other essentials.

From the foregoing discussion of consumer demand one conclusion is clear—consumer behavior is full of complexities. We can express this complex relationship in functional form as follows:

$$Q_x = f(T, P_x, P_0, N, S, F, E)$$

where Q_x is the quantity of the good demanded by the consumer, T is tastes, P is the price of the good, P_0 represents the prices of other goods, N is the income of the consumer, S is socioeconomic factors, F is financial factors, and E is expectations. Of course, the relative importance of these factors in actual buying behavior varies from consumer to consumer and from good to good.

As we point out in our discussion of scientific method, economists, like other scientists, must abstract and simplify in order to understand the behavior of complex phenomena. In the case of consumer behavior, economists have focused primarily on the relationship between the quantity of a good demanded and its price. The other variables are not forgotten; they are simply set aside and stripped of their influence while the relationship between quantity and price is explored. After this task is completed, another variable may be introduced and its influence considered, and so forth, with the analysis growing gradually more complicated. The primary emphasis of the economist on prices stems not only from the relative ease with which prices can be observed and measured, but also—and this cannot be emphasized too strongly—from the important functions that prices perform in a market economy: prices allocate resources, determine production techniques, and distribute the output of the economy.

THE LAW OF DEMAND

In physics the volume and pressure of a gas are related by Boyle's law, which states that the volume of a gas varies inversely with its pressure, if other conditions remain constant. In economics the relationship between quantity purchased and price is expressed by the **law of demand**, which holds that the quantity purchased of a good varies inversely with its price, if other conditions remain constant. This law seems to be in accord with our observations of people's behavior, since most people seem inclined to buy more of a good at a lower price than at a higher price if nothing else is different. But economists, again like all other scientists, are not content to base a theory or law merely on casual observation. They want to explain why quantity and price should be inversely related, and they also want to be able to use carefully measured data to derive statistically the actual relationship, the **demand curve**, for various goods. Explanations of this relationship and of others like it belong to the province of economic theory, whereas the statistical estimation of actual relationships is undertaken in the branch of economics called econometrics.

Economists have developed three major explanations or theories of the demand relationship: utility theory, indifference curve theory, and revealed preference theory. These theories are listed in the order of their historical development. The reasons for this development are indicated as these theories are presented below. The first two theories are discussed in this chapter, and revealed preference theory is developed in Chapter 3.

UTILITY THEORY

The first comprehensive explanation of the demand relationship was developed in the 1870s and was based on the empirically obvious proposition that the possession and consumption of goods yield pleasure or satisfaction, called **utility** in economics, to the consumer. Second, it also appeared indisputable that consumers desire the greatest satisfaction possible from their limited income. Third, observation seemed to indicate that, as more of a good is consumed, each additional unit of this good would give the consumer less satisfaction than the preceding unit; that is, total utility would continue to increase but the utility added—the **marginal utility** (*MU*)—would diminish. This is called the **law of diminishing marginal utility**. Finally, these ideas implied that utility could be measured. These then are the assumptions or postulates of the utility theory of consumer behavior: (1) consumers derive satisfaction from goods; (2) consumers wish to maximize their satisfaction from goods; (3) consumers have limited incomes; (4) consumer satisfaction increases in accordance with the law of diminishing marginal utility; and (5) utility is measurable. If these assumptions are accepted, the law of demand can be explained in terms of consumer behavior as described by these assumptions. How can we derive the law of demand from these assumptions?

Figure 2-1 shows a utility function. The total utility curve consists of the summation of all the additions to utility (the *MU*'s, or marginal utilities) derived from the added units of the good. We can plot the marginal utility for each successive unit of the good and this will give the *MU* curve. Figure 2-2(a) shows the marginal utility curve by

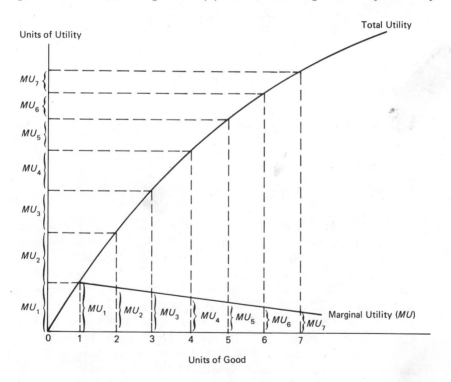

Figure 2-1. Marginal utility function derived from the total utility function.

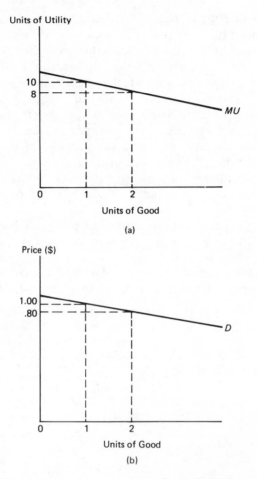

Figure 2-2. The declining demand curve reflects diminishing marginal utility.

itself. Figure 2-2(b) presents a demand curve illustrating that as the price of the good declines, the number of units purchased increases, that is, it depicts the law of demand. These graphs show us that as the units of the good consumed are increased, the units of satisfaction decrease (according to the law of diminishing marginal utility), and therefore each additional unit of the good is worth less to the consumer than the previous unit. This means that an additional unit will be purchased only if the price is reduced. More precisely, if we further assume that the marginal utility of money is itself constant and equal to, say, 10 units of utility per dollar, then the graphs show that if the price of the good is $1, then one unit of the good will give as much utility as the dollar (10 units) and the consumer would just be willing to give up a dollar to get one unit of the good. Suppose he takes the good. Assuming that he wants to maximize utility, he will not buy another unit of this good, since he will derive only eight units of utility; this is less than he would have by keeping the dollar, which yields 10 units. But if the price of the good declines to $0.80, he will be in a position to buy another unit of the good, since at $0.80 the eight units of utility from the good will be equal to the eight units of utility derived from holding the $0.80; that is, if a dollar equals 10 units of utility, then $0.80 equals eight units. Therefore, the price of the good must decline if purchases are to increase, other conditions being constant; the price and quantity vary inversely, which is the law of demand.

A similar line of reasoning can be used to explain consumer demand decisions relative to a large number of different goods and can also be employed to derive the law of demand in terms of each good. We can express the results of the preceding paragraph as follows:

$$\frac{\text{Marginal Utility of the Good}}{\text{Price of the Good}} = \frac{\text{Marginal Utility of Money}}{\$1}$$

When this equality holds, the consumer is in equilibrium: The consumer is maximizing his satisfaction. If the price of the good declines, the first ratio will increase in magnitude and the consumer will respond by buying more of the good; and this will reduce the marginal utility of the good (according to the law of diminishing marginal utility) until the ratios are again equal.

Suppose the consumer is interested in a large number of goods, say, n. Then in equilibrium the ratios of the marginal utility to price P for all the goods would be equal:

$$\frac{MU_1}{P_1} = \frac{MU_2}{P_2} = \frac{MU_3}{P_3} = \cdots = \frac{MU_n}{P_n}$$

If P_1 declined, then

$$\frac{MU_1}{P_1} > \frac{MU_2}{P_2} = \frac{MU_3}{P_3} = \cdots = \frac{MU_n}{P_n}$$

This would mean that the consumer would be receiving more satisfaction per dollar spent on good 1 than he would derive from a dollar spent on any other good. Since we have assumed that the consumer wishes to maximize satisfaction, he can increase his satisfaction by switching purchases from the other goods to good 1. For example, suppose that we start with the following equilibrium position:

$$\frac{12}{\$2} = \frac{6}{\$1} = \frac{3}{\$0.50} = \frac{18}{\$3}$$

The price of good 1 (the left-most term) now declines, so that

$$\frac{12}{\$1} > \frac{6}{\$1} = \frac{3}{\$0.50} = \frac{18}{\$3}$$

Since the consumer derives 12 units of satisfaction per dollar spent on good 1 and only 6 units of satisfaction per dollar spent on each of the other goods, he will shift spending to good 1. As he adds units of this good, the law of diminishing marginal utility tells us, the 12 units of satisfaction will decline, until finally the situation is in equilibrium as follows:

$$\frac{6}{\$1} = \frac{6}{\$1} = \frac{3}{\$0.05} = \frac{18}{\$3}$$

For the sake of simplicity we have ignored the increases in the MU of the other goods, as less is spent on them. But this would only accelerate the adjustment. Again we have demonstrated how the law of demand is explained by utility theory.

It is possible to include consumer savings in the analysis in terms of the following equilibrium condition:

$$\frac{MU_1}{P_1} = \frac{MU_2}{P_2} = \frac{MU_3}{P_3} = \cdots = \frac{MU_s}{\$1}$$

where MU_s is the marginal utility of the last dollar saved. Of course, it is quite possible that the marginal utility of savings is low enough so that the consumer spends his entire income before the marginal utilities per dollar of the goods he buys are reduced to the marginal utility of savings, in which case he does not save and the last term $(MU_s/\$1)$ drops out.

INDIFFERENCE CURVE THEORY

For more than half a century, utility theory was generally accepted by economists. Although criticism appeared before the

1930s, it was not until then that a well-developed alternative was offered. The main objection to utility theory was that utility cannot be measured: to talk about units of satisfaction has little empirical meaning, for satisfaction is a highly personal and emotional experience not given to measurement. The assumption of a constant marginal utility of money was also challenged on the basis that our feelings about money change as we have more or less of it. Another drawback to the theory is that many goods are not divisible—what is the marginal utility of a house? Finally, any attempt to compare the utility derived from a good by one person with that derived by another person is doomed to failure because there is no way of measuring and comparing the feelings of one individual with those of another. These objections and problems led to the development and acceptance of indifference curve theory.

Before considering the assumptions and theorems of this theory, let us see what indifference curves are like. Figure 2-3 shows a typical indifference curve, labeled I_1. An **indifference curve** indicates every combination of two goods that yields the same level of satisfaction to the consumer. Therefore, if it is a matter of indifference to the consumer as far as satisfaction is concerned whether you give him one or another combination, they will both be on the same curve. For example, it would make no difference to the consumer whether he had combination 1 or combination 2 in Figure 2-3, for they both yield the same amount of satisfaction. But if we move to another indifference curve such as I_2, the level of satisfaction changes: It increases as we move from I_1 to I_2. This increase follows from the assumption that the consumer derives more satisfaction if he receives more of a good, everything else remaining the same. For

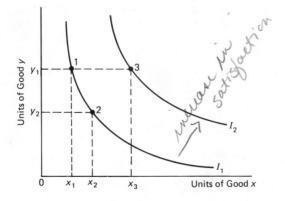

Figure 2-3. Indifference curves.

example, in Figure 2-3 combination 3 is preferred to combination 1 because the consumer has the same amount of y in both cases, but he has more x in combination 3. Since every point on I_2 yields the same level of satisfaction, we see that the consumer prefers every point on I_2 to every point on I_1. It follows that as we move away from the origin the level of satisfaction represented by successive indifference curves increases.

Indifference curves cannot intersect. To show this, we begin with a hypothetical situation (Figure 2-4) in which we suppose that I_1 and I_2 do in fact intersect. At the point of intersection the consumer reaps the same satisfaction from both indifference curves, since they both show the same combination of x and y. As the point of intersection is common to both curves, every other point on I_1 and on I_2 should give equal satisfaction. However, Figure 2-4 shows that below the intersection, I_2 is above I_1 and so yields greater satisfaction, and above the intersection, I_1 is higher and is preferred. But how can $I_1 = I_2$ and $I_1 > I_2$ and $I_1 < I_2$? It is clear that intersecting indifference curves lead to inconsistencies, and therefore we assume that they do not intersect.

Another property of indifference curves to be noted is their shape, which, as shown in Figure 2-4, is usually convex to the origin. There are two possible exceptions to this generalization. An indifference curve may be a straight line, as shown in Figure 2-5(a). This means that the consumer feels as well off with all x or all y, where the line meets the axes, as with any combination of x and y on the line. Such is the case when x and y are perfect substitutes. If I feel that two

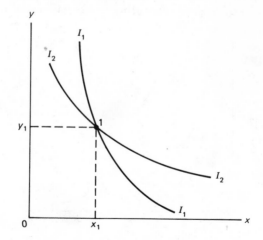

Figure 2-4. Inconsistent indifference curves.

brands of aspirin are alike, I do not care whether I have all of one brand or all of the other or some combination of the two brands. Figure 2-5(b) illustrates the case of perfect complements. Suppose we start with the combination of x and y at the corner of I_1 (x_1, y_1). If we move horizontally along the indifference curve we have the same amount of $y(y_1)$ but more x; yet we are still on the same indifference curve with no change in the level of satisfaction. Such a diagram would apply in the case of a left shoe and a right shoe of the same size and style, generally perfect complements; a consumer's satisfaction would usually not be increased if he had two right shoes to go with one left shoe. But if the consumer received two right shoes and two left shoes, he would move up to a higher indifference curve, such as I_2 in Figure 2-5(b).

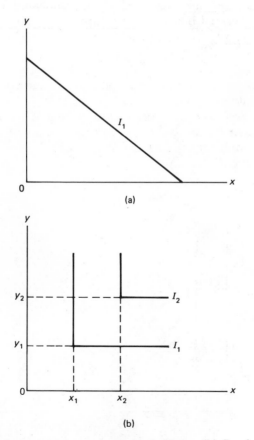

(a)

(b)

Figure 2-5. (a) Goods x and y are perfect substitutes. (b) Goods x and y are perfect complements.

Assumptions

We have now explored the properties of indifference curves. In order to develop indifference curve theory, it is first necessary, as usual, to make a number of assumptions. First, we assume that the consumer's satisfaction increases as he gets more of a good if everything else remains the same, except for an increase in the quantity of one of two perfect complements. Second, the consumer has definite preferences—he knows full well whether he prefers combination 1 to combination 2. Third, if a consumer prefers combination 1 to 2 and if he prefers combination 2 to 3, then he must prefer 1 to 3. By this assumption, preferences are said to be transitive. To these assumptions we add the three assumptions made in connection with utility theory: Consumers wish to maximize their satisfaction, consumers have limited incomes, and the marginal rate of substitution diminishes as defined below (an assumption equivalent to diminishing marginal utility). Actually, the last assumption is implicit in the convex shape of indifference curves.

The **marginal rate of substitution** (*MRS*) of good y and good x is the amount of y necessary to compensate the consumer for the loss of one unit of x so as to maintain his level of satisfaction (stay on the same indifference curve). A **diminishing MRS** means that the more a consumer has of x the less will be the amount of y required to compensate him for the loss of one unit of x. These definitions are illustrated in Figure 2-6. At any point on the indifference curve, the

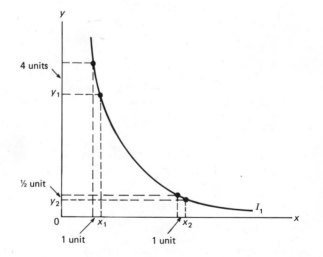

Figure 2-6. The diminishing marginal rate of substitution.

MRS is the slope of the curve at that point. If the consumer has a relatively small amount of x (at x_1 in the graph), he will give up a unit only if he receives four units of y, whereas if he already possesses x_2 he is willing to relinquish a unit of x if he is given only one-half unit of y. The conceptual relationship between diminishing *MRS* and diminishing *MU* is due to the assumption that, as a consumer gets more and more of a good, each additional unit is worth less to him in terms of either money or other goods.

Maximization of Consumer Satisfaction

Given the definitions and assumptions outlined above, how would the consumer maximize his satisfaction? In addition, does this maximization process provide an explanation of the law of demand? The answers to these questions follow from these assumptions, if we also know the consumer's tastes and preferences (expressed as his set of indifference curves), his budget, and the prices of the goods. Figure 2-7 shows the **budget constraint** or **budget line** for the two goods x and y. Suppose that the consumer has allocated N dollars for the purchase of x and y, and that the price of a unit of x is P_x and the price of a unit of y is P_y. Then if he buys x only, he can buy an amount equal to N/P_x units; thus, if N = \$100 and P_x = \$10, the consumer can buy 10 units of x; if P_y = \$20, he can buy five units of y if he buys y only. The straight line connecting N/P_x and N/P_y is the budget constraint, which shows the maximum amounts of x

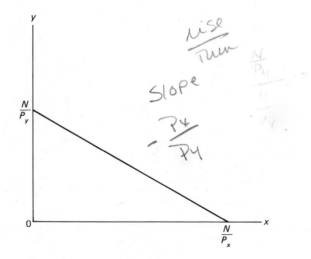

Figure 2-7. The budget constraint.

and y and the combinations of x and y (points on the line) that can be purchased with the given budget. The slope of this line is given by

$$-\frac{N}{P_y} \div \frac{N}{P_x} = -\frac{N}{P_y} \cdot \frac{P_x}{N} = -\frac{P_x}{P_y}$$

which in our example would be $-\$10/\$20 = -\frac{1}{2}$.

Now let us place the consumer's indifference curve system or preference map on a graph showing the budget constraint, as in Figure 2-8. The consumer will now maximize his satisfaction by purchasing combination $x_1 y_1$ with his limited income N, where the budget line is tangent to indifference curve I_2 at point T. This point of tangency of the budget line and an indifference curve represents the highest level of satisfaction attainable with the given budget. This is easily proved by moving away from point T along the budget line either to the right or to the left; in either case we move to points which are below I_2 and must be on indifference curves below I_2 (as intersection with I_1 illustrates) and so must represent a lower level of satisfaction. Therefore point T (combination $x_1 y_1$) must yield the maximum satisfaction with the given budget constraint. Since the slope of the tangent to the curve at any point must equal the slope of the curve at that point, it follows that at point T the MRS is equal to the slope of the budget line, or

$$-P_x/P_y = MRS = -\Delta y/\Delta x.$$

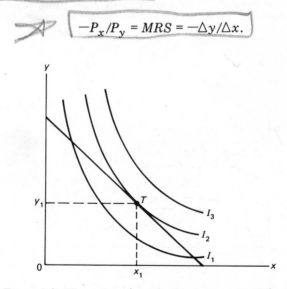

Figure 2-8. The point of maximum consumer satisfaction.

A change in the consumer's budget or in the price of either or both of the goods will of course change the equilibrium position. An increase or decrease in the budget is shown in a graph by moving the budget line up or down, parallel to the original line: The slope of each budget line must be the same, since it is determined by the same price ratio. This is seen in Figure 2-9(a). Figure 2-9(b) traces the satisfaction-maximizing combination of x and y (S, T, U, V) corresponding to different budgets. The **budget consumption curve**, which connects these combinations, shows that more of both x and y is consumed as the budget increases (assuming constant prices).

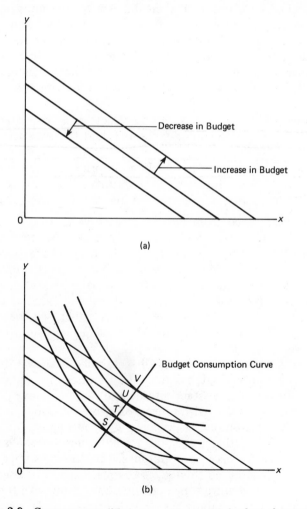

Figure 2-9. Consumer equilibrium positions with budget changes.

A change in the price of either good alters the slope of the budget line. If the price declines, more of the good can be bought on any given budget; and if the price rises, less can be purchased. These shifts are illustrated in Figure 2-10(a). Figure 2-10(b) displays a **price consumption curve** which traces the consumer's reactions to reductions in P_x, i.e., $P_{x1} > P_{x2} > P_{x3}$. Figure 3-10(b) also shows that a decline in price increases the consumer's satisfaction, since each reduction in price places him on a higher indifference curve. Therefore, the effect of a price decline is equivalent to an increase in the consumer's budget (or income), which also shifts him to a higher level of satisfaction. The mechanism of this equivalence is that a price reduction allows the consumer to buy the same amount of the lower-priced good with less money, and the money saved here can be used to buy more of all other goods, including the one that went down in price; in effect, for the consumer it is equivalent to an increase in income, even though his actual money income has not changed.

It is therefore possible to view the effects of a price change as two-fold: the **income effect**, just explained, and the **substitution effect**, which reflects the consumer's purchase of more of the relatively low-priced good (the one that has declined in price) at the expense of the other good. This is illustrated in Figure 2-10(c). The move from T to W is the total effect of a decline in price from P_{x1} to P_{x2}: The consumer has moved from indifference curve I_1 to a higher one I_2. To show the income effect we simply move the new budget line parallel to itself until it is tangent to the original indifference curve I_1 at V. Since at V the consumer's satisfaction is unchanged, the move from V to W is the income effect, because is represents the gain in satisfaction (equivalent to a gain in income) attributable to the price decline. To isolate the substitution effect, we again eliminate the income effect by moving the new budget line back to a tangency with the original indifference curve I_1 at V. The movement from T to V represents the substitution effect, since it shows the substitution of x, the good that has declined in price, for y, assuming no change in the level of satisfaction (level of real income).

The foregoing analysis is in terms of two goods only. A method of dealing with any number of goods involves letting one axis represent one good and the other axis stand for all other goods. This approach can be repeated for each good purchased by the consumer. The slope of an indifference curve then gives the MRS of a single good for all other goods. The assumptions made in connection with the two-good analysis would be the same.

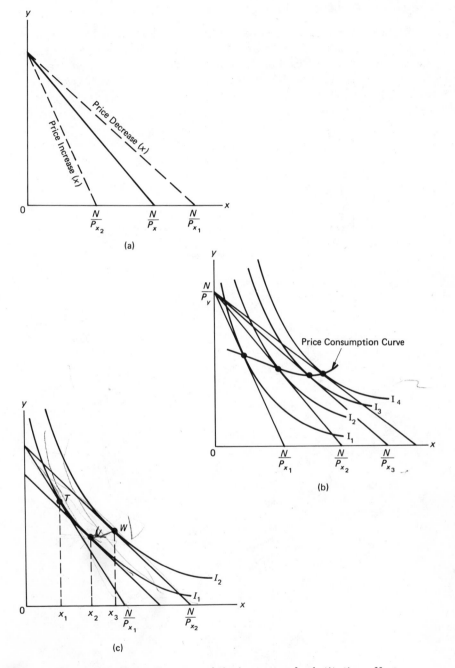

Figure 2-10. Price changes and the income and substitution effects.

The Law of Demand

We have now explored some of the implications of the assumptions made at the beginning of this section. Given these assumptions, the law of demand can be explained by the way in which the consumer behaves. Figure 2-11(a) shows the successive points of maximum satisfaction, T, V, W, corresponding to reduction in the price of good x from P_{x_1} to P_{x_2} to P_{x_3}, that is, $P_{x_1} > P_{x_2} > P_{x_3}$, with the budget held constant at N. In Figure 2-11(b) the quantities of x

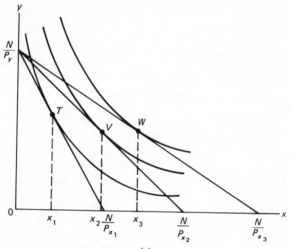

(a)

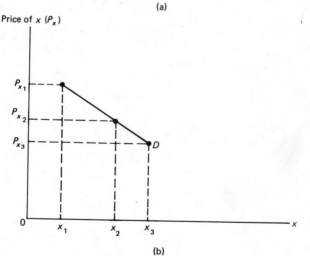

(b)

Figure 2-11. Derivation of the demand curve.

purchased by the consumer at these prices are again shown on the horizontal axis, but the vertical axis now gives the price of x, with $P_{x_1} > P_{x_2} > P_{x_3}$. By plotting on graph (b) the associated prices and quantities from graph (a), such as x_1 at price P_{x_1}, we trace the demand curve for x, and find the inverse relationship between price and quantity given by the law of demand.

We have now explained the law of demand in terms of both utility theory and indifference curve theory. Without these theories the law of demand would merely be an empirical generalization, since it would be based on observations of actual movements of associated prices and quantities, without an explanation of just why they should be inversely related.

INFERIOR GOODS AND GIFFEN GOODS

Ordinarily, a consumer will purchase more of a good when his income increases. If such is the case, the good is called a **normal good**. But consumers will buy *less* of certain goods as income rises. These goods are known as **inferior goods**. For example, a consumer may purchase fewer potatoes and more meat as his income goes up. If this is the case, potatoes are an inferior good and meat is a normal good. In discussing the substitution effect and the income effect, we saw that a decline in the price of a good leads to greater purchases of that good because of both the substitution effect and the income effect [see Figure 2-10(c)]. This is always the case for a normal good. If the price of an inferior good declines, the substitution effect still produces larger purchases of the good, but the income effect results in smaller purchases. On balance, the substitution effect is greater than the income effect, and the consumer buys more of the good as the price declines. This is illustrated in Figure 2-12, where the movement from T to V is the substitution effect and the movement from V to W is the income effect.

There is one exception to the preceding outcome, and this occurs in the case of an inferior good that is also a **Giffen good**. Here the income effect is greater than the substitution effect, and the consumer buys less of the good as its price declines. This is depicted in Figure 2-13. The substitution effect from T to V leads the consumer to buy more of the lower-priced good, but the income effect from V to W outweighs the substitution effect and the consumer ends up by buying less of the good (x_3 as compared with x_1 before the price declines). This result is contrary to the law of demand. Econo-

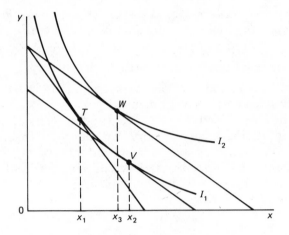

Figure 2-12. Inferior good.

mists have in fact observed rare exceptions to the law of demand. These exceptions are examples of what has been named **Giffen's Paradox**, after Sir Robert Giffen (1837–1910). Giffen noted that the nineteenth-century Irish peasant was sometimes compelled to consume more potatoes when the price rose because potatoes were still the cheapest source of calories. That is, at the higher price of potatoes the consumer was forced to curtail purchases of more expensive foods, which he could not now afford, and buy still more potatoes.

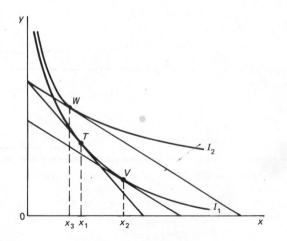

Figure 2-13. Giffen good.

SUMMARY

The main determinants of a consumer's demand for any good or service are the consumer's tastes and preferences, price of the good, prices of other goods, income of the consumer, socioeconomic factors, financial factors, and expectations of the consumer. In the case of consumer behavior, economists are primarily interested in the relationship between the price of a good and the quantity demanded of that good. The other variables influencing consumer demand are held fixed during the analysis of price and quantity.

The relationship between the price of the good and the quantity purchased is expressed by the law of demand. This law holds that the quantity purchased of a good varies inversely with its price, if the other conditions affecting demand remain constant. Economists have developed the following theories to explain this inverse relationship between price and quantity: utility theory, indifference curve theory, and revealed preference theory. The first two theories are discussed in this chapter, and revealed preference theory is developed in the next chapter.

Utility theory is based on the following assumptions: that the consumption of a good yields satisfaction, or utility, to the consumer; that consumers desire to maximize their satisfaction from goods; that consumers have limited incomes; that the law of diminishing marginal utility is valid; and that utility is measurable. Given these assumptions, we can deduce that the consumer will maximize his satisfaction (utility) when the ratios of the marginal utility to the price for all goods consumed are equal. From this it follows that if the price of one of the goods declines, then the consumer would purchase more of this good, which conforms to the law of demand.

Indifference curve theory replaced utility theory largely because of the problems posed in connection with the measurement of utiity. An indifference curve reflects every combination of two goods that yields the same satisfaction to the consumer. Indifference curves are convex to the origin, and they cannot intersect. The assumptions underlying indifference curve theory are the following: (1) The consumer prefers more goods to less goods; (2) the consumer has definite preferences; (3) the consumer's preferences are transitive (i.e., if he prefers combination 1 to 2, and 2 to 3, then he prefers 1 to 3); (4) consumers wish to maximize satisfaction; and (5) consumers have limited incomes. The marginal rate of substitution (MRS) of good y for good x is the amount of y necessary to compensate the consumer for the loss of one unit of x, so as to stay on the same indifference curve. The assumption of convex indifference curves implies a diminishing *MRS*; this means that the more x a consumer has, the less will be the amount of y required to compensate him for the loss of a unit of x.

Given the budget line (or constraint) of the consumer, which determines all combinations of the two goods that can be purchased with the consumer's budget, we can find the combination yielding the maximum satisfaction. The consumer will maximize his satisfaction by consuming that combination of goods represented by the tangency point of the budget line and an indifference curve. If the price of the good changes, the slope of the budget line changes. If the price declines, more of the good can be bought for any given budget, and this puts the consumer on a higher indifference curve. It is possible to distinguish two effects of a price change: the income effect, which is equivalent to a change in income, and the substitution effect, which reflects the consumer's substitution of more of the relatively lower-priced good for the other good. The law of demand, or the inverse relationship between price and quantity, can be explained using indifference curve theory. That is, it can be shown that a decline (increase) in the price of a good results in an increase (decline) in the quantity purchased by the consumer.

Most goods are normal goods, which means that the consumer will purchase more of the good when his income rises. But in the case of an inferior good, the consumer will buy less when his income goes up. The law of demand applies to inferior goods because the substitution effect outweighs the income effect (remember that money income is constant). However, there is a category of inferior goods called Giffen goods, for which the income effect is greater than the substitution effect. This result conflicts with the law of demand; however, Giffen goods are exceedingly rare.

Problems and Questions

1. a. What are the determinants of consumer demand?
    b. Why does the economist hold all of these determinants constant, with the exception of the price of the good?
2. Explain the law of demand in terms of utility theory.
3. Explain the law of diminishing marginal utility.
4. How would indifference curve theory be affected if we permitted indifference curves to intersect?
5. Suppose that the consumer spends his budget on three goods: x, y, and z. The unit prices of the three goods are $7, $6, and $3 for x, y, and z, respectively. The marginal utilities of the goods

are 24 for x, 18 for y, and 9 for z. How should the consumer go about maximizing his satisfaction?

6. Distinguish between the budget consumption curve and the price consumption curve.
7. What is the difference between the income effect and the substitution effect?
8. Explain the law of demand in terms of indifference curve theory.
9. If the *MRS* is $3y$ for x and the prices of y and x are both $1, what should the consumer do to maximize satisfaction?
10. What is the relationship between an inferior good and a Giffen good?
11. Draw a graph, using indifference curves and budget lines, showing how a consumer would respond to a price decline in the case of a Giffen good.

Recommended Reading

Baumol, W. J. *Economic Theory and Operations Analysis*, 4th ed., Chap. 9. Englewood Cliffs, N.J.: Prentice-Hall, Inc., 1977.

Ferber, Robert. "Research on Household Behavior," *American Economic Review* (March 1963), pp. 19-63.

_____ . "Consumer Economics, A Survey," *Journal of Economic Literature* (December 1973), pp. 1303-1342.

Ferguson, C. E. and J. P. Gould. *Microeconomic Theory*, 4th ed., Chaps. 1-3. Homewood, Ill.: Richard D. Irwin, Inc., 1975.

Hicks, J. R. *Value and Capital*, 2d ed., Chaps. 1 and 2. Fairlawn, N.J.: Oxford University Press, 1946.

Marshall, Alfred. *Principles of Economics*, 8th ed., Chaps. 5 and 6. London: Macmillan & Company, Ltd., 1936.

3

Consumer Theory:

Applications and Innovations

THE APPLICATION OF INDIFFERENCE CURVE THEORY

Indifference curve theory can be applied to a large variety of economic problems. In applying the theory it is important to keep in mind the few basic ideas of indifference curve theory. An indifference curve reflects the consumer's preferences only. It does not indicate anything about market value or price. In particular, an indifference curve shows the extent to which a consumer is willing to give up some of his holdings of one good in order to get an amount of another good while feeling no better or worse off after the exchanges. This being the case, indifference curves can be constructed for all sorts of things. For example, most individuals are willing to give up some leisure time in order to work for an income. But as the individual works more hours and has fewer lesiure hours, he will be willing to give up yet another hour of leisure only if he gets paid a greater amount of money for that hour than he received for the preceding hour. Accordingly, an indifference curve can be constructed showing the consumer's preferences for leisure and income, as in Figure 3-1. This indifference curve is discussed later, but here we emphasize that the trade-off between leisure and income is based purely on the preferences of the consumer and does not reflect what the individual would actually be paid if he sacrificed an hour of leisure. With this in mind, let us turn to an application of indifference curve theory, which involves income and leisure.

Income vs. Leisure

Figure 3-1 illustrates how indifference curves can show the relationship between income and leisure. Let the horizontal axis represent hours of leisure and the vertical axis dollars of income. The origin (0) indicates that the individual (Ben) has no leisure, or "all work and no play." This means that when he is off the job he has time for essentials only; that is, he has time for eating, sleeping, and so on, but no leisure time. On the other hand, if Ben does no work, he has the maximum amount of leisure time available, that is, time in excess of that needed for essentials. The maximum amount of leisure is shown on the graph by L^*. Indifference curve I_1 shows the degree to which Ben is willing to sacrifice income in order to gain more leisure, or vice versa. At point 1 on indifference curve I_1, he works long hours, and has much income but little leisure. The curve indicates that he would feel no worse off if his income were reduced to N_2, provided that his leisure were increased to L_2, at point 2. The indifference curve shows all income-leisure combinations that give him the same level of satisfaction. As usual, any point on a higher indifference curve, such as indifference curve I_2 in the graph,

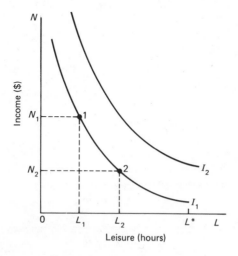

Figure 3-1. Income vs. leisure.

would yield Ben more satisfaction. Before we can determine the point of maximum satisfaction, we need to know the amount of income that Ben can actually earn in an hour, or his hourly wage rate.

Figure 3-2 has the same axes as those in Figure 3-1, which show income and leisure. Any point on the straight line connecting $N*$ and $L*$ shows the attainable level of income (on the vertical axis) corresponding to the time worked (on the horizontal axis); each leisure hour given up means one more hour of work. For example, at point 1, the level of income is N_1 per day, if the graph is scaled on the basis of 24 hours, and hours of work equal $L* - L_1$. The slope of the line $N*L*$ reflects the hourly wage rate. At $L*$, leisure is at a maximum and income is zero. If Ben now gives up one hour of leisure ($L* - 1$), his income must equal the amount that he can earn in an hour (N'), or the hourly wage rate ($ON'/1 = ON*/OL*$). An increase in the hourly wage rate would be shown by a steeper line, such as $N** L*$ on the graph.

By combining Figures 3-1 and 3-2, we can determine how many hours of work would maximize Ben's satisfaction. This is done in Figure 3-3. When the wage rate is such that the relevant line is $N* L*$, the highest level of satisfaction must be indifference curve I_1, which is tangent to $N* L*$ at point 1. A higher indifference curve is not attainable, and a shift to the right or left of point 1 would mean moving to a lower indifference curve. Ben therefore maximizes his satisfaction by working $L* L_1$ hours and receiving N_1 income. By the same reasoning, if the wage rate rises to $N** L*$ he will work more hours ($L* L_2$), have a higher income (N_2), and enjoy a higher level of satisfaction at point 2 on indifference curve I_2.

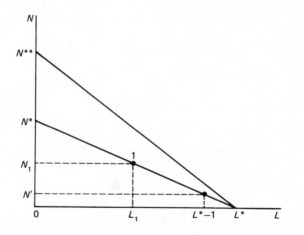

Figure 3-2. The hourly wage rate.

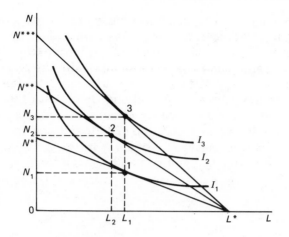

Figure 3-3. Maximizing satisfaction.

It does not necessarily follow that the higher the wage rate, the more hours Ben will work. For example, if the wage rate climbs to $N^{***} L^*$, he would maximize his satisfaction at point 3 on indifference curve I_3, which indicates that he would desire to work fewer hours than was the case at point 2 when wages were lower. This may well occur if wages rise to the point where Ben's total income is high enough so that more leisure is now preferred to still more income. Suppose that he works 36 hours a week when the wage rate is $3 per hour. Thus his total weekly income is $108. If hourly wages move up to $4 he may work a 40-hour week and earn a total of $160. But at $5 an hour he may go back to 36 hours of work a week, since his total income of $180 for the 36-hour week is greater than what he earned for 40 hours at the old rate, and he may now prefer the extra lesiure hours to still more income.

Another Application of Indifference Curve Theory: The Gains from Exchange

Indifference curve theory can be used to demonstrate that each of two individuals can gain from exchange. For example, if both individuals possess apples and oranges, we can show which good should be exchanged by each individual in order to increase his satisfaction. To accomplish this, we need to know the preferences of each individual, that is, his indifference curve system and the quantity of each good in his possession. Given this information, we can depict the preference systems of Ann and Ben for goods x and y in the usual way as in Figure 3-4, graphs (a) and (b). The graphs show that Ann owns x_1 of x and y_1 of y, and Ben has x_2 of x and y_2 of y. We can now construct the so-called **Edgeworth box diagram** by rotating Ben's graph until the origin is diagonally opposite to where it was at the beginning, and then forming a rectangle with the two graphs. The dimensions of the resulting "box" are equal to the combined amounts of x and y owned by Ann and Ben. That is, the horizontal sides of the box are equal to $x_1 + x_2$ and the vertical sides are equal to $y_1 + y_2$, as shown in Figure 3-5. The initial position of both individuals can be represented by point Q in the graph, with Ann on her indifference curve I_{a_1}, and Ben on his curve I_{b_2}.

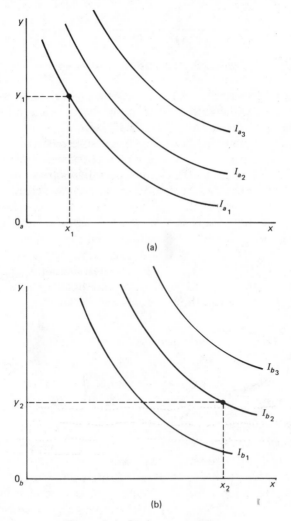

(a)

(b)

Figure 3-4. Preference systems.

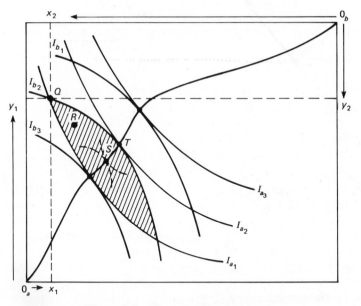

Figure 3-5. The gains from exchange.

How can we tell whether or not exchange would be beneficial to both individuals? Only if exchange moves both Ann and Ben to a higher indifference curve, to a higher level of satisfaction, will exchange lead to mutual gains. This is clearly possible in our illustrative graph. For example, if Ann exchanged some of her y for some of Ben's x, so that the individuals moved to point R in the graph, each would be on a higher indifference curve. In general, a movement, resulting from exchange, from Q to any point in the shaded area bounded by the two intersecting indifference curves, I_{a_1} and I_{b_2}, would lead to greater satisfaction for both individuals. Mutually beneficial exchange could continue until a point is reached where one of Ann's indifference curves is tangent to an indifference curve belonging to Ben such as point S in the graph, which represents the tangency point of the two dashed indifference curves. The line or curve connecting all such tangency points, such as the curve from 0_a to 0_b in the graph, is called the **contract curve**. Once on the contract curve, any further exchange would make one or both of the individuals worse off. For example, a move from S to T would put Ann on a higher indifference curve but would shift Ben to a lower curve, thereby reducing his satisfaction. In this case, Ben would not wish to trade with Ann. On the other hand, a move from S to R would make both individuals worse off, and neither would desire trade. To summarize, mutually beneficial exchange between two in-dividuals is always possible except when a point on the contract curve has been reached, and then it is never possible.

AN APPLICATION OF UTILITY THEORY

Insurance versus Gambling

From time to time, individuals must choose among alternative courses of action that involve different amounts of risk to the in-dividual. For example, an investor must choose between bonds and common stocks, and if the latter, between blue chip stocks and more speculative ones. In choosing an occupation, an individual may choose government service where the salary scale is clearly defined, or he may open a business where income prospects are uncertain but there is a chance that income may be substantial. If someone buys fire insurance on his house, he is accepting a relatively small loss with certainty (the insurance premium), rather than placing himself in the uncertain situation of risking a large loss (in case of fire) in order to save the premium. This person is willing to spend money to avoid an uncertain situation. On the other hand, if an individual buys a lottery ticket, he is spending money to place himself in an uncertain situa-tion. He is uncertain whether he will win a relatively large prize or lose the amount spent on the ticket. The individual could avoid this uncertain situation by simply refusing to buy the lottery ticket. We know that there are many individuals who buy insurance (fire, life, health, etc.) and also gamble (lotteries, horse racing, poker, etc.). How can we explain how the same individual would seek risk and avoid risk at the same time? An answer to this question is provided by the Friedman-Savage hypothesis,[1] by means of the application of utility theory.

The Friedman-Savage Hypothesis

The Friedman-Savage hypothesis holds that as an individual's in-come increases, the utility of that income first increases at a decreas-ing rate, then increases at an increasing rate, and finally again in-creases at a decreasing rate. Friedman and Savage attribute the changes in the rate of increase of utility to the behavior of individ-uals at different levels of income. A low-income individual would certainly reap additional utility from more income, but as he receives more income and the pressures of poverty ease, each additional dollar provides a bit less utility than the preceding dollar. On the other hand, if his income continues to increase, and it becomes possible for him to move into a more prestigious social and economic class, then any additional dollars he earns yield increasing amounts of utility. Finally, once an individual reaches a relatively high income level, and he already possesses most comforts, still more income, while adding to total utility, contributes less utility than the previous addition to income.

In Figure 3-6, individual income is measured on the horizontal axis, and the utility of that income is given on the vertical axis. Suppose that Ben has to decide whether or not to buy fire insurance. Suppose further that his income from work is F. If he buys insurance and pays the premium FD, then his income will be at level D in Figure 3-6, and his utility will be DD'. This is the certain outcome. The outcome is uncertain if he decides not to take the insurance. Suppose that there is a fire, and he has no insurance; then as a result of the loss his income would fall to level A, with a corresponding utility of AA'. If there is no fire, and he has no insurance, then his income would be at level F, since he is not paying the insurance premium. The dashed line from A' to F' gives the expected utility of all possible expected incomes as the probability of a fire varies from 1 to zero. For example, if the probability of a fire were zero, then the expected income with no insurance would be F, with an

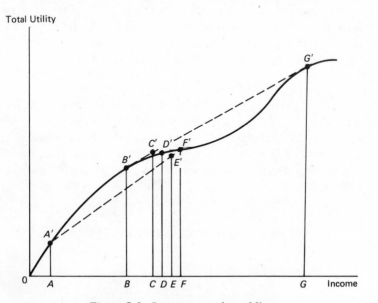

Figure 3-6. Insurance and gambling.

expected utility of FF'. The expected income associated with different probabilities of a fire is found by the following formula:

$$E = (P)A + (1 - P)F$$

where E is the expected income and P is the probability of a fire. For example, suppose that the probability of a fire is 5%, that Ben's income is \$20,000 (F), and that his income as a result of a fire with no insurance drops to \$8,000 (A). Then his expected income would be

$$E = (.05)(8,000) + (.95)(20,000)$$
$$E = 400 + 19,400$$
$$E = \$19,800$$

Ben is now in a position to decide whether or not to buy insurance. If the utility of the certain outcome (with insurance) is greater than the expected utility of the uncertain outcome (with no insurance), then he should buy the insurance. This is illustrated in Figure 3-6, where the certain income D yields a utility DD', which exceeds the expected utility EE' of the uncertain expected income E.

Given that Ben, as illustrated in Figure 3-6, buys insurance, we now must demonstrate that he will gamble at the same time. We know that his income without gambling but with insurance is D. If he gambles and wins, his income will jump to G, with an expected utility of GG'. If he loses, his income will fall to B, where the expected utility is BB'. Once again, the dashed line from B' to G' gives the expected utility of all possible expected incomes as the probability of winning the gamble varies from zero to 1. When we are given the probability of winning the gamble, we can employ our formula to compute the expected income of the gamble. Suppose that it is C, with an expected utility of CC'. The expected utility of the gamble exceeds the utility of the level of income without gambling. Therefore, Ben should take the gamble. This is what we set out to demonstrate: that an individual may buy insurance and gamble at the same time.

INNOVATIONS IN CONSUMER THEORY

Revealed Preference Theory

The third approach to the consumer demand relationship, revealed preference theory, was published just after World War II by M.I.T.

economist Paul A. Samuelson, who is a recipient of the Nobel Prize in economics.[2] The appeal of this theory is that it makes it possible to derive the negatively sloped consumer demand curve with much less information than needed for the other theories. Consumer indifference curves may also be derived by means of revealed preference analysis.

The theory rests on a few straightforward assumptions. First, we assume that the consumer's preferences are transitive: If x is preferred to y, and y is preferred to z, then x is preferred to z. Second, during the analysis the consumer's tastes remain the same and consistent: If x is preferred to y, then y cannot be preferred to x during the analysis. Third, given a low enough price, there is no good that the consumer will not purchase. Fourth, we assume that a consumer always buys a particular combination of goods such as 1, rather than some other combination such as 2, either because 1 costs less than 2 or because he prefers combination 1. Therefore, if we observe that a consumer purchases combination 1 instead of 2, we cannot tell whether this was because 1 is cheaper or whether the consumer actually prefers 1. But if we know that combination 1 costs at least as much as combination 2, then we can infer that it is purchased because it is preferred to 2.

As the name of the theory implies, the consumer reveals his preferences by his actions. Suppose that a consumer has the budget constraint $N/P_y - N/P_x$ as shown in Figure 3-7. We observe that he selects combination 1 consisting of x_1 and y_1. This selection tells us

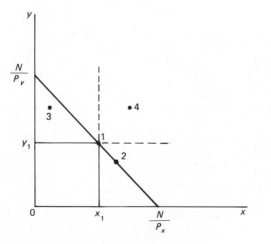

Figure 3-7. Revealed preferences.

that combination 1 is preferred to any other combination on the budget line or within the budget triangle, such as 2 or 3, since it is possible to purchase 2 or 3, but he rejects these combinations. Of course, a combination such as 4, which contains more of both x and y, is preferred to 1, but it is unattainable given the consumer's budget. Given our assumptions, any combination within the dashed-line right angle in Figure 3-7 would be preferred to 1. There are prices that would induce the consumer to purchase a combination such as 4 (third assumption), and the corresponding cost of combination 4, which contains more of x or y or both, would be greater than that of combination 1 (fourth assumption). Therefore, since the consumer could be induced to purchase combinations such as 4, and since the cost would be greater than 1, these combinations must be preferred to 1.

We may now conclude that if combinations in the dashed-line right angle are considered superior to combination 1, and if combinations in the budget triangle are considered inferior to combination 1, then the indifference curve containing combination 1 must fall between these areas, as shown by the striped area in Figure 3-8. By employing mathematical methods, it is possible to determine the exact location of the consumer's indifference curves.

For our purposes, it is sufficient to know that the indifference curve lies in the striped area, because we can now use this information to derive the consumer demand curve. First, let us consider the substitution effect of a decline in the price of x. On eliminating the income effect, the new budget line reflecting a lower price of x can

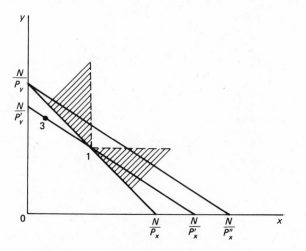

Figure 3-8. Deriving indifference curves.

be shown as $N/P'_y - N/P'_x$ in Figure 3-8. Since this budget line goes through point 1, the consumer has the same amount of x and y, and so is no better or worse off; the income effect has been eliminated.

We now demonstrate that the consumer will never select a combination such as 3 in Figure 3-8. We know that 1 was preferred to 3 before the price change, because the consumer chose 1 even though 3 was cheaper. If the consumer chose 3 after the price change when combinations 1 and 3 are the same price, then 3 would be preferred to 1. But if the consumer did not prefer 3 when it was cheaper than 1, he is being inconsistent, according to our second assumption, in preferring 3 when it is the same price as 1. Since combinations such as 3 will not be chosen, the substitution effect must lead to the choice of a combination located somewhere in the wedge-shaped area between the old and new budget lines. Therefore, a decrease in the price of x will lead the consumer to purchase more of x, confirming the law of demand.

If we include the income effect, as shown by the budget line $N/P_y - N/P''_x$ in Figure 3-8, it is likely that the consumer would purchase more of x when the price of x falls, but to be sure we would have to derive the exact shapes of the indifference curves. There is the possibility that x is a Giffen good, and this cannot be ruled out on the basis of our limited information. The remarkable thing about this analysis is that we have been able to determine so much, given only the consumer's budget and one preferred combination of x and y.

Bandwagon, Snob, and Veblen Effects

In 1950, Harvey Leibenstein, a professor of economics at Harvard University, published an article entitled "Bandwagon, Snob, and Veblen Effects in the Theory of Consumers' Demand."[3] This important contribution to economic theory explores the ways in which consumers interact with one another in their demand for goods and services. The basic theory of consumer demand presented in Chapter 2 ignores this interaction among consumers and assumes that the consumption decisions of a consumer are independent of those of other consumers. Leibenstein recognizes that other economists have been aware of this interdependence, but he has carefully defined the various forms of interdependence, and he has traced the economic consequences of each of these forms.

Perhaps the most familiar way in which consumers are influenced by the actions of other consumers is by means of the **bandwagon** effect. In this case a consumer desires more of a good because he observes other consumers using this good. This may be the case because the consumer wants to be in style, because he admires those who are already consuming the good, or because he feels that the good must be superior if so many other consumers use it. The bandwagon effect leads to a greater consumption of the good at any given price by all consumers than would have been the case in the absence of this effect.

The **snob effect** is the opposite of the bandwagon effect. Here a consumer buys less of a good to the extent that other consumers are buying more of this good. The snob effect reflects the desire of many people to be different, to be exclusive. This type of consumer is turned off as large numbers of other consumers start to use the particular good. The snob effect results in a smaller consumption of the good at any given price by all consumers than would have been the case in the absence of this effect.

The **Veblen effect**, as employed by Leibenstein, refers to a particular kind of conspicuous consumption that is stimulated by high prices. Inherent in this effect is the desire by some people to impress others with their ability to consume high-priced goods, whether they be Cadillacs, caviar, or champagne. Leibenstein distinguishes between the **real price** or the number of dollars actually paid for the good and the **conspicuous price** or the price that other consumers believe was paid for the good by the consumer in question. In some markets, these two prices frequently diverge. If a consumer can buy a Cadillac from his brother-in-law at a 30% discount, then the real price to the consumer is 30% less than the conspicuous price. To the extent that the real price is less than the conspicuous price, the demand for the good due to the Veblen effect will increase. In general, the Veblen effect leads to more consumption of the good by all consumers at higher prices than would have been the case in the absence of this effect.

Leibenstein rounds out his classification of the factors motivating consumers by defining, but not analyzing, **speculative demand** and **irrational demand**. The former refers to the purchase of a good in advance of an expected rise in price, while the latter includes purchases resulting from whims or urges. These two types of demand, unlike the others, do not depend on consumer interdependence. Nevertheless, speculative and irrational demand are still classified along with the bandwagon, snob, and Veblen effects as **nonfunctional** forms of demand, in that all of these forms of demand are not based on qualities inherent in the good itself. The traditional or basic theory of consumer demand is based on **functional** demand, or the demand that is motivated exclusively by the inherent qualities of the good.

Modern Utility Theory

In recent years economists have displayed a renewed interest in utility theory. At first, it appeared as though a method of measuring cardinal utility had been discovered. This new method was proposed by John von Neumann, the famous mathematician, and Oskar Morgenstern, a well-known economist, in their remarkable book *Theory of Games and Economic Behavior.*[4] A controversy soon broke out over whether or not utility was actually being measured. Before reaching any conclusions, let us consider the method.

To arrive at a utility measure or index by means of the new approach, the consumer is required to make choices under conditions involving **uncertainty.** An illustration will clarify how and why uncertainty comes into the picture. Suppose that Ben has the choice of staying home and buying a color TV (T) or going to a vacation resort. If he goes to the resort he may either have a good time (G) or a bad time (B), which introduces an element of uncertainty. Suppose that Ben prefers G to T, but he prefers T to B; that is, $G > T > B$. Then, according to a consistency assumption explained below, we can say that he prefers G to B. This being the case, we are going to arbitrarily assign a higher number to G than to B, that is, the preferred outcome receives a higher number. Suppose that we let G equal 10 and B equal 5. We know that Ben would rather have a good vacation (G) than stay home and buy a color TV (T). But we also know that if he actually goes on vacation there is a chance that he may have a bad time. He is certain that if he stays home he will have a color TV, but he is uncertain about the outcome of his vacation.

Let us now ask Ben what the probability of G would have to be in order to make him feel indifferent between G and T. For example, he may feel that if there were a 90% chance of G he would definitely go, whereas if the chance of a good vacation were only 50%, he would surely stay home and watch his new color TV. Suppose that he decides that if the probability of G occurring were 60% (.6), he would not really care whether he stayed home or went, that is, he is now indifferent between G and T. We can use this information to find the utility number of T by means of the following formula:

$$U(T) = P \cdot U(G) + (1 - P)U(B)$$

where P is the probability of the event, and U stands for utility. We now plug in our information.

$$U(T) = (.6)(10) + (.4)(5)$$
$$U(T) = 6 + 2 = 8$$

The formula tells us that we can assign a utility number of 8 to T.

Let us carry our example one more step. Suppose that Ben is now confronted by the certainty of G, and the uncertainty of staying home and winning either T or a car (C). We ask him what the probability of C must be in order to make him indifferent between G and C. Assume that if there were a 20% chance of winning a car, then he would be indifferent between going on vacation and staying home. We can employ the formula to determine the utility number of C as follows:

$$U(G) = P \cdot U(C) + (1 - P) U(T)$$
$$10 = .2U(C) + .8(8)$$
$$3.6 = .2U(C)$$
$$18 = U(C)$$

We now know that for Ben, C is preferred to G, G is preferred to T, and T is preferred to B, since $18 > 10 > 8 > 5$. Before considering whether or not we have succeeded in actually measuring utility, let us briefly examine the assumptions behind this analysis. There are three basic assumptions. First, we must assume that consumers are consistent in the sense that if good x is preferred to good y, and good y is preferred to good z, then x is preferred to z. Second, the consumer must either prefer x to y, or y to x, or must be indifferent as to x and y. Third, if the consumer prefers x to y and y to z, it must be possible to assign probabilities P and $(1 - P)$ to uncertain outcomes x and z, respectively, such that the consumer is indifferent between the certainty of y and the uncertain outcome consisting of x and z. Obviously, if these basic assumptions did not hold, the analysis would not be possible or would lead to inconsistent results.

We now come to the crucial question: Does this method actually measure utility in terms of the pleasure or satisfaction derived from goods? Unfortunately, this approach does not yield units of actual satisfaction. Recall that we arbitrarily assigned the numbers 5 and 10 to two goods at the beginning of the analysis. This does not imply that one of the goods gives twice the satisfaction of the other, for we could have assigned the numbers 2 and 10 just as easily. But it does mean that goods with higher numbers are preferred to those with lower numbers. In other words, we have here a method of scaling or ordering preferences under conditions of uncertainty. By employing this method we can rank all of a consumer's preferences, but we still have no way of measuring the actual pleasure that a consumer derives from consuming goods. We have not yet captured the phantom of feelings and emotions.

The Technology of Consumption

Kelvin Lancaster proposed a new approach to consumer theory in 1966,[5] which is based on the idea that consumers purchase goods not for the goods themselves, but for their inherent characteristics which in turn provide consumer satisfaction. On a cold day a consumer may buy a cup of coffee because it produces warmth and stimulation. The warmth and stimulation are characteristics of the coffee that lead to the purchase. Another consumer may purchase a glass of milk for its flavor, protein, and vitamin A. It is these characteristics of the good that attract the consumer. Typically, any good will supply a bundle of joint characteristics. It is usually possible for the consumer to obtain the same characteristics from different goods. A consumer can derive warmth and stimulation from either coffee or tea. Moreover, different goods may have the same characteristics but in quantitatively different combinations. For example, some people may find coffee more stimulating than tea. A **consumption activity** is defined in terms of the characteristics obtainable from a unit of a good. The **consumption technology** includes all possible consumption activities available to the consumer.

To illustrate this approach to consumer theory, we assume that Ann may choose among two goods, x_1 and x_2, each possessing two characteristics, c and d. In Figure 3-9 the quantities of the characteristics are measured along the axes. The rays O_{x_1} and O_{x_2} show the quantities of c and d inherent in various amounts of x_1 and x_2. For example, point 1 on the graph may represent five units of x_1, which yields c_1 of characteristic c, and d_1 of characteristic d. The

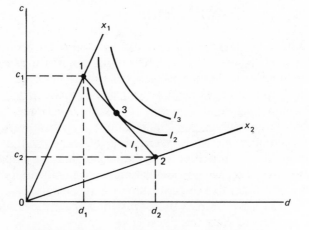

Figure 3-9. Two goods and two characteristics.

slope of a ray reflects the proportions of the characteristics possessed by the good. We also assume that characteristics increase in proportion to an increase in the quantity of a good, that is, twice as much of a good gives twice as much of the good's characteristics. Ann may spend her entire budget on either x_1 or x_2, or on some combination of x_1 and x_2. If the whole budget is used to buy x_1 she will be able to obtain c_1 of characteristic c and d_1 of characteristic d as shown at point 1. If the budget is devoted to x_2, she will have c_2 of c and d_2 of d given at point 2. Points on the line connecting points 1 and 2, called the **budget frontier**, represent all possible combinations of x_1 and x_2, available to Ann, and hence all combinations of characteristics c and d. To determine how she will allocate her budget in order to maximize her satisfaction, we must know her preferences. As usual a consumer's preferences are given by her indifference curves, which in this theory reflect her preferences for the characteristics of the goods. These indifference curves appear as I_1, I_2, and I_3 in the graph. Ann achieves maximum satisfaction at point 3, where I_2 is tangent to the budget frontier running from point 1 to point 2. Any movement to the left or right of point 3 would lead to a lower indifference curve, that is, to a lower level of satisfaction. Therefore, she will buy both good x_1 and good x_2 in order to obtain their characteristics in the proportion that will maximize her satisfaction.

Remember that in our simple example, the consumption technology consists of all of the possible consumption activities available to the consumer, or all of the possible combinations of x_1 and x_2 that the consumer may choose among.

SUMMARY

This chapter is devoted to applications and innovations in consumer theory. One of the more interesting applications of indifference curve theory concerns a consumer's preferences for income and leisure. Indifference curves can be constructed to show the various combinations of leisure and income that yield the same level of satisfaction for the consumer. That is, the consumer is able to maintain his level of satisfaction when sacrificing leisure only if he receives more income. If we construct an income line, with a slope equal to the hourly wage rate, we can determine how many hours of leisure (and work) will maximize the consumer's satisfaction. This is done in the usual manner, by finding the point of tangency between the income line and an indifference curve.

Indifference curve theory can be employed to demonstrate that each of two individuals can gain from exchange, if they each possess some of two goods. To do this, we need to know the indifference curve system of each individual and the quantity of goods each possesses. With this information we can construct an Edgeworth box diagram. Mutually beneficial exchange can occur until a point on the contract curve is reached. The contract curve is the locus of all tangency points of the two individuals' indifference curves. Once on the contract curve, any further exchange would make one or both of the individuals worse off.

Utility theory can be used to explain why an individual might buy insurance (avoid risk) and at the same time gamble (assume risk). The solution of this problem is based on the Friedman-Savage hypothesis, which holds that as an individual's income goes up, the utility of that income first increases at a decreasing rate, then increases at an increasing rate, and finally again increases at a decreasing rate. Friedman and Savage attribute the changes in the rate of increase of utility to the behavior of individuals at different levels of income. The individual's preference for uncertainty or certainty depends on the expected utility of the uncertain outcome as compared with the known utility of the certain outcome. If the utility of the certain outcome (having insurance) is greater than the expected utility of the uncertain outcome (having no insurance), then the individual should prefer the certain outcome (buy insurance). By the same token, if the expected utility of a gamble (lottery tickets) exceeds the utility of the level of income without gambling (no lottery tickets), then the individual should gamble. Given the slope of the Friedman-Savage utility of income function, it can be demonstrated that an individual may buy insurance and gamble at the same time.

Some of the innovations in consumer theory discussed in this chapter are revealed preference theory; bandwagon, snob, and Veblen effects; modern utility theory; and a new approach to consumer theory. Samuelson's revealed preference theory makes it possible to derive the consumer demand curve with much less information than with the other theories. As the name of the theory implies, the consumer reveals his preferences by his consumption behavior. Given the consumer's budget, we need only observe one choice of a combination of two goods in order to demonstrate that the consumer's demand curve has a negative slope.

Leibenstein's bandwagon, snob, and Veblen effects refer to ways by which consumers are influenced by the behavior of other consumers. In the case of the bandwagon effect, a consumer desires more of a good because he observes other consumers using this good. The snob effect is the opposite of the bandwagon effect—a consumer buys less of a good to the extent that other consumers are buying more of this good. The Veblen effect refers to an individual's propensity to buy goods that cost him less than other people think he paid for the good.

Von Neumann and Morgenstern have proposed a new method of measuring utility, which requires an individual to make choices under conditions of uncertainty. Although this method generates utility numbers, and makes it possible to rank a consumer's preferences under conditions of uncertainty, it does not actually measure utility in the sense of the pleasure or satisfaction derived from consuming a good.

Lancaster based his approach to consumer theory on the idea that consumers purchase goods for the characteristics inherent in the good. For example, a consumer buys coffee for such characteristics as flavor and stimulation. Different goods might possess the same characteristics, either in the same or different combinations. A consumption activity is defined in terms of the characteristics obtainable from a unit of the good. The consumption technology includes all possible consumption activities available to the consumer. To determine how the consumer will allocate his budget in order to maximize his satisfaction, we must know his preferences. Although the consumer's preferences are given by indifference curves, in this theory the indifference curves reflect preferences for the characteristics of the goods rather than for the goods themselves.

Notes

1. This hypothesis, which was designed to analyze choices involving risk, was first developed in M. Friedman and L. J. Savage, "The Utility Analysis of Choices Involving Risk," *Journal of Political Economy* (August 1948), pp. 279-304.

2. *Foundations of Economic Analysis*, Chaps. 5 and 6 (Cambridge, Mass.: Harvard University Press, 1947).

3. *The Quarterly Journal of Economics* (May 1950), pp. 183-207.

4. 2d ed. (Princeton, N.J.: Princeton University Press, 1947).

5. "A New Approach to Consumer Theory," *Journal of Political Economy* (April 1966), pp. 132-157.

Problems and Questions

1. According to our indifference curve analysis of income versus leisure, would an increase in the hourly wage rate result in more

or fewer hours of work by the individual?
2. How can we know whether or not two individuals can benefit from exchange?
3. What determines the dimensions of the Edgeworth box diagram?
4. What is meant by expected utility?
5. What assumptions are necessary in connection with the theory of revealed preference?
6. How does the snob effect differ from the bandwagon effect?
7. Distinguish between the real price and the conspicuous price of a good.
8. In what sense does the Von Neuman–Morgenstern theory result in a measure of utility?
9. According to Lancaster's consumer theory, why might wood and blankets be considered similar goods?
10. Explain the Friedman–Savage hypothesis.
11. What is the difference between a consumption activity and a consumption technology?

Recommended Reading

Alchian, A. A. "The Meaning of Utility Measurement," *American Economic Review* (March 1963), pp. 26–50; reprinted in W. L. Breit and H. M. Hochman, eds. *Readings in Microeconomics*, 2d ed., pp. 57–76. New York: Holt, Rinehart and Winston, Inc., 1971.

Baumol, W. J. *Economic Theory and Operations Analysis*, 4th ed., Chaps. 14 and 17. Englewood Cliffs, N.J.: Prentice-Hall, Inc., 1977.

Friedman, M. and L. J. Savage. "The Utility Analysis of Choices Involving Risk," *Journal of Political Economy* (August 1948), pp. 279–304; reprinted in G. L. Stigler and K. E. Boulding, eds., pp. 57–96. *Readings in Price Theory*. Homewood, Ill.: Richard D. Irwin, Inc., 1952.

Lancaster, K. "Change and Innovation in the Technology of Consumption," *American Economic Review* (May 1966), pp. 14–23; reprinted in R. E. Neel, ed., *Readings in Price Theory*, pp. 144–52. Cincinnati: South-Western Publishing Co., 1973.

Leibenstein, H. "Bandwagon, Snob, and Veblen Effects in the Theory of Consumers' Demand," *The Quarterly Journal of Economics* (May 1950), pp. 183–207; reprinted in W. L. Breit and H. M. Hochman, eds., *Readings in Microeconomics*, 2d ed., pp. 111–27. New York: Holt, Rinehart and Winston, Inc., 1971.

von Neumann, J. and O. Morgenstern. *Theory of Games and Economic Behavior*, 2d ed., Chap. 1. Princeton, N.J.: Princeton University Press, 1947.

Samuelson, P. A. "Consumption Theory in Terms of Revealed Preference," *Economica* (November 1948), pp. 243-53.

_____ . *Foundations of Economic Analysis*, Chaps. 5 and 6. Cambridge, Mass.: Harvard University Press, 1947.

4

Market Demand

FROM INDIVIDUAL DEMAND TO MARKET DEMAND

In Chapter 2 we derived the demand curve for the individual consumer. As we saw, this curve is an expression of the law of demand, which holds that the quantity of a good that a consumer will purchase varies inversely with its price, provided that everything else affecting demand stays the same. If we know the demand curve for every consumer of the good, it is an easy matter to find the market demand curve for this good. We need only add up the amounts of the good demanded by all consumers at each price. An example will show how this is done. To simplify, we assume that the entire market consists of two consumers A and B, as shown in Table 4-1. At a price of $5, consumer A demands one unit of the good and consumer B will buy five units, giving a total market demand of six units; when the price is $4, consumer A purchases three units and consumer B takes nine units, for a market demand of twelve units; and so on. This same approach applies to any number of consumers. It follows that if individual demand curves reflect an inverse relationship between the good's price and the quantity bought, then the market demand curve will also reflect this relationship. This can be clearly seen in Figure 4-1, which presents the data in Table 4-1 in graphic form.

Table 4-1. Individual and Market Demand

Price ($)	Quantity Demanded by Consumer A	Quantity Demanded by Consumer B	Market Demand
5	1	5	6
4	3	9	12
3	5	13	18
2	6	17	23
1	7	20	27

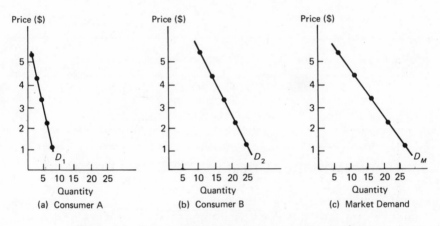

Figure 4-1. From individual demand to market demand.

The **market demand curve** shows the total amount of the good that will be purchased at each and every price during some definite span of time, when all other relevant variables are held constant. This demand relationship between the price and quantity of a good is extremely important to economists because, along with the supply relationship (the supply curve), it determines the good's price. Sellers of the good are also very interested in the demand relationship, because from their point of view consumer purchases of the good at various prices represent sales; that is, dollars actually received by the sellers of the good. This is shown in a more formal way in Figure 4-2, where the shaded area, equal to price (P_{X1}) times quantity (X_1), represents total consumer expenditures and total seller revenues in a market in equilibrium.

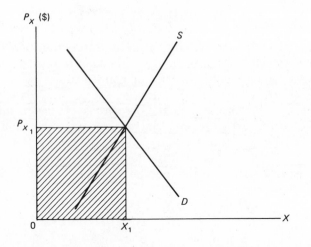

Figure 4-2. Total expenditures and total revenue.

As discussed in Chapter 1, the market demand curve, as well as individual consumer demand curves, may shift to the right or to the left. If the price of the good is constant, the demand curve may shift because of a change in such demand-related variables as tastes and preferences, consumer income, prices of other goods, and consumer expectations. Such demand curve shifts are shown in Figure 4-3. If the price of the good varies, this is always represented by a movement along the demand curve, assuming that the demand-related variables now stay the same.

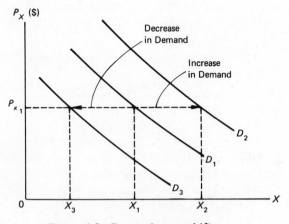

Figure 4-3. Demand curve shifts.

DEMAND ELASTICITIES

We shall first define three demand elasticities and then explain the purposes they serve. **Price elasticity of demand** (e_P) is the ratio of the percentage change in the quantity demanded of a good to the associated percentage change in the price of the good. **Cross-elasticity of demand** (e_{PXY}) is the ratio of the percentage change in the quantity demanded of a good to the associated percentage change in the price of another good. **Income elasticity of demand** (e_N) is the ratio of the percentage change in the quantity demanded of a good to the associated percentage change in the income of consumers. More compactly,

$$e_P = \frac{\Delta X}{X} \div \frac{\Delta P}{P} = \frac{\Delta X}{X} \cdot \frac{P}{\Delta P} = \frac{P}{X} \cdot \frac{\Delta X}{\Delta P}$$

$$e_{PXY} = \frac{\Delta X}{X} \div \frac{\Delta P_Y}{P_Y} = \frac{\Delta X}{X} \cdot \frac{P_Y}{\Delta P_Y} = \frac{P_Y}{X} \cdot \frac{\Delta X}{\Delta P_Y}$$

$$e_N = \frac{\Delta X}{X} \div \frac{\Delta N}{N} = \frac{\Delta X}{X} \cdot \frac{N}{\Delta N} = \frac{N}{X} \cdot \frac{\Delta X}{\Delta N}$$

The symbol Δ stands for a small change in a variable; thus elasticities are simply ratios between percentage changes in variables.

Elasticities are objective measures of responsiveness, and they eliminate misleading appearances caused by differences in units of measurement or in scale. This can best be appreciated by means of an example. Table 4-2 presents a simple, hypothetical demand schedule, or the tabular equivalent of the demand curve. This relationship is plotted in Figure 4-4 in both graph (a) and graph (b), but graph (b) has a somewhat compressed quantity scale that gives the same

Table 4-2. A Hypothetical Demand Schedule

Price ($)	Quantity Demanded (pounds)
9	1
8	2
7	3
6	4
5	5
4	6
3	7
2	8
1	9

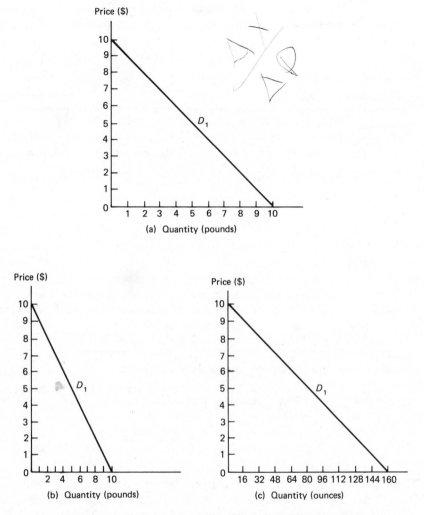

Figure 4-4. The same demand curve differently presented.

demand curve a different appearance. In graph (c), pounds are con-
verted to ounces, and although this does not change the demand
relationship, it may mislead a careless observer. In all three graphs
the price elasticity of demand is the same at corresponding points
on the graph. The elasticity concept also makes it possible to compare the demand relationship for two different goods whose quantities may be expressed in noncomparable units, such as steel (tons)
and gasoline (gallons). The price elasticities of demand calculated

for each of these goods are independent of the units involved and are therefore comparable as elasticities. Although we have been referring to the price elasticity of demand, the foregoing considerations also apply to the income elasticity and cross-elasticity concepts.

Calculating Price Elasticity

Table 4-2 can be used to illustrate how price elasticity is calculated. Since the formula calls for small changes in price and quantity, let us suppose that the price declines from $4 to $3.90 and that the quantity demanded increases from 6 pounds to 6.1 pounds. Then

$$e_P = \frac{\Delta X/X}{\Delta P/P} = \frac{.10/6}{.10/4.00} = \frac{.10}{6} \cdot \frac{4.00}{-.10} = -.67$$

Of course, we could have based our calculations on smaller changes in price and quantity, and this would have produced a different value for e_P. Therefore, our value is only an approximation to the e_P of the curve at the point $4. The inverse relationship between price and quantity means that e_P is always a negative number, but by convention the minus sign is usually omitted.

If we look at Figure 4-4(a), it might appear that the elasticity should be the same at every point on the line. In fact, it is different at every point on all negatively sloped linear demand curves and on all curvilinear demand curves except the rectangular hyperbola. This becomes clear if we reconsider the formula

$$e_P = \frac{P}{X} \cdot \frac{\Delta X}{\Delta P}$$

The $\Delta X/\Delta P$ part does stay constant for all straight-line demand curves, as in our example in Figure 4-4(a), where the demand "curve" is a straight line. But this constant is multiplied by P/X, which is necessarily different at every point on the line, and hence e_P must vary from point to point.

Arc Elasticity of Demand

As the changes in price and quantity, which are used to compute e_P, get larger, e_P becomes less accurate. For large changes (large ΔX and ΔP), it is necessary to compute the **arc elasticity of demand**, instead of the point elasticity that we approximated before. The arc elasticity involves using the average price and the average quantity, rather than the price and quantity, at either end point of the change.

The elasticity formula becomes

$$e_P = \frac{\Delta X}{(X_1 + X_2)/2} \div \frac{\Delta P}{(P_1 + P_2)/2} = \frac{\Delta X}{(X_1 + X_2)/2} \cdot \frac{(P_1 + P_2)/2}{\Delta P}$$

$$= \frac{P_1 + P_2}{X_1 + X_2} \cdot \frac{\Delta X}{\Delta P}$$

Turning again to Figure 4-4(a), suppose we wanted to find the elasticity if we were given a decline in price from \$9 to \$7, and a corresponding increase in quantity from 1 to 3:

$$e_P = \frac{9.00 + 7.00}{1 + 3} \cdot \frac{2}{-2} = \frac{16}{4} \cdot -1 = -4.00$$

For comparison, let us compute the arc elasticity for a price decline from \$9 to \$8, with a quantity increase from 1 to 2:

$$e_P = \frac{9.00 + 8.00}{1 + 2} \cdot \frac{1}{-1} = \frac{17}{3} \cdot -1 = -5.67$$

However calculated, the numerical value of e_P can range from 0 to $-\infty$. As we pointed out, the minus sign is usually ignored, and the elasticities of demand curves are classified as follows: elastic, if $e_P > 1$; inelastic, if $e_P < 1$; and unit elasticity, if $e_P = 1$. If $e_P = 0$ the demand curve is a vertical line and is called perfectly inelastic; if $e_P = \infty$ the curve is a horizontal line and is called perfectly elastic. A single demand curve may range from $e_P > 1$ to $e_P = 1$ to $e_P < 1$, as shown in Figure 4-5.

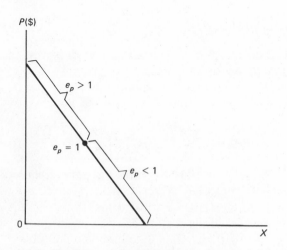

Figure 4-5. Elasticity of demand changes from point to point.

Elastic and Inelastic Demand

Some generalizations can be made regarding the relationship between price elasticity and the nature of the good. If a good is in the elastic range of its demand curve, a 1% increase in price will result in a decrease in the quantity demanded in excess of 1%. We can expect the demand for the good to be increasingly elastic to the extent that it has numerous and close substitutes. For example, if a gasoline refiner increases the price of his regular gas much above that of his competitors, it is likely that his sales will fall off rather sharply as drivers start switching to the other similar gasolines. Another factor that influences price elasticity is the number of different uses for a good. In general, if a good can be put to many uses it will tend to be elastic because, as the price declines, additional markets for the product will open up. Finally, if the cost of a good represents a negligible proportion of the consumer's total income, fairly large changes in price might not change the quantity purchased very much since the cost to the consumer would be relatively minor both before and after the change. In this case, the demand would tend to be inelastic. Note that it is frequently misleading to apply these characteristics pertaining to elasticity in isolation. For example, water has many uses, such as for drinking, washing (people, clothes, cars, etc.), cooking, lawns, and swimming pools. This implies an elastic demand. However, in most of its uses water has few or no substitutes, which implies an inelastic demand. Thus, it is necessary to take all factors into account, and to weigh the relative importance of each before concluding that the demand for a product is elastic or inelastic. Often, this can be decided only after a careful empirical investigation.

Cross-Elasticity of Demand

Let us turn to another of our elasticity measures, the cross-elasticity of demand. We defined cross-elasticity as the ratio of the percentage change in the quantity demanded of one good (say X) to the percentage change in the price of another good (say Y)—that is,

$$e_{PXY} = \frac{\Delta X}{X} \div \frac{\Delta P_Y}{P_Y} = \frac{P_Y}{X} \cdot \frac{\Delta X}{\Delta P_Y}$$

Unlike price elasticity, which measures a negative relationship, cross-elasticities may be negative or positive, depending on whether the two goods are complements or substitutes; therefore the sign of the relationship must be indicated. Recall that two goods are complements if they are used together, like crackers and cheese. A decline in the price of crackers results in a larger consumption of crackers and in additional purchases of cheese to go with the crackers, if everything else remains unchanged. Therefore, the cross-elasticity would be negative. For example, if the purchase of cheese increased 1% with a 1% decline in the price of crackers, the cross-elasticity would be −1.

Two products are good substitutes to the extent that they both can satisfy the same need, like butter and margarine. The cross-elasticity of demand for substitutes is positive. For example, an increase in the price of butter would lead consumers to buy less butter and more margarine, thereby resulting in an increase in both the price of butter and the quantity of margarine purchased.

Income Elasticity of Demand

Income elasticity of demand measures the change in the demand for a good relative to a change in income:

$$e_N = \frac{\Delta X}{X} \div \frac{\Delta N}{N} = \frac{N}{X} \cdot \frac{\Delta X}{\Delta N}$$

Note that, in the case of income elasticity, it is the price of the good that is held constant while income varies. Income elasticity is positive, and larger purchases are associated with a rise in income, except in the case of inferior goods. The consumer purchases less of an inferior good when income rises; for example, potatoes are an inferior good for many consumers who prefer less starch in their diet as their income rises, and so they switch from potatoes to other foods.

Elasticity and Total Expenditures

If we know the price elasticity of the market demand curve, we can predict how a price change will affect the total amount of money spent on the good. Since the total expenditures on a good constitute the total revenue or receipts of the firm or firms selling this good, the way in which a price change affects spending is important. Recall that total expenditure equals price times quantity. If the demand for the good is elastic ($e_P > 1$), a given percentage decline in price will be associated with a greater percentage increase in the quantity purchased and therefore total expenditures (= total business receipts) will increase. This result can be seen in Figure 4-6(a). At price P_1 consumers purchase X_1 of the good, and the total amount spent on the good is equal to $P_1 \cdot X_1$; at price P_2 the quantity demanded

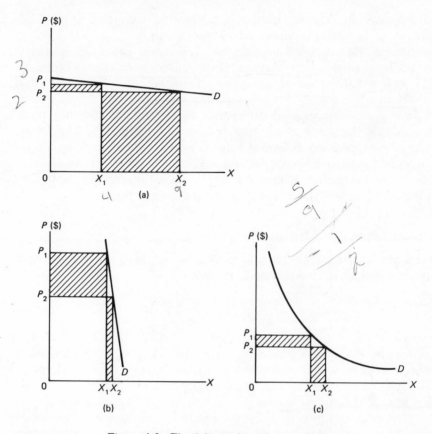

Figure 4-6. Elasticity and total expenditures.

increases to X_2, and total expenditures are $P_2 \cdot X_2$. On the graph it is easy to see that $P_2 \cdot X_2 > P_1 \cdot X_1$. Another way of seeing that a price reduction leads to greater spending on the good when demand is elastic is to compare the amount of spending lost (equal to the area of the small rectangle with vertical lines) because of the price decline with the gain in spending (area with horizontal lines). Of course, just the opposite is true in the event of a price increase.

On the other hand, if the demand for the good is inelastic, a price decrease leads to smaller total spending on the good, as in Figure 4-6(b). The decline in price from P_1 to P_2 results in a loss of spending equal to the area of the rectangle with vertical lines, but the corresponding gain due to the increase in quantity from X_1 to X_2 is smaller (area with horizontal lines), and so total spending and business revenue fall. In the case of a demand curve having unitary elasticity at all points, which occurs only if the demand curve assumes the shape of a rectangular hyperbola, as shown in Figure 4-6(c), a change in price up or down does not change total expenditures.

Another way of depicting the relationship between elasticity and total revenue is illustrated in Figure 4-7. The demand curve described in Figure 4-5 is shown along with the corresponding total revenue curve. Throughout the elastic portion of the demand curve, a decline in price is associated with rising total revenue; whereas total revenue falls as we move down the inelastic stretch of the demand curve. The total revenue curve attains a maximum at the point of unitary elasticity, where the demand curve changes from elastic to inelastic.

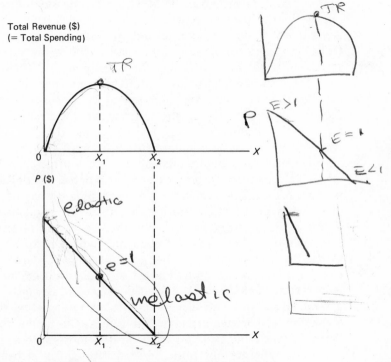

Figure 4-7. Relationship between elasticity and total revenue.

APPLICATION: MEASURING ELASTICITIES

Price Elasticity of Demand

Price elasticity of demand is the primary measure of the demand relationship between price and quantity of a good. Therefore, it is not surprising that economists have employed various statistical techniques for the purpose of determining actual elasticities. The statistical problems associated with finding empirical elasticities are part of an area of economics known as econometrics, which ties together economic theory, mathematics, and statistics. There are numerous technical problems, here, but we must ignore them as they would carry us too far afield.

Elasticity values are of interest not only to economists; they are also important to businessmen and to government policymakers. As we have already seen in this chapter, whether total dollar expenditures and receipts rise or fall with a price change hinges on elasticity. This kind of information is vital to a businessman contemplating a change in the present or future price for his good, as well as to a government body considering such policies as price supports or controls. But measures of elasticity must be used with caution. There are statistical problems involved in finding them, and for the same good they tend to vary from one country to another, and from time to time in the same country. For example, consumers would respond differently to a change in the price of wine in France, where wine is an everyday drink, from the way they would in the United States, where wine is considered more of a luxury. Also, if consumers are allowed sufficient time to adjust fully to a price change, then price elasticity will tend to be greater as compared with elasticity associated with initial adjustment.[1] The foregoing discussion accounts for differences in the price elasticity of a specific good because of variations in time and place. On the other hand, the factors that determine whether the demand for a good will tend to be elastic or inelastic, as compared with other goods, were considered earlier in this chapter under the heading "Elastic and Inelastic Demand."

A review of the factors that influence the price elasticity of a good at any given time and place is helpful in interpreting the sample of estimated elasticities given in Table 4-3. The staple food products listed in the table have an inelastic demand relationship, indicating that consumers cannot find good substitutes for such basic foods as milk, flour, sugar, and eggs; since their purchases do not change greatly with price changes, demand for them is inelastic. But expenditures on such items as restaurant meals and shoe maintenance can be cut back more readily in the event of a price rise; that is, demands tend to be elastic in these cases.

Income Elasticity of Demand

Recall that income elasticity of demand refers to the percentage change in the quantity demanded associated with a given percentage

Table 4-3. Some Estimated Price Elasticities of Demand

Good	Price Elasticity
Milk	− .20*
Cheese	− .20*
Beef	− .50*
Pork	− .45*
Flour	− .15*
Sugar	− .35*
Eggs	− .43†
Beer	− .87†
Cigarettes	− .39†
Shoes	− .91‡
Medical Care	− .31‡
Motion Pictures	− .87‡
Restaurant Meals	−2.27‡
Shoe Cleaning and Repairs	−1.31‡
Tableware	−1.54‡

SOURCE: *H. Wold and L. Jureen, *Demand Analysis* (New York: John Wiley & Sons, Inc., 1953); †R. Stone, *The Measurement of Consumers' Expenditure and Behaviour in the United Kingdom, 1920–1938,* Vol. 1 (Cambridge: Cambridge University Press, 1954); ‡H. S. Houthakker and L. D. Taylor, *Consumer Demand in the United States: Analysis and Projections,* 2nd ed. (Cambridge, Mass.: Harvard University Press, 1970).

change in consumer income. A **normal good** is one that has a positive income elasticity, whereas an **inferior good** is defined as a good with a negative income elasticity. Some actual income elasticities for Sweden are given in Table 4-4. There are two inferior goods in the table, flour and margarine; that is, if income rises by 1.0%, consumers will buy 0.36% less flour and 0.20% less margarine. Explanations for these results might be that consumers bake less of their own bread as they become more affluent, and they substitute butter for margarine to put on their bread. The other goods in the table are all normal goods with elasticities ranging from 0.07 for milk and cream to 1.48 for restaurant meals. In general, normal goods with low income elasticities tend to be necessities, whereas high elasticities are usually associated with luxuries. For example, the 0.07 value for milk and cream indicates that consumers will purchase about the same amount of these essentials as income varies, but they will vary the luxury of dining out proportionately more or less as their income goes up or down.

Cross-Elasticity of Demand

Cross-elasticity of demand shows the ratio of the percentage change in the quantity demanded of a good to the percentage change

Table 4-4. Some Estimated Income Elasticities of Demand
for Sweden

Good	Income Elasticity
Cheese	0.34
Eggs	0.37
Milk and Cream	0.07
Flour	−0.36
Bread	0.24
Butter	0.42
Margarine	−0.20
Liquors	1.00
Tobacco	1.02
Restaurant Meals	1.48

SOURCE: H. Wold and L. Jureen, *Demand Analysis* (New York: John Wiley & Sons, Inc., 1953).

in the price of some other good. As such this measure indicates whether the two goods are substitutes (a positive cross-elasticity) or complements (a negative cross-elasticity). Table 4-5 presents some estimated cross-elasticities of demand for the United Kingdom. Most of these cross-elasticities indicate substitute goods. For example, margarine and butter are good substitutes, as are imported meat and domestic meat; however, butter and cheese show a complementary relationship, as do fresh fruit and sugar.

Table 4-5. Some Estimated Cross-elasticities of Demand

Good	Cross-elasticity, with Respect to the Price of	Cross-elasticity
Margarine	Butter	+1.01
Cheese	Butter	−0.61
Imported Beef and Veal	Domestic Beef and Veal	+1.57
Imported Beef and Veal	Fresh Fish	+0.33
Condensed Milk	Fresh Milk	+2.25
Sugar	All Fresh Fruit	−0.28
All Food	Drink and Tobacco	+0.23

SOURCE: R. Stone, *The Measurement of Consumers' Expenditure and Behaviour in the United Kingdom, 1920–1938*, Vol. 1 (Cambridge: Cambridge University Press, 1954).

SUMMARY

The market demand curve is simply the summation of all individual demand curves. That is, the total quantity of the good demanded at any given price is the total amount demanded by all consumers of the good at that price. Since we demonstrated in Chapter 2 that individual demand curves have a negative slope, it follows that the market demand curve also has a negative slope. The market demand curve is important to economists because, along with the market supply curve, it determines the equilibrium price of the good, as well as the total quantity of the good that is bought and sold at that price. As with individual demand curves, the market demand curve may shift to the right or to the left. A shift in the curve is caused by a change in demand-related variables other than the price of the good. Such variables include consumer tastes and preferences, consumer income, prices of other goods, and consumer expectations.

Demand elasticities are objective measures of consumer responsiveness. We defined three different elasticities of demand: price elasticity of demand, cross-elasticity of demand, and income elasticity of demand. Price elasticity of demand (e_P) is the ratio of the percentage change in the quantity demanded of a good to the associated percentage change in the price of the good. A demand curve, or any portion thereof, is called elastic if $e_P > 1$; inelastic, if $e_P < 1$; unitary elasticity, if $e_P = 1$; perfectly elastic, if $e_P = \infty$; and perfectly inelastic, if $e_P = 0$. Generally, the demand for a good is increasingly elastic to the extent that it has numerous and close substitutes. In addition, the price elasticity of a good will determine how a price change will affect total expenditures on the good. If the demand for the good is elastic, a decline in its price will result in an increase in total expenditures on the good, and a price increase will lead to a decline in total expenditures. If demand is inelastic, a price decline will bring about a decline in total expenditures, and a price increase will yield greater total expenditures.

Cross-elasticity of demand (e_{PXY}) is the ratio of the percentage change in the quantity demanded of a good to the associated percentage change in the price of another good. Unlike price elasticity, which measures a negative relationship, cross-elasticity of demand may be negative or positive, depending on whether the two goods are complements or substitutes. If two goods are used together, they are complements, and their cross-elasticity is negative. If two goods can be used to satisfy the same need, they are substitutes, and their cross-elasticity is positive.

Income elasticity of demand (e_N) is the ratio of the percentage change in the quantity demanded of a good to the associated percentage change in the income of consumers. For most goods, income elasticity is positive, meaning that consumers will buy more of the good if their income rises. But in the case of inferior goods, consumers will purchase less of the good if their income goes up.

Economists employ various statistical techniques for the purpose of measuring actual elasticities of demand. These measures of elasticity must be used with caution because of the statistical problems involved in finding them; and because for the same product, elasticities tend to vary from place to place and also from the short run to the long run. As examples of empirical elasticities, economists have found that staple food products, such as milk, flour, sugar, and eggs, display inelastic demand relationships. On the other hand, demand is elastic in the case of restaurant meals and shoe maintenance. Studies have shown that income elasticities are positive for such goods as milk and restaurant meals, but negative for flour and margarine. Measures of actual cross-elasticities of demand indicate that although butter and margarine are good substitutes, butter and cheese show a complementary relationship.

Problems and Questions

1. You are given the following demand relationship:

Price ($)	Quantity Demanded (Units)
5.00	1
4.75	2
4.50	3
4.25	4
4.00	5

a. Suppose that the price declines from $5.00 to $4.75. How would you calculate the price elasticity of demand?
b. Now calculate the price elasticity if the price falls from $4.75 to $4.50.
c. How do you account for the different results in questions (a) and (b)?

2. You are given the following information on goods X and Y:

Price of X ($)	Quantity Demanded of X	Quantity Demanded of Y
3.00	10	12
2.85	11	13
2.75	12	16
2.65	13	20

Are these good substitutes or complements? Explain your answer.

3. What information would you need in order to determine whether or not a good is an inferior good?
4. What is the relationship between price elasticity of demand and total expenditures on the good? Why is this relationship important?
5. If the price elasticity of demand for a good were very inelastic, what would you conclude about the nature of this good?
6. Why must empirical studies of elasticities be interpreted with care?
7. Define cross-elasticity of demand. What would you conclude if two goods have a negative cross-elasticity of demand?
8. What causes a demand curve to shift to the right?

Note

1. For example, see H. S. Houthakker and L. D. Taylor, *Consumer Demand in the United States: Analysis and Projections*, 2d ed., Chap. 3. Cambridge, Mass.: Harvard University Press, 1970.

Recommended Reading

Houthakker, H. S., and L. D. Taylor. *Consumer Demand in the United States: Analysis and Projections*, 2d ed., Chaps. 1-3. Cambridge, Mass.: Harvard University Press, 1970.

Marshall, Alfred. *Principles of Economics*, 8th ed., Book 3, Chap. 4. London: Macmillan and Co., Ltd., 1920.

Robinson, Joan. *The Economics of Imperfect Competition*, pp. 29-40. London: Macmillan & Co., Ltd., 1933.

Schultz, Henry. *The Theory and Measurement of Demand*, Chaps. 1-4. Chicago: The University of Chicago Press, 1938.

Wold, H., and L. Jureen. *Demand Analysis*, Chaps. 1-3 and 16-18. New York: John Wiley and Sons, Inc., 1953.

5

The Theory of Production

The major objective of the preceding chapters about the consumer was the derivation of the market demand curve, which, together with the market supply curve, determines the price of a good. We now turn our attention from the demand side of economics to the supply side, with the derivation of the market supply curve as our goal. To understand the forces at work behind supply, it is necessary to start with the theory of production, the subject of this chapter. The theory of production explores the relationship between productive inputs, like labor and capital, and the associated output of a good or service. The behavior of the firm's input-output relationship is essential to the explanation of how costs vary with the output of the good or service; that is, in explaining the cost of production. Costs, in turn, play a vital role in the determination of the firm's output and hence of the supply of the good. We start with the business firm, since this is where production takes place.

THE CONCEPT OF THE FIRM

The business firm is the basic unit of production in our economic system, and as such it is the subject of intensive study by economists.

In recent years the behavior of the firm has attracted the attention of sociologists, statisticians, mathematicians, and other specialists, all of whom view the firm as a fertile field wherein to apply the tools of their trade. Economists of course stand to benefit greatly from this interdisciplinary activity, because the firm is in reality a complex entity and it is becoming increasingly clear that the very simple abstractions formulated by economists in the past have rather severe limitations. Although these new developments and insights do indeed add to our understanding of the firm, in the following analysis we shall concentrate on the basic theory of the firm as developed over the decades by economists. In fact, many of the recent contributions to the theory have taken the form of alterations, revisions, substitutions, or additions to the basic theory. Therefore, a thorough understanding of this basic theory remains a prerequisite for further work.

The firm as we shall view it is an economic unit which transforms productive inputs into goods and services demanded by other economic units; these may include consumers, other firms, units of the government, or foreign purchasers. The firm's transformation process is conducted by a risk taker called an entrepreneur, whose risk involves the possibility of monetary loss. To induce the entrepreneur to assume this risk of loss there must also be a possibility of profit. The entrepreneur always prefers more profit to less profit, and therefore he attempts to maximize the profit of the firm. Much of the criticism directed toward the theory of the firm concerns this fundamental assumption of the traditional theory: that the entrepreneur strives to maximize profit under all conditions. Nevertheless, we shall retain this assumption in order to present the basic theory of entrepreneurial behavior.

Before we can determine how the entrepreneur goes about maximizing profit, or even what we mean by profit, it is necessary to examine the nature and behavior of production and costs.

THE PRODUCTION FUNCTION,
THE SHORT RUN, AND THE LONG RUN

The production function expresses the relationship between various combinations of the firm's productive inputs—labor, capital, land, and management—and the maximum associated outputs during a specified period of time. The production function is really a technological relationship, which specifies the maximum amount of output obtainable per unit of time from any given combination of inputs. We are referring to physical units of input and output, not dollar amounts. Mathematically, the production function can be expressed in the same form as any other functional relationship. If X denotes quantity of output, and L_1, L_2, L_3, and so forth stand for inputs, then the production function can be written as

$$X = f(L_1, L_2, L_3, \cdots, L_n)$$

This brings us to another important set of concepts in microeconomic theory, the short run and the long run. In the **short run**, one or more of the inputs is assumed to be constant and one or more of the inputs is allowed to vary. In the simplest case of only two inputs, say capital and labor, capital is usually held fixed and labor is variable; hence, capital is called the **fixed input** and labor is the **variable input**. In the **long run**, all inputs are assumed to be variable. Note that the distinction between the short run and the long run does not depend on calendar time, such as months or years, but only on the variability of the inputs. For example, suppose we are considering a factory with 10,000 square feet of working area, and we are interested in the behavior of output as more workers are employed: This would be a short-run problem. Suppose now that we double the size of the factory, and we also double the number of workers, and then consider the effect on output. Assuming that capital and labor are the only inputs, we have now varied all the inputs and so are now dealing with a long-run problem.

The Short Run and the Law of Diminishing Returns

Just as the law of demand is basic to the theory of the consumer, the **law of diminishing returns** is fundamental to the theory of production. We can state this law as follows: If successive identical units of one productive input are added to a fixed amount of one or more other inputs, then beyond a certain point (called the point of diminishing returns) the corresponding successive increments of the output will get smaller and smaller.

As usual, certain definite assumptions must be made if this "law" is to be satisfied. First, we must assume that the different inputs can be combined in variable proportions, rather than only in a rigidly fixed relationship such as one unit of labor to one unit of capital; sometimes the law is referred to as the law of variable proportions. Second, the state of technology is fixed; that is, the law will only be valid, and we can only observe or test the operation of the law if technology is not allowed to change during the process. Third, all but one of the inputs must be held constant or fixed. Fourth, the units of the variable input are identical, both quantitatively and qualitatively.

Why the law is believed to hold under these conditions is best demonstrated by a method of logic called a *reductio ad absurdum*, a reduction to an absurdity. Let us start by assuming that the law is false. If it is really false, we should be able to continue indefinitely to add units of an input to a constant amount of another productive input, and the resulting increments of the good will never get smaller. To use an example that has become familiar to all economists, we could continue to plant units of wheat seed in a flower pot and the resulting additions to our wheat crop would never decrease. But this is absurd, for if it were possible we could in fact grow the world's wheat requirements in one flower pot.

On the basis of numerous similar empirical situations the empirical generalization called the law of diminishing returns has been formulated. If we could use theories or other laws to explain why diminishing returns must always occur under the specified conditions, then we would indeed possess a law. But the theories necessary to accomplish this objective are those of physical science, since diminishing returns refers to a relationship between physical entities.

The connection between the short run and the law of diminishing returns should now be clear. The law of diminishing returns explains the behavior or shape of the production function in the short run, when only one input is allowed to vary, the other inputs being held constant. The production function under these conditions can be written as

$$X = f(L_1, \overline{L}_2, \overline{L}_3, \cdots, \overline{L}_m)$$

where a bar over an L indicates that it is held constant.

The typical short-run production function, reflecting the law of diminishing returns, is illustrated in Figure 5-1(a). As units of the variable input are added to the fixed input, total output or product (*TP*) first increases at an increasing rate, meaning that the additions to total product are getting larger and larger. This continues until the point of diminishing returns D is reached, after which each additional unit of input results in smaller and smaller additions to total product. Notice that total product keeps growing even after the point of diminishing returns, but it finally reaches a maximum at point M.

The additions to total product are plotted in Figure 5-1(b) and the resulting curve is called the marginal product curve. The **marginal**

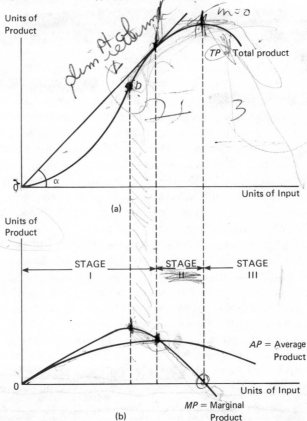

Figure 5-1. The production function and the law of the diminishing returns.

product (MP) is defined as the change in total product corresponding to a unit change in input. The marginal product curve is at its maximum at the point of diminishing returns. It becomes zero when the total product curve reaches its maximum, and less than zero thereafter, indicating that an additional unit of input results in a reduction of total product, or the marginal product is negative.

In Figure 5-1(b) we have drawn an **average product** (AP) curve that shows, at any input, the total product divided by that input. The maximum point on the AP curve can be derived from the TP curve. First, draw a straight line or ray which starts at the origin and is tangent to the TP curve. Next, drop a perpendicular from the point of tangency to the axis, at which input the AP is at a maximum. The angle α formed by this ray and the horizontal axis is at its maximum, which is to say that the tangent of α, or total product divided by total input, is maximized. Note that $MP = AP$ where AP is at a maximum.

Table 5-1 presents a hypothetical example of this short-run input-output relationship with one variable input, that is, the same kind of situation as we have in Figure 5-1. The table shows that MP continues to increase until four units of input have been added but starts to decline when the fifth unit is added. Therefore, with the fifth unit we encounter diminishing returns, even though the total product continues to increase until the ninth unit of input is employed. When the ninth unit is added the total product declines, which means that MP is negative, as the table shows.

Turning back to Figure 5-1(b), we see that there are three stages of production indicated on the graph. First, consider stage III, in which MP is negative. If the firm wished to maximize profits, it would never carry production into stage III, even if the variable input were costless, because the total product would actually be decreased by the negative contribution of these units. It is shown below in the section "Isoquants and the Stages of Production" that in stage I the marginal product of the fixed input is negative, and hence the firm would not operate in stage I. Therefore, if production is to take place, it will occur somewhere in stage II. But we simply have not developed our theory far enough at this point to determine exactly where production will occur within stage II. In fact, much of our attention in the following chapters is directed to this problem.

Table 5-1. Hypothetical Short-Run Production Schedule

Units of Input	Total Product	Average Product	Marginal Product
1	10	10	10
2	24	12	14
3	39	13	15
4	56	14	17
5	65	13	9
6	72	12	7
7	77	11	5
8	80	10	3
9	72	8	− 8

MULTIPLE VARIABLE INPUTS AND ISOQUANTS

So far we have examined the behavior of total output, as successive units of one variable input are added to a constant input. Generally, however, the firm finds that it must consider adding more than one variable input. Figure 5-2 shows such a situation, assuming that two inputs (e.g., labor and capital) are added to a constant amount of land. The curve in Figure 5-2 is called an **isoquant**: Every point on such a curve represents the same level of output (e.g., 10 units). The isoquant shows that the same output can be produced by using different combinations of the inputs; that is, the 10 units of output could be produced with L_1 and K_6, or with L_2 and K_5, and so on. It is therefore apparent that the same output can be produced with a smaller amount of capital only if the quantity of labor is increased. The rate at which one input can be substituted for another while maintaining the same level of output is called the **marginal rate of technical substitution.**

The isoquant in Figure 5-2 is drawn convex to the origin. In terms of isoquants, this is called the **diminishing marginal rate of technical substitution.** If we start off by assuming a relatively large amount of labor combined with little capital, say L_6 and K_1, and then remove one unit of labor, a relatively small amount of additional capital will maintain output at 10 units. This is because there is little capital, and hence a little additional capital will give output a big enough boost to compensate for the loss of one unit of labor. But as more capital is added and labor withdrawn, the initial highly beneficial effects of the capital are gradually exhausted and it takes larger amounts of capital to offset the loss of labor. If we reverse this process we see that the withdrawal of diminishing increments of capital is called for as additional units of labor are employed.

The relationship between the marginal rate of technical substitution and the marginal products of labor and capital can be easily demonstrated. If we remove a unit of labor, output falls by an amount equal to the marginal product of labor. To maintain output

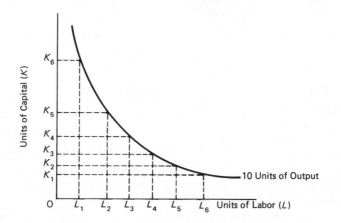

Figure 5-2. Diminishing marginal rate of technical substitution.

at 10 units, we must add enough capital so that its marginal product will make up for the lost marginal product of labor. For example, suppose that the *MP* of one unit of labor at some point on the curve is two units of output; then we must add an amount of capital such that its *MP* will be two units, for otherwise output will fall and we will move off the isoquant. Let us assume that the *MP* of one unit of capital at this point is one unit of output. Therefore, two units of capital must be added to compensate for the two units of output lost when the one unit of labor was removed. This relationship can be written as follows:

$$MRTS_{K,L} = \frac{MP_L}{MP_K} = \frac{2}{1}$$

or

$$MRTS_{K,L} \cdot MP_K = MP_L$$
$$2 \cdot 1 = 2$$

Therefore, the marginal rate of technical substitution of capital for labor is 2, which is the same as the ratio of the marginal product of labor to the marginal product of capital; or, which is the same thing, enough capital must be added so that its *MP* exactly offsets the loss of the *MP* of a unit of labor.

Suppose that we wish to use isoquants to represent higher levels of output. Given that the firm is employing the most efficient technology, greater output requires the use of more of either of the inputs or more of both inputs. This being the case, more output would be reflected by an isoquant further from the origin. This is shown in Figure 5-3, where output is increased from 10 units to 20 units by increasing both labor and capital (moving from point 1 to point 2); or by holding labor constant and increasing capital sufficiently (moving from point 1 to point 3). It is even possible to increase output when one of the inputs is decreased, provided that the other input is increased enough, as in the move from point 1 to point 4 on the graph.

Suppose now that two inputs can be efficiently employed in only one fixed ratio. For example, one worker is required to operate one machine, so that the ratio of workers to machines is always 1 : 1. In this case, the isoquant will be a right angle, as shown in Figure 5-4(a). This is known as a **fixed proportion production function**. In order to increase the level of output, both inputs must be increased in the same proportion, as shown in the graph. The slope of the ray from the origin represents the ratio of the inputs. Figure 5-4(b)

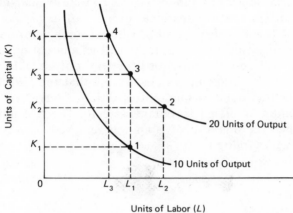

Figure 5-3. Higher levels of output.

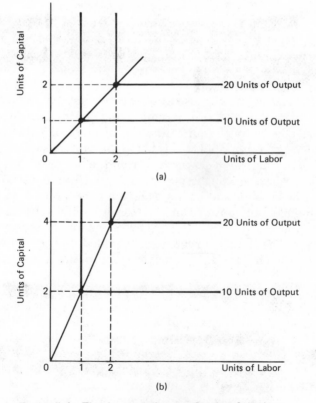

Figure 5-4. Fixed proportion production functions.

depicts another fixed proportion production function, but here the proportion of capital to labor is 2 : 1. In contrast, the isoquant approach implies a **variable proportion production function**, since a movement along an isoquant means that the firm is able to substitute one input continuously for another and maintain the same level of output; that is, at every point on the isoquant the ratio of the inputs is different.

Between the fixed proportion production function and the continuous isoquant are intermediate forms. Figure 5-5 shows a case where there are three possible ways to combine the inputs; these are usually called **processes**. Process I is a fixed proportion production function using relatively much capital and little labor for any output, whereas process III uses relatively more labor than capital. For example, the graph shows that the firm has the option of producing 10 units of output using process I (K_3 and L_1), or process II (K_2 and L_2), or process III (K_1 and L_3). The resulting isoquant is not a smooth curve, but takes on an angular shape, as shown in the graph at the 10-unit and the 20-unit levels of output.

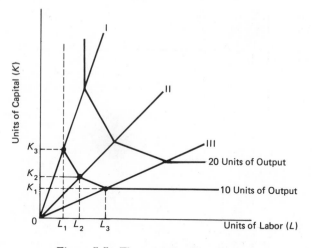

Figure 5-5. Three production processes.

Isoquants and the Law of Diminishing Returns

Assume now that the firm has only two inputs, capital and labor. Bear in mind that if both inputs can be varied, we are considering a long-run problem. But it is also possible to depict the operation of the law of diminishing returns (the short run), in terms of isoquants, by holding one of the inputs constant and allowing the other input to vary. Figure 5-6(a) shows three different isoquants representing successively higher levels of output: 10, 20, and 30 units, respectively. In Figure 5-6(b) the horizontal axis remains the same as in Figure 5-6(a), but the vertical axis now represents units of output. Assume that capital is held constant at level $\overline{K}$ in graph (a), thereby making labor the only variable input. We are now able to translate the isoquant approach into the short-run production function approach. Both graph (a) and graph (b) show that one unit of labor adds 10 units of output. In order to produce 20 units of output, it is necessary to add two more units of labor; and to increase output to 30 units, five additional units of labor are required. In other words, for each additional 10 units of output, it is necessary to employ successively larger increments of labor, which is another way of expressing the law of diminishing returns. In graph (a) this is reflected by the increasing distance between the isoquants; in graph (b), the total product curve follows the usual diminishing returns pattern of increasing at a decreasing rate.

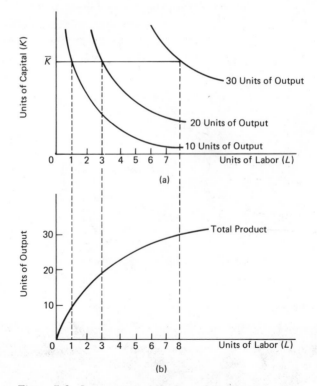

Figure 5-6. Isoquants and the law of diminishing returns.

Isoquants and the Stages of Production

Isoquants can be used to derive the economic region of production, or stage II, as explained earlier in this chapter. Figure 5-7 shows two isoquants representing 10 and 20 units of output, respectively. By holding capital constant at $\bar{K}$, we can see what happens to output if only labor is increased (short run), as we did in Figure 5-6. If labor is increased from L_1 to L_2, output rises, since there is a movement from the lower partial isoquant drawn at L_1 to the higher 10-unit isoquant. But if labor is again increased from L_2 and L_3, output falls from the 10-unit isoquant to the lower partial isoquant drawn at L_3. Since we find that the additional labor leads to less output, the marginal product of this added labor is negative. Therefore, any labor added to $\bar{K}$ beyond L_2 corresponds to stage III for labor (stage I for capital). In general, stage III is reached at the point where the isoquant changes slope from negative to positive, as shown at point 1 in the graph. In our example, the 10-unit isoquant stopped falling from left to right at input L_2 (and started to rise from left to right), so input L_2 represents the border between stage II and stage III. This border occurs at point 2 on the 20-unit isoquant. If we connect all such border points, the loci of these points form a curve called a **ridge line**. The ridge line resulting from our analysis in Figure 5-7 is *OP*.

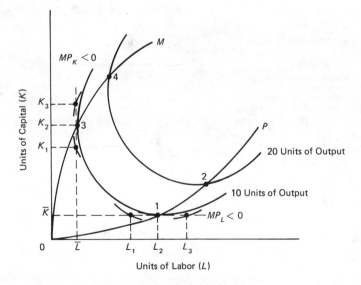

Figure 5-7. Isoquants and the economic region of production.

Now we can hold labor constant and vary capital, thereby determining the location of stage III for capital (stage I for labor). In Figure 5-7, labor is held constant at $\overline{L}$. As capital is increased from K_1 to K_2, output rises from the partial isoquant at K_1 to the higher 10-unit isoquant. But an increase in capital from K_2 to K_3 results in lower output, as shown by the lower partial isoquant at K_3. Therefore, the marginal product of capital is negative beyond point 3, and so point 3 is the borderline between stage II and stage III for capital. We can form another ridge line, OM, which is the locus of all points such as 3.

The **economic region of production**, or stage II, consists of the area within the two ridge lines OM and OP.

THE LONG RUN: RETURNS TO SCALE

We have defined the long run as meaning that all inputs are variable. Therefore, it must be emphasized that in the long run the law of diminishing returns, which assumes one or more fixed inputs, does not apply. In the long run we are concerned with the problem of how output changes when all inputs are varied in the same proportion, which is called **returns to scale**.

Suppose that capital and labor are the only inputs. We now change the amounts of capital and labor in the same proportion. Output can be affected in three possible ways. First, output can change in the same proportion as the change in capital and labor. For example, if both capital and labor are doubled, output would also double; this is referred to as **constant returns to scale**. Second, output can change by more than in proportion to the change in capital and labor. For example, a doubling of both capital and labor would increase output by more than double. This is called **increasing returns to scale**. Third, output may change by less than in proportion to the change in capital and labor. For example, if we were to double capital and labor, the increase in output would be less than double. This is known as **decreasing returns to scale**.

These long-run production relationships are illustrated in Figure 5-8, in which we again assume that there are only two inputs, capital and labor. Constant returns to scale are shown in Figure 5-8(a). The straight lines from the origin to E_1 and E_2 are called **expansion paths**. If we go from point 1 to point 2 on expansion path E_1, we use twice as much labor (L_1 to L_2) and twice the amount of capital (K_1 to K_2) to produce double the output (10 units to 20 units). The slope of an E line is determined by the ratio of capital to labor, which is constant all along the line; for example, along E_1 in the graph about one unit of capital must be employed with every two units of labor. A steeper slope indicates that more capital must be used relative to labor: E_2 shows a capital-to-labor ratio of 1 : 1.

Figure 5-8(b) illustrates a long-run production function yielding increasing returns to scale up to combination K_3L_3 at point 1, and decreasing returns to scale beyond this point. For example, if labor is doubled from L_1 to L_3 and capital is doubled from K_1 to K_3, output triples from 10 units to 30 units, which indicates increasing returns to scale. On the other hand, if labor and capital are doubled from L_4 to L_6 and K_4 to K_6, respectively, the increase in output from 40 units to 60 units is less than double, signifying decreasing returns to scale.

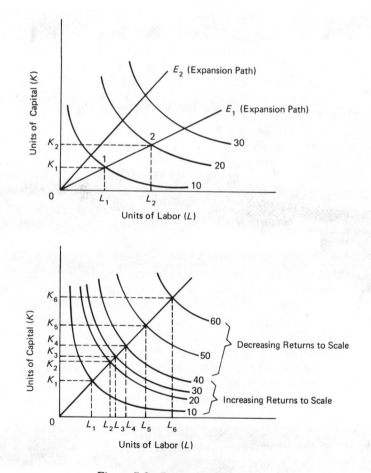

Figure 5-8. Return to scale.

Explanations of Returns to Scale

Economists have not been content merely to observe and describe returns to scale in the real world; they have also offered general explanations for returns to scale. The advantages of specialization have long been recognized by economists as being important in the development of increasing returns to scale. As a business firm grows larger, greater division of labor and more specialization become possible. This yields benefits to workers and managers in the form of greater skills, better dexterity, and more knowhow. Larger size may also make it feasible to replace certain all-purpose machinery or equipment with more specialized machines, which are usually more productive as they are specifically designed to perform a particular job in the most efficient manner.

A second factor in the explanation of increasing returns to scale is the change of techniques made possible by growing size. As a firm expands, a different and more efficient technology may become feasible. For example, certain types of advantageous mass-production techniques and equipment may not be applicable until a certain large size has been achieved. In addition, growing firms may benefit simply from changing the proportions of their operations. For example, a 100- X 100-foot factory has 10,000 square feet of floor space, whereas, if the outside dimensions are doubled to 200 X 200 feet, the floor space is quadrupled to 40,000 square feet. Many similar examples can be found. Finally, the large firm often gains from its sheer size through quantity discounts on purchases, better banking connections, more elaborate research facilities, and the ability to support basic research where the payoff may be distant but substantial.

Decreasing returns to scale generally result from problems associated with the management and coordination of very large enterprises. Beyond a certain point, which varies from industry to industry, the advantages of size finally give way to the ever-growing difficulties of managing a big business. As the firm expands, managerial systems must be developed, authority must be delegated, paperwork proliferates, communication networks grow, and red tape abounds. It is no wonder that businessmen show such keen interest in computers, copying and duplicating machines, and private airplanes as means of coping with these problems, and, perhaps, putting off the onset of decreasing returns to scale.

There is, finally, the possibility of a balance between increasing returns to scale and decreasing returns to scale which may prevail over a considerable range of output. If this is the case, in effect there will be constant returns to scale.

APPLICATION: EMPIRICAL PRODUCTION FUNCTIONS

Economists not only want to explain the relationship between inputs and their associated output in theoretical terms (the theoretical production function discussed in this chapter), but they also wish to determine how this relationship behaves in specific cases. They want to define and measure production functions for specific firms or industries, or even whole economies. There are three main methods employed in the measurement of production functions.

The first method relies on information supplied by engineers and technicians who are familiar with the production process being analyzed and measured. A well-known example of this approach is the study of crude oil pipelines by Leslie Cookenboo, Jr.[1] Cookenboo used engineering data to derive production functions for oil pipelines. His production functions consist of two inputs: the diameter of the pipeline and the horsepower needed to pump the oil through the pipeline. The output, referred to as **throughput**, is the amount of oil that goes through the pipeline during a specific period of time, e.g., thousands of barrels per day. Cookenboo found that for any given throughput, horsepower can be substituted for pipeline diameter; within limits, diameter can be decreased if horsepower is increased. This gives rise to output (throughput) isoquants similar to those shown in Figure 5-9. The engineering explanation of the substitution of horsepower for pipeline diameter has to do with friction. As oil travels through the pipeline, friction is generated by the oil that touches the inside surface of the pipeline. Horsepower is needed to overcome this friction. As the diameter of the pipeline gets smaller, more oil touches the inside surface relative to the volume of oil passing through, hence more horsepower is required for any given throughput as the diameter gets smaller.

From the above relationships, Cookenboo found that if pipeline diameter is held constant and horsepower is increased, then the throughput curve will reflect increasing returns over a considerable range. Finally, if both the pipeline diameter and the horsepower are increased by the same proportion, throughput would expand by more than this proportion. In other words, there are increasing returns to scale for crude oil pipelines.

A second method of measuring production functions involves the application of statistical techniques to cross-section data. The cross-section data of interest to the microeconomist consist of measurements of the input-output relationship for firms in an industry for a specific time period. By measuring the production functions for numerous firms in the industry, the economist may then be able to

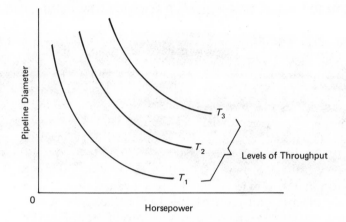

Figure 5-9. Pipeline production function.

derive a production function for the industry statistically. The functional form generally employed in these empirical studies is known as the **Cobb-Douglas function.** It has the following form:

$$X = AL^{\alpha}K^{\beta}$$

where X is output; L and K are inputs; and A, α, and β are parameters that are determined from the data. This function has some interesting characteristics. The exponent α indicates the percentage increase in output that would result from a one percent increase in L, assuming K is held constant. Likewise a one percent increase in K, with L held constant, will increase output by β%. The exponents α and β are called **output elasticity coefficients.** The sum of the exponents, $\alpha + \beta$, can be interpreted in terms of returns to scale: $\alpha + \beta = 1$ denotes constant returns to scale; $\alpha + \beta > 1$ signifies increasing returns to scale; and $\alpha + \beta < 1$ means decreasing returns to scale.

Table 5-2 presents some estimates of the Cobb-Douglas coefficients α and β from various cross-section studies. The table shows, for example, that if the labor input (L) had been increased by 1% in the Indian coal industry in 1951, then output would have increased by 0.71%. Similarly, if the capital input had been increased by 1% in this industry, then output would have risen by 0.44%. Since $\alpha + \beta > 1$, there were increasing returns to scale in the Indian coal industry at that time.

The third method of measuring production functions makes use of time series data, which give the input-output relationship for a particular industry for each year in a series of years. In this approach,

Table 5-2. Values of Cobb-Douglas Coefficients

Industry	Year	Country	α	β	$\alpha + \beta$
Cotton	1951	India	.92	.12	1.04
Jute	1951	India	.84	.14	.98
Sugar	1951	India	.59	.33	.92
Coal	1951	India	.71	.44	1.15
Paper	1951	India	.64	.45	1.09
Chemicals	1952	India	.82	.40	1.22
Electricity	1951	India	.20	.67	.87
Gas	1945	France	.83	.10	.93

SOURCE: A. A. Walters, "Production and Cost Functions," *Econometrica*, Vol. 31 (Jan.-April, 1963), pp. 1–66.

for example, data would be collected on the annual amounts of labor and capital employed to produce the associated annual output of the Canadian automobile industry for each year from 1918 to 1930. This study was actually carried out and it was found that α = 0.96 and β = 0.41.[2] Since $\alpha + \beta$ = 1.37, the industry exhibited increasing returns to scale during this period. Compared to cross-section studies, there are relatively few time series studies for specific industries. In general, the results of these studies have been somewhat disappointing and this method has been applied with more success to groups of industries or sectors of the economy.[3]

Innovation: The Concept of X-Efficiency

At the beginning of this chapter, we defined the production function as a technological relationship that determines the maximum amount of output obtainable per unit of time from any specific combination of inputs. This definition implies that the theoretical production function is efficient, since it includes only the maximum output associated with each input combination. This is called **technical efficiency**. In like manner, producing an output with more than the minimum amount of inputs necessary to produce that output represents an inefficient combination of inputs.

Professor Harvey Leibenstein published an article in 1966 in which he explained another kind of efficiency (and inefficiency), labeled X-efficiency (and X-inefficiency).[4] Professor Leibenstein points out that in many real-world firms, neither labor nor management work as hard or as effectively as they might. If this is the case, then output is not at a maximum relative to these inputs, which is what Leibenstein calls X-inefficiency. The major reason why labor and management might not maximize their effort is lack of *motivation*. When people and organizations are not sufficiently motivated, whether because incentives or competitive pressures are lacking, they will not function at maximum efficiency. Leibenstein explains that the members of a firm have some degree of discretion over the amount of effort they expend, largely because labor contracts are incomplete and therefore allow firm members to interpret the extent of their jobs up to a point. Without adequate motivation of one form or another, labor and management will choose not to exert themselves as much as they could, and hence X-inefficiency will exist.

Professor Leibenstein has produced empirical evidence to support his concept of X-efficiency. For example, he cites the case of two Egyptian petroleum refineries within one-half mile of each other, wherein the labor productivity of one was twice that of the other for many years.[5] When new management was brought into the inefficient refinery, efficiency improved spectacularly with the same labor force. Leibenstein also points to a variety of studies which demonstrate that a change in worker incentive plans can increase worker productivity considerably.[6] Indeed, the so-called Hawthorne Studies have shown that even if management shows a greater interest in a group of workers, this alone can lead to increased output.[7] In general, Leibenstein believes that much of the increase in efficiency found in these studies can be traced to improvements in worker and management motivation.

More recent information in support of Professor Leibenstein's ideas can be found in an article titled "Productivity Gains from a Pat on the Back," which appeared in a leading business publication.[8] According to this article, motivational methods of increasing productivity are being used by such companies as Frito-Lay, B. F. Goodrich, Minnesota Mining & Manufacturing Co., Addressograph-Multigraph, and Warner-Lambert. The methods employed are designed to provide employees with a sense of belonging and accomplishment, and include liberal amounts of praise for a job well done. In most cases, companies using these methods to stimulate worker motivation have experienced large gains in worker productivity along with the associated reductions in costs. For example, Western Air Lines, Inc. found that when supervisors praised those employees who asked people to make reservations when they called the airline, the ratio of sales to calls rose from one in four to two in four.[9] At Collins foods International, Inc. clerical employees were praised when their reports contained fewer than the average number of errors, and the error rate fell sharply.[10] It appears that X-inefficiency is a real problem, and that businesses are now beginning to recognize the potential gains to be made in reducing X-inefficiency.

SUMMARY

The production of goods and services takes place in the business firm. The entrepreneur, who operates the firm, assumes the risk of incurring a loss in order to make a profit. We assume that the entrepreneur strives to maximize the profit of the firm. The production function is a technological relationship, which specifies the maximum amount of output of a good or a service obtainable per unit of time from any given combination of inputs, where both inputs and outputs are measured in physical units rather than dollar amounts. Production may occur in either the short run or the long run. The short run is defined as meaning that there is at least one fixed input and one variable input. In the long run it is assumed that all inputs are variable. Therefore, the distinction between the short run and the long run depends on the variability of the inputs, not on calendar time.

In the short run, the relationship between the inputs and the output of the good is governed by the law of diminishing returns. This fundamental law states that if successive identical units of one productive input are added to a fixed amount of one or more other inputs, then, beyond a certain point (called the point of diminishing returns), the corresponding successive increments of the output will get smaller and smaller. This law is based on the assumptions that the inputs can be combined in variable proportions, that the state of technology does not change, that all but one of the inputs are fixed, and that the units of the variable input are identical. Because of the law of diminishing returns, as units of the variable input are added to the fixed input, total output first increases at an increasing rate, and then at a decreasing rate until a maximum is reached. The change in total output corresponding to a unit change in input is called the marginal product, and the marginal product reaches a maximum at the point of diminishing returns.

A curve that is convex to the origin, called an isoquant, can be used to show the relationship between two variable inputs. Every point on an isoquant represents the same level of output, meaning that different combinations of the variable inputs can be used to produce the same amount of output. The rate at which one input can be substituted for another, while maintaining the same level of output, is called the marginal rate of technical substitution. If there is only one way of combining the variable inputs, then the isoquant will be a right angle, and it is called a fixed proportion production function. If there are a limited number of ways of combining the variable inputs, then each way is called a process, and the resulting isoquant has an angular shape. Isoquants can be used to demonstrate the law of diminishing returns, as well as the stages of production and the economic regions of production.

In the long run, we are concerned with the problem of how output changes when all inputs are varied in the same proportion, which is called returns to scale. If all inputs are changed in the same proportion, then output can be affected in three possible ways. First, output may be changed in the same proportion as the change in inputs, which is called constant returns to scale. Second, output may change by more than the change in inputs, which is called increasing returns to scale. Finally, output may change by less than the change in inputs, which is called decreasing returns to scale. The explanation of increasing returns to scale is based largely on the advantages of specialization of both workers and machines as the firms grow larger. As the firm expands, greater division of labor and more specialization become possible, and more specialized and efficient machinery can be used. On the other hand, decreasing returns to scale result from the difficulties associated with managing and coordinating a large business.

There are three methods used in measuring production functions. The first method relies on information supplied by engineers and technicians who are familiar with the production process being analyzed and measured. A second method involves the application of statistical techniques to cross-section data, which consist of measurements of the input-output relationship for firms in an industry for a specific time period. The third method of measuring production functions makes use of time series data, which give the input-output relationship for a particular industry for each year in a series of years.

Professor Harvey Leibenstein introduced the concept of X-efficiency in 1966 to explain real-world situations in which labor or management do not work as hard or as efficiently as they might. If this is the case, then output is not at a maximum relative to these inputs, which is what Leibenstein calls X-inefficiency. Recall that in our theoretical production function we assumed that each input combination produced the maximum output possible for that combination. According to Leibenstein, the main reasons why labor and management may not maximize their output is because they are not sufficiently motivated. Empirical evidence suggests that in many cases methods used to stimulate worker motivation have resulted in greater efficiency, with corresponding gains in productivity and reductions in costs.

Problems and Questions

1. Assume a short-run production function in which capital is the fixed input and labor is the variable input. On the basis of the information given below, calculate the average product and the marginal product.

Units of Labor	Total Product	Average Product	Marginal Product
1	50		
2	150		
3	300		
4	440		
5	570		
6	690		
7	805		
8	905		

   a. Identify the point of diminishing returns.
   b. Does the average product reach its maximum before or after the maximum point of the marginal product?
   c. Is the marginal product rising or falling when the average product is at its maximum point?
   d. At what point are the marginal product and the average product the same? Why are they equal at this point?
   e. Draw a graph of these relationships.
2. Do you believe that the distinction between the short run and the long run is helpful in analyzing real-world problems? First, define the short run and the long run, and then apply these definitions to various types of business (e.g., a bakery or a producer of shoes).
3. What is the purpose of the isoquant approach to production? Can this approach be used in long-run analysis as well as in short-run analysis?
4. Draw an isoquant and demonstrate how the marginal rate of technical substitution is found at some specific point on the curve.
5. What are the three stages of production? Why would the firm refrain from producing in stages I and III?
6. What is the difference between diminishing returns and decreasing returns to scale?
7. How would you explain constant returns to scale?
8. Use isoquants to show increasing returns to scale, constant returns to scale, and decreasing returns to scale. Can you employ this same graph to demonstrate the law of diminishing returns? If so, how. If not, why not?

9. What is the difference between the conventional concept of economic efficiency and X-efficiency?
10. What is a production function? What is the difference between a fixed proportion production function and a variable proportion production function?
11. What is a Cobb-Douglas production function?
12. How would you define the business firm?

Notes

1. *Crude Oil Pipe Lines and Competition in the Oil Industry* (Cambridge, Mass.: Harvard University Press, 1955).
2. A. A. Walters, *An Introduction to Econometrics* (New York: W. W. Norton & Co., Inc., 1970), p. 334.
3. See ibid., pp. 332–37.
4. "Allocative Efficiency vs. 'X-Efficiency,' " *American Economic Review* (June, 1966), pp. 392–415.
5. Ibid., p. 398
6. Ibid., p. 401.
7. Ibid.
8. *Business Week* (January 23, 1978), pp. 56–62.
9. Ibid., p. 56.
10. Ibid.

Recommended Reading

Douglas, P. H. "Are There Laws of Production?" *American Economic Review* (March, 1948), pp. 1–41.

Henderson, J. M., and R. F. Quandt. *Microeconomic Theory*, 2d ed., Chap. 3. New York: McGraw-Hill Book Company, 1971.

Leibenstein, Harvey. "Allocative Efficiency vs. 'X-Efficiency,' " *American Economic Review* (June, 1966), pp. 392–415.

Walters, A. A. *An Introduction to Econometrics*, Chap. 10. New York: W. W. Norton & Co., Inc., 1970.

6

The Theory of Cost

In the preceding chapter we were concerned with the relationship between physical inputs and physical output under varying conditions, with no consideration being given to the costs involved. But the cost incurred to produce a good is a prime concern for businessmen; costs, along with prices, are the major elements that determine the profitability and perhaps even the survival of the enterprise. Therefore, a careful consideration of the meaning and behavior of costs is a necessary prelude to an examination of the market behavior of the firm. The latter leads to the supply curve of the firm and of the market, which together with the market demand curve determines the price of the good.

THE MEANING OF COST IN ECONOMICS

Opportunity Cost

Of fundamental importance in cost theory is the concept of **opportunity cost**, or **alternative cost**, as it is also called. This concept holds that the cost of a good is measured in terms of the unproduced

111

goods that could have been produced with the inputs used to produce the good in question. If a variety of goods could have been made with these inputs, the opportunity cost consists of the most preferred foregone good. From the point of view of society, the cost of using certain inputs to produce a post office might be a portion of highway that must be sacrificed in order to obtain the inputs for the post office. For a farmer, the opportunity cost of using his land for growing wheat would be the corn that could have been grown on this land, assuming that corn is his next best crop.

The idea of opportunity cost can be applied in other ways. For example, the cost to a student of an hour spent studying might be an hour that could have been spent on the tennis court, if playing tennis was the best alternative to studying during the hour in question. In general terms, opportunity cost refers to what must be given up in order to obtain something else.

Explicit and Implicit Costs

Explicit costs consist of all the monetary outlays and expenses incurred by the firm in the production process. These costs include payment for such inputs as labor, raw materials, electricity, equipment, and for any other input not actually owned and supplied by the owner of the firm. But suppose that a businessman has invested some of his own money in his enterprise, and suppose that he also works there himself performing various jobs. Certainly his own money should earn interest and his own labor should be rewarded. Even if some businessmen do not explicitly recognize these costs of owned inputs, the economist always does. They are called implicit costs.

Implicit costs raise the question of how to determine the amount that a businessman should charge his firm for the use of his own money or labor or other inputs. To solve problems like this, economists apply the opportunity cost concept. According to this concept, the businessman should count as implicit cost an amount equal to the maximum return that his inputs could earn if he put them to work outside his firm in the best alternative employment. For example, if the businessman could get a job paying $25,000 performing the same services that he performs in his own firm, then $25,000 would be the implicit cost of his services to his firm.

Private Costs, External Costs and Benefits, and Social Costs

We have been discussing **private costs**, the costs of a privately owned business, and we have explained that the economist's approach includes both explicit and implicit costs. But there may be other costs that accrue to the society when the firm produces its output. Suppose that a factory emits acrid smoke in the process of production. As a consequence, people living near the factory suffer from eye irritations and must visit their doctors more often. This is a cost to these people stemming from the production of the good, but it is ignored by the factory. Such a cost is called an **external cost**, since it is external to the firm. In order to determine the social cost of production, it is necessary to add any external costs to the private cost of producing the good. On the other hand, a firm may also benefit society as a result of its production process and not charge society for these benefits. If so, there is an **external benefit**. For example, a firm may clear a smelly, mosquito-ridden swamp to make room for a parking lot. If the factory is otherwise clean and quiet, people living near the factory will now feel better off without the smells and mosquitoes. In the case of external benefits, social cost is less than private cost; that is, social cost equals private cost minus external benefits. These external effects, both costs and benefits, are generally referred to as **externalities**. They are discussed in greater detail in connection with welfare economics in the last chapter of this book.

SHORT-RUN COSTS

The basic distinction between the short run (a variable input and one or more fixed inputs) and the long run (all inputs variable) discussed in Chapter 5 is applied in the analysis of costs of production. Since short-run analysis assumes at least one fixed input and at least one variable input, short-run costs are divided into fixed costs and variable costs. **Total fixed cost** (TFC) is defined as all costs attributable to the fixed inputs, and as such these costs do not vary as output varies, Examples of fixed costs would include rent, property taxes, interest on debt, and basic maintenance expenses for plant and equipment. **Total variable cost** (TVC) is the total cost of the variable input or inputs, which means that this cost varies as output varies. Total variable cost could refer to such items as wages, material costs, and electricity used in the production process.

TVC is influenced by the law of diminishing returns through the short-run production function. The relationship between the production function and short-run variable cost can be seen in Figure 6-1. Graph (a) shows the usual short-run production function (see Figure 5-1a), but here we have reversed the axes: units of input are now measured on the vertical axis and units of output are shown on

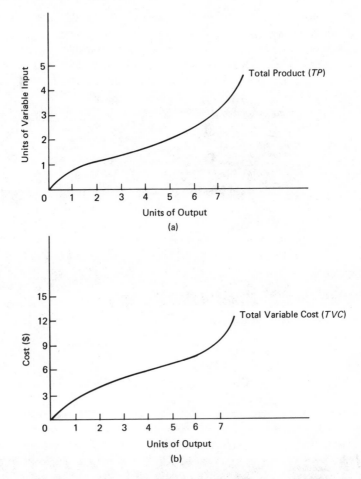

Figure 6-1. The production function and total variable cost.

the horizontal axis. For the sake of simplicity, let us assume that a single variable input is available to the firm at a constant cost per unit, say $3 per unit. By placing units of output on the horizontal axis in both graph (a) and graph (b), it can be seen that the shape of the TVC curve in graph (b) reflects the shape of the total product (TP) curve in graph (a), since the vertical axis in graph (b) is a constant multiple (input unit cost) of the vertical axis in graph (a). That is, one unit of the variable input costs $3, two units cost $6, three units are $9, and so forth.

Since TFC is constant regardless of output, it is shown as a straight horizontal line in Figure 6-2. We have defined all costs as being either

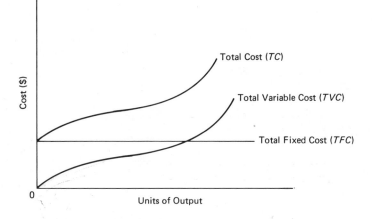

Figure 6-2. Total fixed cost, total variable cost, and total cost.

fixed or variable; therefore **total cost** (TC) must be the sum of TFC and TVC, or $TC = TFC + TVC$. In Figure 6-2, it can be seen that the shape of the TC curve is really the same as the shape of the TVC curve; that is, the TC curve is merely the TVC curve shifted upward by the amount of the constant TFC.

For analytical purposes, it is frequently desirable to express total cost in average and marginal terms, that is, cost per unit of output. In Figure 6-3, we therefore show the typical shapes of the three average cost curves as well as the marginal cost curve, in relation to the total cost curves. **Marginal cost** (MC) is the cost of producing one more unit of output, or to put it differently, the change in TC (or TVC) divided by the change in output: $MC = \Delta TC/\Delta x = \Delta TVC/\Delta x$. The shape of the MC curve is determined by the rate of increase (or shape) of the TC curve, which, as we have noted, is the same as that of the TVC curve. When these curves are increasing at a decreasing rate the MC curve is falling, and when they are increasing at an increasing rate the MC curve is rising. Therefore, the minimum point of the MC curve corresponds to the inflection points of the TC and TVC curves—points 1 and 2 in Figure 6-3(a).

The other curves shown in Figure 6-3(b) are simply curves expressing averages derived from the three total cost curves in Figure 6-3(a). The **average fixed cost** (AFC) of any output x is the TFC divided by that output: $AFC = TFC/x$. Since TFC is constant, AFC must get smaller and smaller as output increases. TVC divided by total output yields **average variable cost** (AVC): $AVC = TVC/x$.

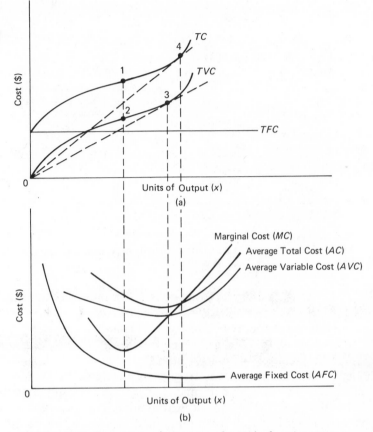

Figure 6-3. Derivation of average and marginal cost curves.

Average total cost (AC) is TC divided by total output: $AC = TC/x$; or, what is the same thing, $AC = AFC + AVC$.

Note that in Figure 6-3(b) the MC curve intersects the AVC curve and the AC curve at their respective minimum points. This is perhaps best understood in terms of an example. If your average grade is 80 and you receive a 75 on your next exam (the marginal grade), your average grade goes down, say to 78. That is, whenever the marginal grade (or cost) is below the average grade (or cost), the marginal pulls the average down. If the next grade (cost) is 78 (equal to the average), then the average stays the same. But if the following grade (cost) is above the average, say 82, then the average grade (cost) moves up. In short, when MC is below AVC or AC, it pulls them down; when MC is above AVC or AC, it pulls them up;

therefore, MC must cross AVC and AC at their respective minimum points.

Table 6-1 presents some hypothetical figures designed to further illustrate these definitions and relationships. The first two columns show the relationship between units of input and units of output, or the production function. TFC is assumed to be $60, as shown in column 3, and the next column indicates that each unit of the variable input costs $10; that is, TVC increases by $10 for every unit of variable input added. The information contained in the first four columns of the table can be used to derive the values in the next five columns, showing TC, AFC, AVC, AC, and MC, respectively. The relationships among these concepts are given at the tops of the columns, and checking the entries provides a good exercise in fitting these concepts together.

LONG-RUN COSTS

First, recall the results of our discussion of returns to scale. We know that in the long run all inputs can be varied. As the size of the firm gets larger, it will experience increasing returns to scale up to a point, largely because of greater specialization and the use of more efficient technology. This implies that the long-run average cost per unit of output will decline. For example, assume that a firm produces 100 units of output with an input cost of $100, giving a long-run average cost of $1 per unit of output. Now suppose that the firm doubles its inputs and therefore must spend $200 for inputs. But let us further suppose that, because of increasing returns to scale, output increases to 400 units. Long-run average cost would now be only $.50 per unit of output. We must emphasize that the analysis is here concerned with the behavior of costs per unit of output, not with the costs or prices of units of input. The prices of the inputs are assumed to be constant. We also assume that the long-run production function does not vary during the analysis; that is, even though the firm may change its technology as it grows, the existing range of technological possibilities is known and does not change during the analysis.

As long as the firm enjoys increasing returns to scale, long-run average cost will decline. Eventually, the benefits of growing size will give way to the costly problems of coordinating a large enterprise, and long-run average cost will rise. Although management, along with all other inputs, must by definition be variable in the long run, it is not possible simply to enlarge the mangement as the firm grows while maintaining the same degree of managerial effici-

Table 6-1. Hypothetical Table Showing Derivation of Cost Curves

Units of Input	Total Product (TP)	Total Fixed Cost (TFC)	Total Variable Cost (TVC)	Total Cost (TC) (TFC + TVC)	Average Fixed Cost (AFC) (TFC ÷ TP)	Average Variable Cost (AVC) (TVC ÷ TP)	Average Total Cost (AC) (AFC + AVC)	Marginal Cost (MC) (ΔTC ÷ ΔTP)
1	$10	$60	$10	$ 70	$6.00	$1.00	$7.00	$1.00
2	24	60	20	80	2.50	.83	3.33	.71
3	39	60	30	90	1.54	.77	2.31	.67
4	56	60	40	100	1.07	.71	1.78	.59
5	65	60	50	110	.92	.77	1.69	1.11
6	72	60	60	120	.83	.83	1.66	1.43
7	77	60	70	130	.78	.91	1.69	2.00
8	80	60	80	140	.75	1.00	1.75	3.33

ency. Just as the technology suitable for the firm usually changes with size, so the relationship of the management to the firm changes with size and becomes less efficient: decisions become increasingly complex, authority must be delegated, lines of communication get longer and more involved, and the decision-making process becomes more time-consuming.

The construction and shape of the long-run average cost curve (LAC) are illustrated in Figure 6-4. The LAC, also called a **planning curve** or **envelope curve**, is merely a curve that is tangent to all the short-run average cost curves (SAC). As the firm expands and is capable of greater output, this is represented by a SAC further to the right in Figure 6-4(a). The LAC encompasses all of the most efficient SAC available to the firm in the long run for each possible output. Production must actually take place in one specific SAC, so that the LAC is a planning curve in the sense that it displays all the SAC available to the firm in the long run.

Shown in Figure 6-4(a) are five SAC; as we move from SAC_1 to SAC_5 the firm is expanding its size and output. The lowest

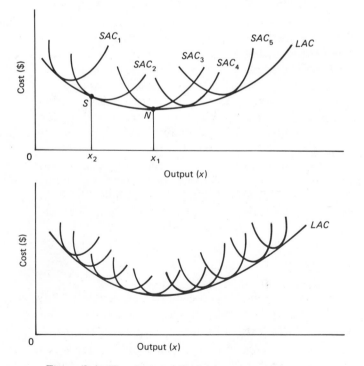

Figure 6-4. The shape of the long-run average cost curve.

possible average cost in the long run for all potential outputs occurs at point N on SAC_3 corresponding to output x_1; up to this point the firm experiences economies of scale, and beyond it diseconomies of scale take over. Although the LAC is tangent to every SAC, it is tangent at the minimum point of only one SAC, the SAC with the minimum cost for all possible outputs, namely point N.

In general, the minimum cost for any specific output in the long run is given by the point on the LAC corresponding to that specific output. For example, the minimum cost of producing output x_2 is shown by point S, where the LAC is tangent to SAC_2; note that the tangency is to the left of the minimum point of SAC_2. It is always the case that to the left of the minimum point on the LAC, the LAC is tangent to all SAC to the left of their minimum points; and to the right of the minimum point on the LAC, the LAC is tangent to all SAC to the right of their minimum points. If we include all possible SAC, the LAC is automatically traced out, as in Figure 6-4(b).

Figure 6-5(a) shows a **long-run total cost curve** (LTC). Just as the LAC is an envelope curve of all the SAC, so the LTC is an envelope curve of all the short-run total cost curves (STC). For any output, say x_1, $LAC = LTC/x_1$, or $LTC = LAC \cdot x_1$, which means that the LTC can be derived from the LAC, or vice versa. The **long-run marginal cost curve** (LMC), which is drawn in Figure 6-5(b), shows the increase in LTC resulting from the production of an additional unit of output in the long run. The minimum point on the LMC is where the LTC curve changes from increasing at a decreasing rate to increasing at an increasing rate. The LMC crosses the LAC at the minimum point on the LAC, for the same reason that any short-run marginal cost (SMC) intersects its corresponding SAC at its minimum point, which we explained earlier in this chapter.

Let us pursue the relationships between long-run costs and short-run cost a bit further. At any output, such as x_1, where Figure 6-5(a) shows that STC_1 is tangent to LTC, SAC must also be tangent to LAC: at the tangency point, $STC_1 = LTC$, and hence

$$\text{SAC}_1 = \frac{STC_1}{x_1} = \frac{LTC}{x_1} = LAC$$

In addition, at any tangency point of LTC and STC the slope of LTC equals the slope of STC, and therefore the $LMC = SMC$ (see Figure 6-5). Note that at the minimum point on the LAC, and only at this point, $LAC = LMC = SAC = SMC$. If we take any other output, such as x_1, then $SAC = LAC$ and $SMC = LMC$, but $SAC = LAC \neq SMC = LMC$.

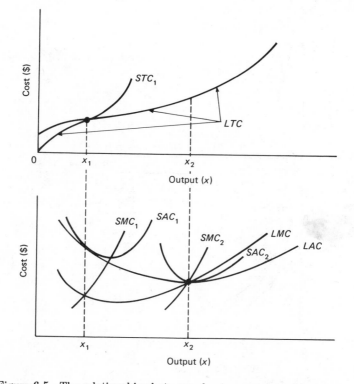

Figure 6-5. The relationships between short-run costs and long-run costs.

ISOQUANT AND ISOCOST ANALYSIS

Isoquant and isocost analysis can be employed to determine the minimum total cost of producing any level of output in the long run. Figure 6-6(a) presents an isoquant which shows the various com- binations of labor and capital that could be used to produce x_1 units of output. Graph (a) also displays an isocost line, which traces the different combinations of inputs that can be purchased for some fixed money outlay. Suppose that a firm is going to spend an amount M_1 (say $1000) for the purchase of labor and capital. If the price of a unit of labor is P_L (say $10) and that of capital is P_K (say $5), then for an expenditure of $1000 the firm can purchase either M_1/P_L units of labor ($1000/$10 = 100 units) or M_1/P_K units of capital ($1000/$5 = 200 units). The line connecting these two points contains all the possible combinations of labor and capital available for outlay M_1. In like manner an isocost line can be con-

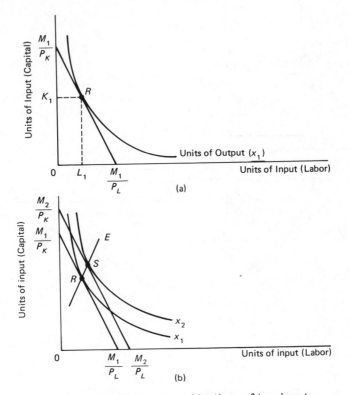

Figure 6-6. Least-cost combinations of two inputs.

structed for any other total outlay. The slope of an isocost line is equal to the ratio of the input prices P_L/P_K. Assuming fixed input prices, all isocost lines are parallel.

If the firm wants to produce a specific level of output such as x_1 at the lowest possible cost, it will employ that combination of inputs indicated by the tangency point of an isocost line and the isoquant representing the desired level of output (such as x_1). In Figure 6-6(a) this point is R and the input combination is $L_1 K_1$. That the tangency point is the least-cost combination of inputs for the given output can be seen as follows: A movement away from the tangency point R in either direction along the isoquant would result in a movement to a higher isocost line and hence the desired output would cost more.

We know that the slope of the isoquant is equal to the slope of the isocost line at the tangency point. Since the slope of the isoquant is equal to $\Delta K/\Delta L = MP_L/MP_K$, and the slope of the isocost line is

P_L/P_K, at the tangency point $MP_L/MP_K = P_L/P_K$ or $MP_L/P_L = MP_K/P_K$. In other words, the firm will purchase its inputs in such a way that the last dollar spent on each input will bring forth the same amount of output. For example, with P_K = \$5 and P_L = \$10, a solution could be 5/\$5 = 10/\$10 or 1/\$1 = 1/\$1, which means that a dollar spent on capital yields as much output as a dollar spent on labor. If this were not the case then the solution would not be at least-cost one for the output in question.

Figure 6-6(b) shows the least-cost solution for a higher level of output, x_2, to be point S. If we connect points R and S and other similar points we derive line E, called the **expansion path**, which shows all the least-cost combinations of inputs for all levels of output at constant input prices. It is an easy matter to derive the long-run total cost curve from the expansion path. Since the LTC shows the lowest cost for each output in the long run, every point on the expansion path corresponds to a point on the LTC. For example, point R on the expansion path in Figure 6-6(b) denotes that the lowest total cost attainable for output x_1 is M_1, and for output x_2 the lowest total cost is M_2 (point S). By plotting the total cost and output given by all points such as R and S, we derive the LTC in Figure 6-7.

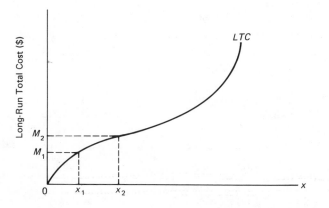

Figure 6-7. The LTC derived from the expansion path.

APPLICATION: EMPIRICAL COST FUNCTIONS

Numerous empirical studies have been made in an effort to determine the actual (real-world) behavior of costs.[1] As with production functions, economists have studied cost functions by using both the cross-section approach and the time-series approach, and by employing engineering studies. Data have been drawn from cost accounting records, engineering sources, and questionnaires. Let us consider some of the results of these cost function studies.

Table 6-2 shows the type of study, the time period, and the results of 19 studies of manufacturing in general and also of many specific industries. The most glaring departure of the empirical results from our theory is the constant marginal cost found in many of the specific industry studies. According to cost theory, marginal cost should be rising over the relevant range of output in the short run. Although some studies do indeed show increasing marginal cost, how can we explain the constant marginal cost in others?

Critics of these studies claim that they tend to be biased in the direction of constant marginal cost, and that without these biases marginal cost would tend to rise. The biases arise largely from the use of accounting data, and from the way in which the data are treated statistically. Accounting data are generally accumulated for periods longer than the short-run period of economic theory, and as a result there is an averaging effect that tends to produce constant marginal cost when a short-run period is under examination. In the case of time-series studies, it is claimed that the correction for input price changes introduces a bias toward constant marginal cost. In addition to these general biases, some of the studies were further biased toward constant marginal costs because their observations covered outputs far below plant capacity, where marginal costs would not normally be rising very sharply.

Table 6-2. Results of Studies of Cost Curves: Industry Studies

Study	Industry	Type	Period	Result
Bain (1956)	Manufacturing	Q	L	Small economies of scale of multiplant firms.
Eiteman and Guthrie (1952)	Manufacturing	Q	S	MC below AC at all outputs below "capacity."
Hall and Hitch (1939)	Manufacturing	Q	S	Majority have MC decreasing.
Lester (1946)	Manufacturing	Q	S	Decreasing average variable cost to capacity
Moore (1959)	Manufacturing	E	L	Economies of scale generally.

Table 6-2 (continued).

Study	Industry	Type	Period	Result
T.N.E.C. Mon. 13	Various industries	CS	L	Small or medium size *plants* usually have lowest costs. Blair (1942) draws different conclusions.
Alpert (1959)	Metal	E	L	Economies of scale to 80,000 lbs/month; then constant returns.
Johnston (1960)	Multiple product	TS	S	"Direct" cost is linearly related to output. MC is constant
Dean (1936)	Furniture	TS	S	MC constant. SRAC "failed to rise."
Dean (1941)	Leather belts	TS	S	Significantly increasing MC. Rejected by Dean.
Dean (1941)	Hosiery	TS	S	MC constant. SRAC "failed to rise."
Dean (1942)	Dept. store	TS	S	MC declining or constant.
Dean and James (1942)	Shoe stores	CS	L	LRAC is U-shaped. (Interpreted as *not* due to diseconomies of scale.)
Holton (1956)	Retailing (Puerto Rico)	E	L	LRAC is L-shaped. But Holton argues that inputs of management may be undervalued at high outputs.
Ezekiel and Wylie (1941)	Steel	TS	S	MC declining but large standard errors.
Yntema (1940)	Steel	TS	S	MC constant.
Ehrke (1933)	Cement	TS	S	Ehrke interprets as constant MC. Apel (1948) argues that MC is increasing.
Nordin (1947)	Light plant	TS	S	MC is increasing.

Code: Q = questionnaire, E = engineering data, CS = cross-section, TS = time series, S = short-run, L = long-run, MC = marginal cost, AC = average cost, SAC = short-run average cost, and LAC = long-run average cost.

Reprinted from A. A. Walters, "Production and Cost Functions: An Econometric Survey," *Econometrica*, Vol. 31 (Jan.–April, 1963), pp. 48–49.

INNOVATION: NEW DIMENSIONS IN COST ANALYSIS

Conventional cost theory relates cost to the level of output per unit of time. That is, the standard cost curves show how costs increase as more and more output is produced during some time period such as a day or a week. But other characteristics of production may influence cost. Perhaps the best systematic discussion of these other characteristics of production can be found in a paper by Armen A. Alchian called "Costs and Outputs."[2] In this paper, Alchian identifies two major characteristics that affect costs, in addition to the level of output. One characteristic is the total contemplated volume of output. The other is the programmed time schedule of availability of output; this includes the initial delivery date, as well as the length of the interval over which the output is made available.

Given the level of output, costs will be influenced by the contemplated overall quantity or volume that eventually will be produced; it will make a difference whether the firm intends to produce a thousand units or a million units of the good. Clearly, costs will increase as volume expands, but they will increase at a decreasing rate and the cost per unit of total volume will decrease. This is because the method of production is largely a function of volume. If a secretary can type a hundred copies of a letter per day, and this output is required only one day per month, then a typewriter may be all the capital equipment needed for this purpose. But if a hundred copies are needed every day, costs could be reduced by acquiring a copying machine. In other words, if the volume increases from 100 to 3000 letters per month, the typewriter will give way to the copying machine, and the cost per letter will decline.

The time schedule of the availability of output will influence costs. Here we are referring to the time between the decision to make the good and the time when the good is actually delivered. Delivery may occur at some one time or, more commonly, according to some delivery schedule over a period of time. Costs will increase as the time interval between the decision to produce and initial delivery gets shorter, given the rate and volume of output. This is the case because a variety of inputs must be purchased in order to produce the output; if these inputs are purchased at a faster rate, the sellers of these inputs must step up their rate of output, and hence their costs will rise as a result; and this leads to higher costs for the buyer of these inputs.

As a consequence of his analysis of costs, Alchian challenges the traditional distinction between the short run and the long run. In his own words:

> For any given output program there is only *one* pertinent cost, *not* two. Unambiguous specification of the output or action to be costed

makes the cost definition unambiguous and destroys the illusion that there are two costs to consider, a short- and a long-run cost for any given output. There is only one, and that is the *cheapest* cost of doing whatever the operation is specified to be. To produce a house in three months is one thing, to produce it in a year is something else. By uniquely identifying the operation to be charged there results one cost, not a range of costs from immediate to short- to longer-run costs.[3]

SUMMARY

Costs are important to the firm because the level of profit depends on costs and revenues, as we explain further in the next chapter. A basic concept in cost theory is that of opportunity cost, also called alternative cost. This concept holds that the cost of a good is measured by the best alternative good that could have been produced with the inputs used to produce the good in question. That is, opportunity cost is measured in terms of the good that must be sacrificed in order to obtain the good in question. Another distinction in cost theory is that between explicit costs and implicit costs. Explicit costs refer to the actual monetary outlays incurred by the firm in the production process. Implicit costs refer to the value of inputs supplied by the owner of the firm; even though these inputs are not purchased in the market, they must be recognized as a part of total costs. Finally, social cost must be distinguished from private cost. The latter includes explicit and implicit cost, but to determine social cost we must add external costs to private costs. External costs are costs to society attributable to the production of a good that are not recognized by the firm as part of its private costs. Such is often the case with air and water pollution.

The analysis of the firm's costs of production is divided into the short run (one variable input and one or more fixed inputs) and the long run (all inputs are variable). In the short run, there are fixed costs as a consequence of the fixed inputs, and variable costs as a result of the variable input. Total fixed cost does not vary with output, since the fixed inputs are independent of output (by definition). The behavior of total variable cost depends on the law of diminishing returns, and therefore this cost first increases at a decreasing rate (before the point of diminishing returns) and then increases at an increasing rate (after the point of diminishing returns). Total cost is the sum of total fixed cost and total variable cost. Short-run cost can be expressed in both average and marginal terms. Marginal cost is the addition to total cost caused by producing one more unit of output. The shape of the marginal cost curve is determined by the rate of change of the total cost curve, which is the same as the rate of change of the total variable cost curve. When these curves are increasing at a decreasing rate the marginal cost curve is falling, and when they are increasing at an increasing rate the marginal cost curve is rising. Average fixed cost for any output is total fixed cost divided by that output. Average variable cost for any output is total variable cost divided by that output. Average total cost is the sum of average fixed cost and average variable cost.

In the long run, all costs are variable. The long-run average cost curve, or envelope curve as it is also called, first declines because of increasing returns to scale, and then rises as a result of decreasing returns to scale (which were discussed in the preceding chapter). The expansion of the firm in the long run is represented by short-run average cost curves that are further to the right on the graph, which reflect the greater output that larger firms are capable of producing. Production must actually take place in one specific short-run plant, so that the long-run average cost curve is really an envelope curve tangent to all possible short-run average cost curves. The minimum cost for any specific output in the long run is given by the point where a short-run average cost curve is tangent to the long-run average cost curve at that output. Long-run marginal cost represents the increase in long-run total cost resulting from the production of an additional unit of ouput in the long run. The long-run marginal cost curve crosses the long-run average cost curve at the minimum point on the long-run average cost curve.

Isoquant and isocost analysis can be used to determine the minimum total cost of producing any level of output in the long run. Since we are analyzing the long run, where there are no fixed inputs, the isoquant must represent two variable inputs. In terms of this approach, the lowest possible cost in the long run for any specific output is given by the isocost line that is tangent to the isoquant representing that specific output. The expansion path shows the least-cost combinations of inputs for all possible levels of output at constant input prices. The long-run total cost curve can be derived from the expansion path.

Economists employ statistical methods in order to derive empirical cost functions. As with production functions, they use engineering data, the cross-section approach, and the time-series approach. The most glaring departure of the empirical results from cost theory is the constant marginal cost found in many studies. But many critics of these studies claim that the studies tend to be biased in the direction of constant marginal costs, largely because of an averaging effect produced by accounting data.

Conventional cost theory relates cost to the level of output per unit of time. Armen Alchian has identified two other factors that affect cost, in addition to the level of output. One factor is the total contemplated volume of output; the other is the programmed time schedule of availability of output. Although total cost will increase as volume increases, it will increase at a decreasing rate, and the cost per unit of total volume will decrease. Costs will increase as the time interval between the decision to produce and initial delivery gets shorter, given the rate and the volume of output.

Notes

1. This section relies heavily on an excellent article by A. A. Walters that reviews production and cost functions and discusses the many theoretical and statistical problems involved in this area: "Production and Cost Functions: An Econometric Survey," *Econometrica* (January-April 1963), Vol. 31, pp. 1-66.
2. Originally printed in Moses Abramovitz et al. *The Allocation of Economic Resources* (Palo Alto: Stanford University Press, 1959); reprinted in W. Breit and H. M. Houchman (eds.), *Readings in Microeconomics*, 2d ed. (New York: Holt, Rinehart and Winston, Inc., 1971), pp. 159-171.
3. Ibid., p. 167.

Problems and Questions

1. Calculate the entries in the following table.

Total Product	Total Cost	Average Fixed Cost	Average Variable Cost	Marginal Cost
0	100			
10	120			
24	140			
39	160			
56	180			
65	200			
72	220			
77	240			
80	260			
81	280			

2. What is the relationship between the short-run average cost curve and the long-run average cost curve?
3. Why does the short-run average cost curve have a U shape?
4. Why does the long-run average cost curve have a U shape?
5. Why do you suppose that economists consider the concept of opportunity costs to be of such fundamental importance?
6. What are external costs and how do they enter into the distinction between private costs and social costs?
7. Why does the marginal cost curve intersect the average variable cost curve and the average total cost curve at the minimum point of each curve?
8. Draw a graph containing isoquants and isocost lines, and show how an expansion path is derived.
9. Explain how a long-run total cost curve can be derived from an expansion path.
10. What did Armen Alchian contribute to cost theory, and why is it important?
11. Do empirical studies of cost functions support cost theory?

Recommended Reading

Alchian, A. A. "Costs and Outputs," *The Allocation of Economic Resources*, Moses Abramovitz et al., eds., pp. 23–40. Palo Alto: Stanford University Press, 1959.

Clark, J. M. *The Economics of Overhead Costs*. Chicago: University of Chicago Press, 1923.

Henderson, J. M., and R. E. Quandt. *Microeconomic Theory*. 2d ed. New York: McGraw-Hill Book Company, 1971.

Viner, Jacob. "Cost Curves and Supply Curves," *Zeitschrift für Nationalökonomie*, Vol. III (1931), pp. 23–46, Reprinted in G. J. Stigler and K. E. Boulding, eds., *Readings in Price Theory*. Homewood, Ill.: Richard D. Irwin, Inc., 1952.

Walters, A. A. "Production and Cost Functions: An Econometric Survey," *Econometrica*, Vol. 31 (Jan.–April, 1963), pp. 1–66.

7

The Theory of

Perfect Competition

ASSUMPTIONS

In Chapter 1 we divided all market structures into four basic types: perfect competition, monopoly, monopolistic competition, and oligopoly. In this chapter and in the following three chapters, we examine the way in which the firm and the industry function in each of these market structures. Our main interest concerns how the price and output of the good are determined by both the firm and the industry; remember, prices control the allocation of resources in our economy, and they also perform the other functions discussed in Chapter 1.

To have a perfectly competitive market, we found that it was necessary to make the following four assumptions. First, there must be enough small (relative to the size of the total market) sellers and buyers of the good to eliminate the possibility that any single seller or buyer could influence the price of the good. Second, the good produced by each seller must be identical to that made by every other seller, which is the same as saying that the good is homogeneous. Third, firms, as well as all resources and inputs, must be mobile in the sense that there are no barriers or impediments preventing them from entering or leaving the industry. Fourth, there must be perfect knowledge, meaning that all participants in the economic process must know all costs and prices in which they have an economic interest, and they must know the outcome of all economic events pertaining to them.

We shall now add a fifth assumption that is a characteristic not so much of the market as of the behavior of the seller. This is the assumption of profit maximization, which holds that the seller strives to make as much profit as possible. We shall apply this assumption to all four market structures because it greatly simplifies the analysis of the market behavior of the firm. Much controversy has revolved around the realism of this assumption: One side of the argument contends that it is too unrealistic to lead to satisfactory theories, and the other side claims that it is a reasonable and useful abstraction. We shall employ this assumption for the sake of simplicity and because it yields relatively accurate results. The firm has been analyzed on the basis of other behavioral assumptions, but those analyses and results are not as widely accepted as those based on profit maximization. In any case, complications can always be added to the analysis after the simplified theory is developed.

We now define the **total profit** (including both normal and abnormal, or economic, profit, as explained here) derived from any output as the difference between the total revenue (or income) of the firm and total cost, including both explicit and implicit cost. Therefore, when this difference is maximized, total profit is maximized.

The analysis of how price and output are determined by the firm and the industry is divided into three categories: the very short run, the short run, and the long run. The very short run is any time interval during which the supply of a good is fixed; therefore, production cannot take place in the very short run. The concepts of the short run and the long run are the same as they were in the analysis of production and cost. The short-run period is one in which the supply of the good can be increased by the firm, and hence by the industry, by adding a variable input to one or more fixed inputs. In the long run all inputs are variable. These three periods are conceptual and do not depend on calendar time. We shall first consider equilibrium conditions in the very short run and then go on to the analysis of the short run and the long run.

VERY SHORT-RUN EQUILIBRIUM

There are two ways of handling the very short run. In the first approach, not only is the supply fixed, but the entire amount is offered for sale at once. As an example, consider the plight of a coastal fisherman who ties up his fish-laden boat at the dock in the morning of a hot day. He has no refrigeration and no market outlets except his own dockside fish stand. Under these circumstances his entire catch will be put on the market; and the sooner it sells, the better. What is true of the one fisherman would be true of any number under these conditions, and the market supply would simply be the total of the amounts possessed by all individual fishermen. The market supply curve would consist of a vertical line, representing a fixed supply, as in Figure 7-1. The equilibrium market price would be P_1 if the market demand curve happened to be D_1, that is, where D_1 and S intersect, making demand equal to supply. If demand increased from D_1 to D_2 the new intersection would yield a higher price, P_2; and if demand decreased to D_3, price would decline to P_3. Therefore, given a fixed supply, the price will depend on the level of demand.

The other approach to the very short run assumes that the seller may withhold a portion of his fixed supply from the market. The extent to which supplies would be withheld from the market, depends on such considerations as the perishability of the product, the cost of storage, and the price expectations of the seller. For example, a nonperishable good might be held for a fairly long time, but not if storage costs are high, and surely not if the seller expected the price to decline in the future. But if the price is currently below a certain level and the seller expects it to rise in the future, he may withhold his supply from the market and offer all of it or part of it for sale once the price exceeds the minimum level, which is called his reserva-

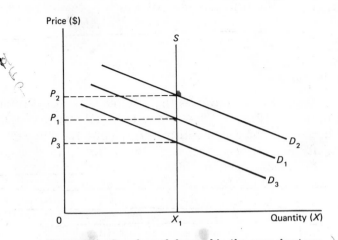

Figure 7-1. Supply and demand in the very short run.

tion price. Since different sellers are likely to have different reservation prices, larger amounts of the good will be offered for sale by all sellers at higher prices, and the supply curve in the very short run will then have a positive slope.

SHORT-RUN EQUILIBRIUM OF THE FIRM AND INDUSTRY

Perf. Comp. firm

Revenue Curves

One of the assumptions of pure competition is that the number of firms is so large and each one is so small that any firm can sell as much as it desires without influencing the price of the good. In other words, the firm can sell its entire output at the prevailing market price. If each additional unit of output sold by the firm adds the same amount (= price) to total revenue (TR), then the total revenue curve of the competitive firm must be linear, that is, a straight line, as shown in Figure 7-2(a). Therefore, the marginal revenue (MR), which is defined as the addition to TR resulting from the sale of an additional unit of output, must be equal to the price. This is shown in Figure 7-2(a), in which we suppose that the change in output from x_1 and x_2 represents a unit increase, and therefore the corresponding change in TR or $\Delta TR = P = MR = AR$. The average revenue (AR) is also equal to $P = MR$, since the constant P means that the average receipt or revenue of the firm must be the same as P. Figure 7-2(b) shows the demand curve for the output of the firm, as perceived by the firm. From the viewpoint of the firm, any output can be sold at the prevailing market price and so the demand curve appears as a horizontal line to the firm, the level of which is determined by the price level. Since $P = MR = AR$, the competitive firm's horizontal demand curve also denotes MR and AR.

Profit Maximization   *Total Profit = TR − TC*

We have defined total profit as the difference between total revenue and total cost. Figure 7-3(a) shows the total revenue curve and the total cost curve of a competitive firm. Total revenue equals or exceeds total cost for any output from x_S to x_T, and therefore these are the boundaries of profitable operation. Given this range, the firm will maximize total profit when producing output x_M, where the slope of the total cost curve equals that of the total revenue curve; this occurs at point V, where the tangent to the TC curve is parallel to the TR curve, and total profit is VW.

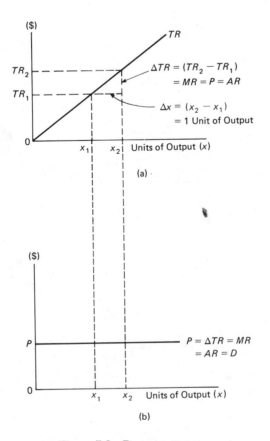

($)

TR

TR_2

$\Delta TR = (TR_2 - TR_1)$
= MR = P = AR

TR_1

$\Delta x = (x_2 - x_1)$
= 1 Unit of Output

0

x_1 x_2 Units of Output (x)

(a)

($)

P

$P = \Delta TR = MR$
= AR = D

0

x_1 x_2 Units of Output (x)

(b)

Figure 7-2. Revenue curves.

That profit is maximized at output x_M can be seen by supposing that output is less than x_M, in which case the slope of the TC curve would be less than that of the TR curve and the two curves would diverge, indicating that profits would increase with greater output. On the other hand, if output were greater than x_M the slope of the TC curve would exceed that of the TR curve and the curves would converge, meaning that total profits would be decreasing as output increased beyond x_M. Therefore, the firm will maximize total profits, or the distance between the TR and TC curves, if it expands output to x_M but not beyond.

The same result can be expressed in terms of average and marginal cost and revenue curves. This is shown in Figure 7-3(b) where, as before, profits are maximized when output x_M is produced. At this

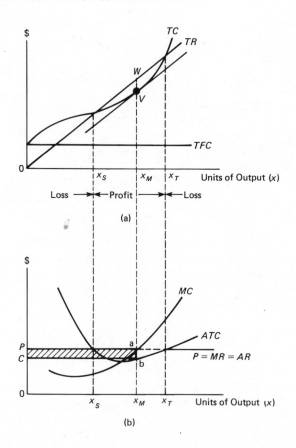

Figure 7-3. Competitive short-run profit maximization.

output $MC = MR$, which is the condition for profit maximization or, as we shall see, loss minimization. When $MC = MR$ the rate of increase in total costs equals that of total revenue, since the marginal curves express the rate of change of the total curves, that is, $MC = \Delta C/\Delta x$ and $MR = \Delta R/\Delta x$. Therefore, the slope to the TC curve is equal to the slope of the TR curve when $MC = MR$, so that in effect the same condition for profit maximization applies in both Figure 7-3(a) and Figure 7-3(b). In (b) it is apparent that, if less than x_M is produced, then $MR > MC$, and therefore more could be added to total revenue than to total cost by increasing output. However, if more than x_M is produced, then $MC > MR$, indicating that the additional output beyond x_M is reducing total profit; hence a decrease in output toward x_M is called for. If, to increase profit, output should be increased when it is less than x_M and decreased when it is more than x_M, profits must be maximized at exactly x_M. In Figure 7-3(b), at output x_M average profit per unit is equal to the distance ab, which is the difference between the average cost and average revenue or price. If we multiply the average profit per unit times the number of units x_M (i.e., $ab \cdot x_M$), we find the total profit, which is equal to the area of the rectangle $abcP$ and which is also equal to the distance VW in Figure 7-3(a).

If TR is less than TC at all outputs, meaning that the firm cannot make a profit, it will minimize its loss by following the $MC = MR$ rule. Figure 7-4 illustrates this case. Graph (a) shows that TR is tangent to the TVC curve at point Y. This means that, although variable costs are fully covered by total revenue, total fixed costs are not returned at all. Even so, the best output is x_L because, if less or more than x_L is produced, then TR would lie below TVC, and TVC would not be fully covered. Graph (b) shows the equivalent position in terms of average and marginal curves. The loss is equal to the hatched area $abPc$, the average loss per unit (ab) times the number of units x_L, which equals YZ in graph (a).

The firm suffers a loss whenever the price is below average total cost (AC). If the price falls to the point where it is equal to the minimum point of the average variable cost (AVC) curve, as in graph (b), the firm has reached a critical juncture. At this price, variable costs are just returned by the sale of the output, but fixed costs are not recouped at all. But this would also be the case if the firm produced nothing, that is, fixed costs must be paid even at zero output. By producing x_L the firm must pay all its revenue to the variable inputs, and it loses an amount equal to fixed costs; by producing zero output the firm finds that it is no worse off, since it still loses fixed costs. Therefore, when $P = AVC$ the firm is on the borderline of operating or shutting down and this is called the **shut-down point**. If price should fall below AVC it would definitely shut down, and if P is above AVC, it would definitely pay to operate.

The supply curve of the competitive firm therefore is that part of the MC curve above the AVC curve, since this portion of the MC curve relates market prices to the quantities supplied by the firm. The market price is determined by the intersection of the market demand curve and the market supply curve. This is the price that the competitive firm regards as given and fixed; as we have seen, it therefore appears as a horizontal demand curve for the firm, meaning that the firm can sell any quantity it desires at the prevailing market price. Figure 7-5 illustrates these relationships. Graph (a) shows the equilibrium market price P_1 and graph (b) shows that the firm

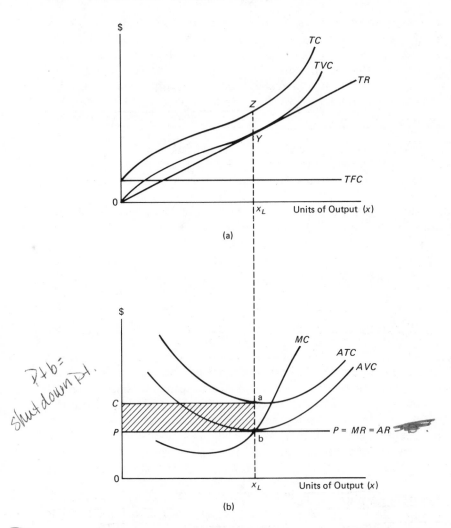

Figure 7-4. Competitive short-run loss minimization.

responds to the price by producing x_1, the quantity that maximizes profits at this price, that is, where $MR = MC$. The firm is therefore in equilibrium at price P_1 and quantity x_1.

We can now see that the market supply curve shows the total quantity offered for sale by all firms at each price. This is a case of mutual determination, for, given the demand curve, the market supply curve determines the price. This price determines the amount supplied by each firm, which when summed constitutes the market

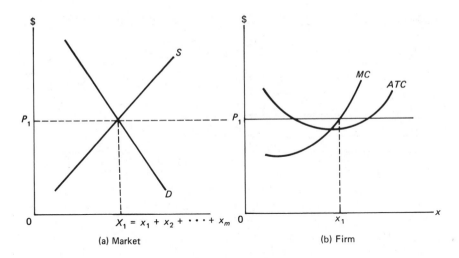

Figure 7-5. The market and the competitive firm.

supply. Note that we are assuming that the cost curves for each individual firm do not change or shift when all firms expand or contract output, although this will probably occur. Although any single firm can expand its output without affecting the prices of its inputs, when the entire industry increases output the concerted demand for inputs will bid up input prices. This in turn is reflected in an upward shift of the cost curves of the firms. Each firm will now produce a smaller output, and the market supply curve will shift to the left, resulting in a higher price and less total output.

LONG-RUN EQUILIBRIUM OF THE FIRM AND INDUSTRY

Recall that the long run is defined as meaning that all inputs are variable, which implies that firms can expand or contract or they may enter or leave an industry. The decision to enter into or exit from an industry is based on whether there are abnormal profits or losses in the industry. If $TR > TC$ for firms in the industry then new firms will enter the industry; if $TR < TC$ (loss) firms will exit; and if $TR = TC$ firms will neither enter nor exit. In the latter case, the firms and the industry are in long-run equilibrium, provided that the typical firm is operating at the minimum point on its long-run average cost curve.

When $TR = TC$, total costs are fully covered by total revenue, and this includes a normal return to all the inputs, including labor, land, capital, and management. The normal returns to the inputs are equal to what could be expected in accordance with the opportunity cost doctrine; that is, what might be called the going market rate, which includes a normal return or normal profit to the entrepreneur for the management function. In this light, when $TR > TC$ (for the typical firm) there exists an abnormal profit, or economic profit, for firms in the industry, in excess of these normal returns. Hence, other firms outside this industry are attracted to this more lucrative industry.

Figure 7-6(b) shows the firm in a long-run equilibrium position at price P_1, at the minimum point of the long-run average cost (LAC) curve. P_1 is established by the intersection of the market supply and demand curves in Figure 7-6(a). When the firm is in long-run equilibrium the following set of equalities holds: $P(= MR) = SMC = SAC = LMC = LAC$, where SMC is short-run marginal cost, SAC is short-run average cost, and LMC is long-run marginal cost. When this is the case, the firm is operating at the minimum point of both the short-run and long-run average cost curves. The firm is in equilibrium because there is no tendency to change since this position cannot be improved upon by the firm; nor will other firms be attracted to this industry. If new firms did enter the industry then the supply would be increased (S would shift to the right); the price would fall, and subnormal profits (losses) would result, as the price would then be below the SAC and LAC curves; and the firms would leave the industry, thereby restoring the price to P_1.

Long-Run Adjustments

Now let us suppose that this equilibrium position is disturbed by an increase in market demand: D_1 shifts to D_2 in Figure 7-6(a), and the price rises to P_2. In the short-run the typical firm will maximize profit by equating P_2 and SMC_1 and producing output x_{M1}. Market output will rise to x_1' from x_1. Next, assume that the firm increases its output to x_{M2} in the long run because it can now maximize profits by using a larger plant SAC_2 where $P_2 = SMC_2 = LMC$. This output yields maximum abnormal profits for the firm, equal to the number of units produced (x_{M2}) times the abnormal profit per unit, which is always measured by the distance between the SAC and the price at the output produced. Note that we are ignoring the shift of the supply curve to the right caused by the increase in output from x_{M1} to x_{M2} by all firms, for the sake of simplicity.

When the firm does expand to SAC_2 it is in for an unpleasant surprise. The abnormal profits of the typical firm in the industry

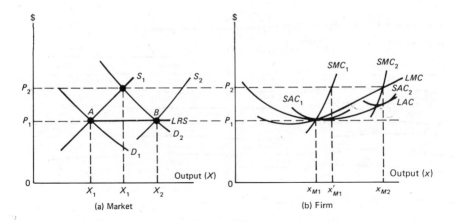

Figure 7-6. Long-run supply curve for a constant-cost industry.

attract additional firms to this industry, which would be the case even if the firm produced x_{M1}. If we assume that the same cost curves apply to the new firms, we see that the entering firms tend to construct plants equal to SAC_2 and produce output x_{M2} so that they too may maximize profits. But as the new firms enter the industry, the total market supply will increase (the S_1 curve shifts to the right) and the market price will decline. As the price declines, a smaller-sized plant will now lead to greater profits because of the profit maximization condition that $P = SMC = LMC$. Therefore, the existing firms would contract, and new firms entering would build smaller plants. These adjustments will continue in this manner until the supply is increased to the point where the price declines back to P_1, because of the shifting of the supply curve from S_1 to S_2. At this point each firm is again in long-run equilibrium producing x_{M1}, but there is a larger number of firms, so that total industry output is now X_2.

CONSTANT-, INCREASING-, AND DECREASING-COST INDUSTRIES

The Constant-Cost Industry

The long-run supply curve for the industry can now be constructed by connecting the long-run market equilibrium points A and B in graph (a). This long-run supply curve (LRS) indicates that, in the long run, additional amounts of product will be supplied by this industry at price P_1, which is equal to the minimum long-run average cost. Here we are assuming that, when the industry expands (or contracts), the LAC curve of each firm will not shift up or down but will remain unchanged. This is the case of the **constant-cost industry**. But the LAC curve of each firm may shift upward as new firms enter and the industry expands, in which case the long-run supply curve of the industry would rise; or if the LAC curve shifts downward with the growth of the industry, then the LRS curve would decline. Let us now consider these cases.

The Increasing-Cost Industry

The case of the **increasing-cost industry**, or a rising LRS curve for the industry, is shown in Figure 7-7. Starting with a long-run equilibrium position for the firm and market at price P_1, with output x_M for the firm and X_1 for the industry, we again assume that the market demand curve shifts from D_1 to D_2. The resulting rise in price from P_1 to P_2 makes for abnormal profits, and let us now suppose that there is an immediate influx of new firms. In other words, the entire industry expands, and this expansion causes (1) the LAC curve to rise from LAC_1 to LAC_2 for reasons we explain below, and (2) the short-run market supply curve to shift from S_1 to S_2. The upward shift of the LAC curve, and the shift to the right of the S curve, will stop when the shifting S curve lowers the price to the point P_3 where it is again equal to the minimum point on the rising LAC curve, i.e., the minimum point on LAC_2 in Figure 7-7(b). At

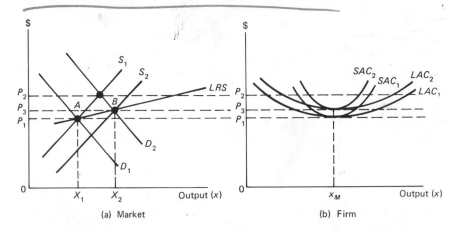

Figure 7-7. Long-run supply curve for an increasing-cost industry.

price P_3 there are no longer any abnormal profits, so new firms stop entering the industry, and equilibrium is reestablished. The *LRS* curve connects all long-run equilibrium points such as A and B, and it shows that in the long run the industry can supply additional amounts of the product only at higher prices because of the rising *LAC*. Again, this is the case of the **increasing-cost industry,** and the explanation of the upward-rising *LAC* curve runs in terms of what we shall call **industry diseconomies** (also called **external diseconomies**).

Industry Diseconomies

Industry diseconomies are changes that occur because of the expansion of the industry, and that raise the cost of inputs to the firms in the industry. For example, as the industry grows, it may become necessary to resort to more costly ores or other natural resources; or higher labor expenditures may be necessary to attract additional workers for the expanding industry, even though a single firm could have hired additional workers at the going market rate; or the expanding industry may cause enough pollution of water and air to necessitate the installation of costly control devices; and so forth. We must emphasize that these changes do not determine the shape of the *LAC* curve but cause the entire *LAC* curve to move upward, as shown in Figure 7-7(b).

The Decreasing-Cost Industry

Finally, the *LRS* curve declines in the case of the **decreasing-cost industry.** Figure 7-8 illustrates this case. Again, we begin with a long-run equilibrium position for the firm and the market at price P_1.

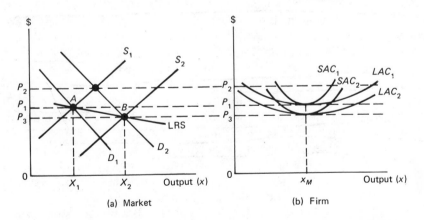

Figure 7-8. Long-run supply curve for a decreasing-cost industry.

We again assume that demand increases from D_1 to D_2, thereby increasing the price to P_2 and creating abnormal profits for the firm. This leads to the entry of new firms, which causes (1) the supply curve to shift to the right and, in this case, (2) the LAC curve to shift downward. The entry of new firms continues until the price declines to P_3, where it is again equal to the minimum point on the LAC curve, and a new long-run equilibrium is achieved. By connecting the long-run equilibrium points A and B we trace the LRS curve, which now declines as a result of the downward movement of the entire LAC curve.

Industry Economies

The LAC curve shifts downward because of **industry economies** (also called **external economies**), changes that lower the cost of inputs to the firm as the entire industry expands. For example, as an industry grows, independent trade schools may spring up to earn a profit by training workers to meet the industry's growing need for skilled labor, thereby reducing the firm's outlays for costly in-plant training programs; or transportation costs may decline as the public carriers adapt their facilities to the needs of the industry, and so forth. Eventually, as the industry gets larger, these industry economies are gradually exhausted, and the declining LRS curve gives way to a horizontal or rising LRS curve.

Shifts in Demand

In our analysis of constant-cost, increasing-cost, and decreasing-cost industries, we assumed that an initial long-run equilibrium position was disturbed by an increase in demand. In all three cases, new firms entered the industry because of abnormal profits. On the other hand, if we assume a decrease in demand, the effect is a decline in price below the minimum point on the firm's LAC curve. This means that losses will occur, firms will leave the industry in the long run, and the industry will get smaller. As the output of the industry shrinks, the supply curve will shift to the left. The LAC curve will stay in the same position, will move upward, or will shift downward, depending on whether the industry is one of constant, decreasing, or increasing costs, respectively. Referring to the preceding three pairs of graphs, the movement is now from point B to point A, from the second set of curves in each case to the first set. We are of course assuming that the growth process is exactly reversible. If this is not the case, the LRS curve will have one slope when the industry expands, but a different slope when it contracts.

APPLICATIONS: SOME REAL-WORLD CONSIDERATIONS

We have seen how shifts in demand and supply curves change the price of a good. A change in price will affect the output of the firm in the short run, and in the long run it will lead to an expansion or contraction of the number of firms in the industry. If the industry expands, more resources will be used in this industry; if it contracts, fewer resources will be needed. In this fashion, demand and supply determine prices, which serve to allocate resources throughout the economic system.

But suppose that prices are prevented from responding to changes in demand and supply? What then? Such is the case when the government introduces any form of price control that sets the price of a good at a predetermined level, either below or above the equilibrium price that would be established by demand and supply. If the government fixes the price below the equilibrium price and prevents it from rising to the equilibrium price, it is called a **price ceiling**. Examples of price ceilings are maximum prices set on natural gas, and rent controls (which are discussed in Chapter 1). If the price of a good is fixed at a level above the equilibrium price and the government does not allow the price to go down to equilibrium, this is known as a **price floor** or a **price support**. Minimum wages and agricultural price supports are examples of price floors. The government establishes price ceilings and price floors for various reasons, but chiefly to try to help consumers, to aid the poor, and to satisfy the demands of specific interest groups such as farmers.

The government's intentions may be good, but the natural gas industry provides an excellent example of how price ceilings lead to shortages. Since 1960 the government, through the Federal Power Commission, has effectively controlled the price of natural gas transported from one state to another. Gas sold in the state in which it is produced is not subject to federal control. The price of interstate gas has been regulated at a level below the equilibrium price for many years. According to our theory, what would we expect from such a policy? Figure 7-9 shows a hypothetical situation, in which the price of gas is set below the price that would be established by demand (D_1) and supply (S). If the price is regulated at P_R, below the equilibrium price (P_E), then demand (X_2) will exceed supply (X_1) by an amount $X_2 - X_1$. That is, more will be demanded at the abnormally low price (P_R) than will be supplied, and there will be a shortage equal to the difference between the quantity demanded and the amount supplied at the regulated price. This is what our theory tells us would happen, and this is what actually did happen.

By the late 1960s, it became clear that people were not able to obtain all the natural gas they desired.

In the early 1970s, shortages become more acute; not only were regular consumers unable to obtain all the gas they wanted, but many of those desiring natural gas for the first time had to wait to be hooked up. By the mid-1970s, the shortage of natural gas had become a national issue, and it was obvious that the gas situation was part of the energy crisis. It was also apparent that if the price of gas remained low relative to other fuels, then demand would increase and the shortage would get worse. In Figure 7-9 this is illustrated by a shift of the demand curve from D_1 to D_2, which increases the shortage from $X_2 - X_1$ to $X_3 - X_1$. At the same time, the search for greater supplies of gas is discouraged by the abnormally low controlled price.

In recognition of this situation, Congress passed a natural gas deregulation bill toward the end of 1978 that provides for the gradual decontrol of the price of new gas between 1979 and 1985. According to our theory, this should stimulate the search for new gas, as well as curb the demand for gas, thereby relieving the shortage of natural gas.

The economic consequences of price floors (or price supports) can be clearly seen by examining governmental intervention in agricultural markets. Since the depression of the 1930s the government has tried to help the farmer by means of price support programs designed to maintain the prices of various farm products above the levels dictated by demand and supply. Higher farm prices mean higher farm incomes and less farm poverty. Sounds good, but what are some of the other consequences of these price floors?

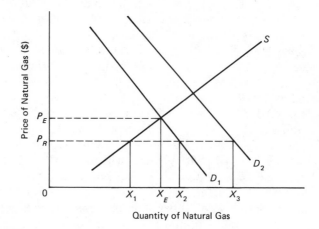

Quantity of Natural Gas

Figure 7-9. Price ceiling on natural gas.

Figure 7-10 shows a hypothetical demand and supply curve for any one of the many farm products, such as corn, tobacco, wheat, or cotton, that has been supported by the government. The equilibrium price in the graph is P_E, where demand equals supply. The support price is set above the equilibrium price at a level such as P_R. At the higher price P_R, farmers will be encouraged to grow more of the commodity, whereas consumers will consume less because of the higher price. Therefore, at the support price farmers will want to sell more of the commodity than consumers will want to buy, and there will be a surplus, equal to $X_2 - X_1$ in the graph. In order to maintain the price at P_R the government must purchase this surplus; otherwise farmers will attempt to sell it in the market, thereby driving the price back down to P_E. The cost of the surplus to the government is represented by $P_R(X_2 - X_1)$ in the graph. But it is the taxpayer who really pays this cost in the end, for the government uses taxpayer dollars to buy the surplus. In addition, taxpayers must also bear the cost of storing the surplus commodities. Consumers must pay a higher price for the commodity, and as a result they are not able to consume as much. Finally, resources are misallocated to the extent that they are employed to produce surplus commodities.

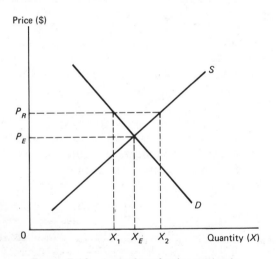

Figure 7-10. Agricultural price supports.

INNOVATION: LINEAR PROGRAMMING

Linear programming has been called "one of the most important postwar developments in economic theory."[1] Strictly speaking, it is a mathematical method, which was developed in 1947 by the mathematician George Dantzig. Although it was developed to help the U.S. Air Force plan its various activities, it was not long before the technique was applied to other aspects of management and to economic theory in general. Although problems containing hundreds of variables and equations can be solved using high-speed computers, we shall employ graphical methods to present some simple illustrative programming problems with just a few variables.

In this chapter and in the previous one, we have seen how the firm minimizes cost or maximizes profit, given various assumptions. One such assumption holds that if the firm employs two variable inputs such as capital and labor, it can continuously substitute one for the other and maintain a given level of output. This approach, as developed in Chapter 6, is shown in Figure 7-11(a), where output x_1 can be produced by any one of an infinite number of combinations of capital and labor, such as $K_1 L_2$ (combination 1) or $K_2 L_1$ (combination 2). Recall that the shape of the x_1 isoquant reflects a diminishing marginal rate of input substitution.

In linear programming, on the other hand, we assume that there are only a limited number of ways in which inputs can be combined to produce a good. Each combination is called a **process**. For example, a tree may be felled by two men using a double-handled saw, or by one man with a power saw; the former process is more labor-intensive than the latter. Figure 7-11(b) illustrates a situation where only two processes, G and H, are available for the production of a good. Output x_1 can be produced with combination 1 or combination 2 only, as contrasted with the infinite number of combinations possible in graph (a).

Even when there are but two processes, there is a degree of flexibility in the employment of inputs through the simultaneous use of both processes. Figure 7-11(b) shows the output x_1 can be produced by using a combination of capital and labor denoted by point 3. But combination 3 really means that half of x_1 is produced by process G and the other half by process H. This result can be demonstrated after noting that a process represents what is called a linearly homogeneous production function. This production function has the following characteristic: If inputs are changed in some proportion, then the output is changed in the same proportion. For example, if inputs are doubled, output is doubled; if inputs are halved, output is halved; and so forth. Looking at graph (b), we see that by cutting process G inputs in half we cut x_1 in half. The same cutting operation is next applied to process H. We now add the half of x_1 produced by process H to the half of x_1 of process G, and again we are

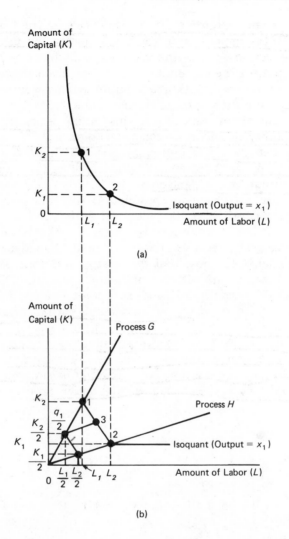

Figure 7-11. Continuous input substitution and process analysis.

producing x_1. Only now we are at point 3 on isoquant x_1, using $L_1/2 + L_2/2$ labor and $K_2/2 + K_1/2$ capital, denoting the simultaneous employment of process G and H.

Constant Prices and the Least-Cost Combination of Inputs

Another assumption underlying linear programming is exactly the same as in conventional analysis, namely, that the prices of all the firm's inputs and outputs are not influenced by the firm. In other words, there is competition in the input market and in the product market. We can now derive the least-cost combination of inputs for a given output, or the maximum output for a given cost. Figure 7-12 shows three processes: G, H, and J. Suppose relative input prices and total outlay were such as to yield isocost line C_1, as derived in Chapter 6. The maximum output for this outlay is x_1, since C_1 just reaches a corner of the x_1 isoquant at point 2 of process H; or we could say that C_1 is the minimum cost that must be incurred to produce output x_1. To produce to the left or right of point 2 would mean less output for the same cost.

The linearly homogeneous production function assures us that, with given input prices, if we double our outlay, then we double our output. In Figure 7-12 the new isocost line is C_2—twice the outlay of C_1. Process H is again optimum at point 2′ and output x_2 (= $2x_1$) is attainable. Suppose that the relative input prices change. Let us assume that we start with isocost line C_1 and that relative prices change in such a way as to produce isocost line C_1', for which we wish to maximize output. The maximum output would again be x_1, but since the isocost line coincides with the edge of the isoquant between corners 1 and 2, we can equally well use process G or H or any combination of the two. On the other hand, if the isocost line were C_1'', then process G at point 1 would be employed.

Figure 7-13 compares a change in relative input prices in the

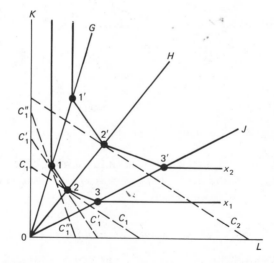

Figure 7-12. Changes in outlay and changes in relative input prices.

conventional continuous isoquant approach of graph (a) with the linear programming analysis in graph (b). With the same output x_1 and the same isocost line C_1 in both cases, graph (a) indicates an optimum at combination 4 and graph (b) at combination 3. Now suppose that relative input prices shift, such that the new isocost line is C_1' in both cases. In the conventional graph (a), combination 2 will now be best, but graph (b) shows that combination 3 and process H will still be used. We can conclude that if there are few available processes, the linear programming model would be less sensitive to changes in input prices than the conventional model.

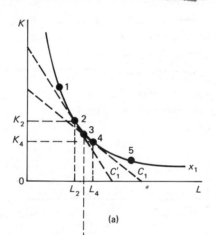

(a)

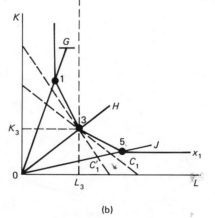

(b)

Figure 7-13. A change in relative input prices: conventional analysis and linear programming.

The Use of Constraints

We now come to a third major assumption encountered in linear programming problems, in addition to the assumptions of linearity and constant price. This involves the use of constraints. A firm may at any given time have only a limited amount of capital or labor skills available, or it may be confronted by a fixed amount of floor space or other facilities. Indeed, as we pointed out earlier, the iso-cost line could be viewed as a constraint, in which case the problem is to maximize output subject to a given outlay. Figure 7-14 illustrates a case in which there is a capital limitation of K_1 and a labor limitation of L_1. Isocost line C_1 shows that input combination 1 using process H yields output x_1 for the minimum outlay. But combination 1 requires more of input L than there is available; L_2 exceeds constraint L_1. Therefore, combination 1 is unattainable even though K_2 is well within the K constraint. In fact, the only possibility of producing x_1 under the constraints is by combining process G and process H to produce at point 2, but this would involve an outlay in excess of C_1.

Another type of linear programming problem is one in which the firm must determine the most profitable combination of goods to produce, given various production constraints. For example, imagine a pin factory that produces safety pins and straight pins. The factory has three departments: one to make safety pins, another to produce straight pins, and a third to package and ship the output of the two other departments. Each department has an upper limit to its output and these limits are the constraints. Figure 7-15 is a linear program-

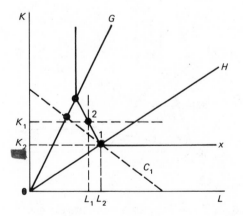

Figure 7-14. Input constraints.

ming representation of this situation. Let good A be safety pins and good B be straight pins. R_1 is the maximum output of the safety-pin department; R_2, the upper limit of the straight-pin department; and $R3$, the various maximum combinations of the two goods that can be handled by the packing and shipping department. Given these constraints, the firm is capable of producing and shipping any combination of goods A and B found on the boundary or interior of the figure 0-A_1-1-2-B_2, which defines the so-called feasible region.

Our problem now is to find the most profitable combination of A and B, given these constraints. Suppose that each package of A sold yields a profit of $\$a$, and each sale of a pack of B returns a profit of $\$b$. Therefore, the total profit (π) will equal $\$a$ times the total amount of A sold plus $\$b$ times the total quantity sold of B, or $\pi = aA + bB$. This equation is called the **objective function, and it must be maximized subject to the constraints.** This profit equation is linear and is therefore represented by a straight line on the graph, with a slope determined by the profit ratio. If the profit on a pack of A happened to be twice that of B, the profit equation or isoprofit line would have a slope similar to line π_1 on the graph. As total profit gets larger, the isoprofit line moves upward parallel to itself. Clearly, profit maximization is achieved by moving the isoprofit line as high as the constraints will permit. In our graph, isoprofit line π_2, just touching the constraint boundary at corner 1, is the highest line attainable. Hence the most profitable, or the optimum, combination of goods A and B is A_1 and B_1. Suppose that the isoprofit line happened to coincide with constraint R_3. If this were the case, any

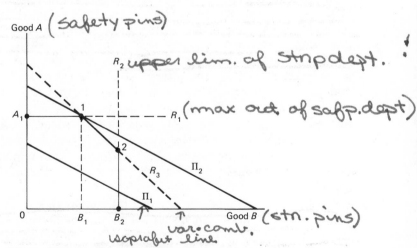

Figure 7-15. Profit maximization with constraints.

combination of A and B between and including points 1 and 2 would represent the same (maximum) profit and would be optimal.

In general, linear programming is a mathematical approach to problems that involve maximizing or minimizing an objective function subject to various constraints. These constraints usually take the form of inequalities. For example, the shipping department can handle an amount of the good equal to or less than so many units. The constraints, as well as the objective function, are linear in form, and the idea is to program or plan some activity for an optimal solution, hence the name *linear programming*.

SUMMARY

Perfect competition is a theoretical market structure based on the following assumptions: (1) there must be a large number of small sellers and buyers in order to assure that the influence of any single seller or buyer on the price of the good is negligible; (2) the good produced by each seller must be exactly the same as that produced by every other seller; (3) all firms and inputs must be completely mobile in the long run; (4) there must be perfect knowledge by all market participants; (5) all sellers must strive for maximum profits. Total (normal and abnormal) profit is defined as the difference between total revenue and total cost, and it is this difference that is maximized.

The analysis of price and output determination by the firm and industry is divided into three categories: the very short run, the short run, and the long run. In the very short run production cannot take place, and hence the supply of the good is fixed. Therefore, the market supply curve is a vertical line, assuming that sellers do not withhold any supplies from the market. In this case, the price of the good is determined by the intersection of the market demand curve and the vertical supply curve. It is possible that the entire supply may not be offered for sale at once, depending on cost of storage, perishability, and price expectations. In this case, the market supply curve would have a positive slope, indicating that more of the supply would be offered for sale as the price rose. The market price and output are determined by the intersection of the market demand and supply curves.

In the short run, the supply can be increased, since more or less of the variable input can be added to one or more fixed inputs in the short run. The firm will produce the output that will maximize its total profit, that is, maximize the difference between total revenue and total cost. This difference is maximized when these two curves have the same slope. Another way of expressing the same results is that total profits are maximized when marginal revenue (the slope of the total revenue curve) equals marginal cost (the slope of the total cost curve). If total revenue is less than total cost, the firm will minimize its loss by equating marginal revenue and marginal cost. In the case of a perfectly competitive firm, marginal revenue is always the same as the market price of the good, so that the firm maximizes profit by equating price and marginal cost. Therefore, the supply curve of the firm in the short run is the marginal cost curve; more precisely, that portion of the marginal cost curve above the average variable cost curve (the shut-down point). The market supply curve is found by summing the supply curves of all the firms in the industry. The market price and output are determined by the intersection of this supply curve and the market demand curve.

In the long run, all inputs are variable, and firms may enter or leave an industry. Firms will enter if there are abnormal profits being earned by firms already in the industry, and firms will leave the industry when less than normal profits exist. Long-run equilibrium is reached when the price of the good is equal to the minimum point on the long-run average cost curve. When this is the case, all firms are earning normal profits. The shape of the long-run supply curve depends on whether the industry is a constant-cost industry, an increasing-cost industry, or a decreasing-cost industry. In the case of a constant-cost industry, the long-run supply curve is a horizontal line, indicating that the industry is able to supply more or less of the good at a constant price in the long run. In the case of an increasing cost industry, the entry of new firms leads to higher input prices as a consequence of industry diseconomies, causing the long-run average cost curves of all firms to move upward. This in turn results in an upward-sloping long-run supply curve for the industry. In the case of a decreasing-cost industry, new firms bring about declining long-run average cost curves because of industry economies, and the long-run supply curve slopes downward.

The equilibrium market price of a good under perfect competition is determined by the intersection of the demand curve and the supply curve. In this chapter, we analyzed the consequences of government interference with the market price. If the government controls the price at a level below the equilibrium market price, this is called a price ceiling, and price ceilings are associated with shortages. If the price is controlled at a level above the equilibrium price, this is called a price floor and results in a surplus, as in the case of agricultural surpluses. In general, price ceilings and price floors prevent the pricing mechanism from allocating resources in the most efficient way.

Linear programming is a mathematical approach to problems that involve maximizing or minimizing an objective function subject to various constraints. Unlike conventional theory, in linear programming we assume that there is only a limited number of ways in which inputs can be combined to produce a good. Each combination is called a process, and a process is represented by a linearly homogeneous production function. This production function is such that if inputs are changed in some proportion, then output is changed in the same proportion. Using high-speed computers, linear programming can be used to solve a variety of problems in which a maximum or minimum is sought, subject to constraints.

Note

1. R. Dorfman, P. A. Samuelson, and R. M. Solow, *Linear Programming and Economic Analysis* (New York: McGraw-Hill Book Company, 1958), p. vii.

Problems and Questions

1. Under what circumstances would the industry supply curve not be a vertical line in the very short run?
2. a. Discuss how the supply curve of the firm is determined in short run.
   b. Assume that the price of the good is $10, how would you use the following table to find the firm's profit-maximizing output?

Output (Units)	Total Cost ($)
1	100
2	105
3	112
4	122
5	135

3. How would the firm determine how much to produce if the price fell below short-run average variable cost? Explain.
4. How would you explain the difference between normal and abnormal profits?
5. How is the long-run supply curve derived in an increasing-cost industry?

6. What is the difference between industry economies and industry diseconomies?
7. Why do we assume that there are large numbers of both sellers and buyers in a perfectly competitive industry?
8. What is the difference between the consequences of a price floor and a price ceiling?
9. How does the firm perceive its demand curve? Why?
10. What is a linearly homogeneous production function?
11. How does linear programming differ from the conventional analysis of the firm?

Recommended Reading

Dorfman, R., P. A. Samuelson, and R. M. Solow. *Linear Programming and Economic Analysis*, Chapters 1, 2, and 6. New York: McGraw-Hill Book Company, 1958.

Dorfman, Robert. "Mathematical, or 'Linear,' Programming: A Nonmathematical Exposition," *American Economic Review*, Vol. 43 (December, 1953), pp. 797–825.

Henderson, J. M., and R. E. Quandt. *Microeconomic Theory: A Mathematical Approach*, 2d. ed., Chap. 4. New York: McGraw-Hill Book Company, 1971.

Marshall, Alfred. *Principles of Economics*, 8th ed., Book 5, Chaps. 4 and 5. London: Macmillan & Co., Ltd., 1920.

Stigler, G. J. "Perfect Competition, Historically Contemplated," *Journal of Political Economy*, Vol. 65 (February, 1957), pp. 1–17.

The Theory of Monopoly

INTRODUCTION

A monopolistic industry is the extreme opposite of a competitive industry. In a competitive industry there is a large number of small sellers, whereas a monopoly consists of only one seller—it is a one-firm industry. In a competitive industry we assume easy entry into and exit from the industry in the long run, but in a monopolistic industry entry is completely blocked; otherwise, additional firms might enter, in which case the monopoly would be destroyed. In a competitive industry every firm produces the same good, but the monopolist produces a unique good having no satisfactory substitutes anywhere in the economy. To put it another way, the need the good serves cannot be satisfied by any other good, except perhaps in a very inferior manner. There are not many goods like this because most goods are simply not that unique. An example of a unique good, or service, is provided by the telephone. The telephone company serving a particular community may be said to have a monopoly on all telephone calls in the community. Still, even the telephone has substitutes. Instead of making a long-distance call, an individual can send a telegram or a letter and can substitute direct contacts and letters or telegrams for local telephone calls. At one time, the Aluminum Company of America was the only producer of aluminum in the United States, although now there are several aluminum producers. But even aluminum has substitutes in many of its uses in the form of plastics and other metals.

Although it may be difficult to find a pure monopoly, in the sense that there are no substitutes available, there are many companies that enjoy a high degree of monopoly. Usually this is found in a large multiproduct corporation with correspondingly large research expenditures. A new discovery may give the firm an exclusive position in a particular good until other firms catch up. A drug company may discover a new drug unlike anything available, or an electronics firm may develop a unique device. If the new good or process is patented, then the company will control the market for this particular good or process until the patent expires or other companies develop substitutes.

Another means of monopoly power is through control of essential resources. For example, for many years the Aluminum Company of America had exclusive rights to almost all the domestic bauxite ore, from which aluminum is made, and this resource position effectively excluded potential rivals. Monopoly may also arise because the market for the good is of such size that it can support only one low-cost firm; only one firm can make profits. If another firm entered the industry with another large plant, then output would be so large relative to demand that both firms would be unprofitable.

When we turn to the kind of monopoly possessed by telephone, gas, electric power, and water companies, we find that these are regulated monopolies. Although there may be only one firm supplying an essential, almost unique good, the community or state generally regulates the monopoly to the point where the firm's power over prices and profits is very limited and subject to frequent investigation by a regulatory commission. Aside from these regulated public utilities, a firm is prevented from monopolizing an industry by the antitrust laws. The Sherman Antitrust Act of 1890 prohibits a firm from attempting to monopolize an industry. If the Sherman Act did not exist, it is likely that the economist would be able to observe real-world monopolies in action. For example, it is conceivable that IBM would have emerged as our only computer company.

SHORT—RUN EQUILIBRIUM

Revenue Curves

Since a monopoly is an industry with only one firm, it follows that the market demand curve is also the demand curve for the output of the monopolist. This means that the monopolist's demand curve is negatively sloped, unlike the horizontal demand curve facing the perfectly competitive firm. As a result, the monopolist must reduce his price if he wishes to increase his sales. This implies that his marginal revenue (MR), the addition to total revenue (TR) from selling one more unit of output, will always be less than the price. This important proposition is demonstrated in Figure 8-1. At price P_1 the monopolist finds that X_1 units of his product will be demanded, yielding a TR equal to areas a and b in the graph, or $TR_1 = P_1 \cdot X_1$. By lowering his price to P_2 he can sell one more unit of product, $X_1 + 1$, giving him a TR of a plus c, or $TR_2 = P_2 \cdot (X_1 + 1)$. If he started out with a TR of only area a and added area c when he sold the additional unit, then the MR would equal price P_2, as in a competitive firm. But actually we must subtract from P_2 (= area c) the amount represented by area b in order to find the MR. In other words, the monopolist adds to his TR an amount equal to the price of the additional unit of product, but he must at the same time sacrifice an amount of revenue because he now has to sell all the other units (X_1) at the lower price, or P_2 instead of P_1. Therefore, MR must be less than price, and since the demand curve indicates the price at which varying amounts of product can be sold, the MR curve must be below the demand curve. In addition, the declining MR curve implies that the TR curve increases at a decreasing rate, reaches a maximum, and then declines.

Figure 8-2 shows the relationship between price elasticity of demand (e), MR, and TR. When demand is elastic ($e > 1$), MR is positive and TR is increasing, as illustrated in graphs (a) and (b). When $e = 1$,

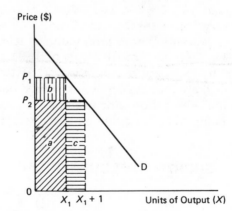

Figure 8-1. Marginal revenue is less than price.

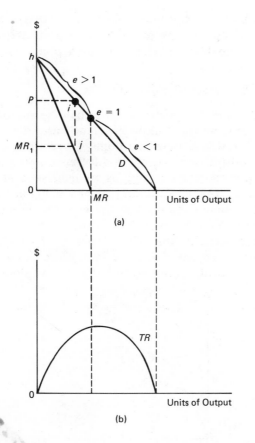

Figure 8-2. Relationship between elasticity, marginal revenue, and total revenue.

this means that the percentage change in the quantity demanded is equal to the percentage change in price, and there is no addition to TR, making $MR = 0$. For $e < 1$, MR is negative, indicating that TR is declining, or a negative amount is added to TR. Also, we can express the relationship between MR, P, and e as $MR = P - P/e$. Thus, when $e = 1$, then $MR = P - P = 0$, as shown in Figure 8-2.

A method of plotting the MR curve is shown in Figure 8-2(a). If the D "curve" is a straight line, the distance from the vertical intercept (h) to the price, distance hP, is measured down vertically from the point on the D curve corresponding to the price ($i = P$), or $hP = ij$, and this gives a point on the MR curve, MR_1. If the demand curve is a curve, the same approach can be employed by placing tangents to the curve. Another method of finding a point on the

MR curve is to bisect the horizontal distance from the vertical axis to the demand curve. For example, in Figure 8-2(a) the point k, which bisects the horizontal line Pi, is a point on the MR curve.

Maximizing Short-Run Monopoly Profits

Figure 8-3 shows that if we assume that the monopolist wishes to maximize profits, he will follow the same basic rule for maximizing his short-run profit as does the competitive firm. That is, he will produce that output for which the difference between total revenue and total cost is the greatest and, as we have seen in the case of the competitive firm, this is equivalent to producing at the point where $MR = MC$. The main difference in the case of the monopolist is the behavior of the total revenue curve, which, as we pointed out above, is no longer a straight line. The shapes of the cost curves of the monopolist are essentially the same as those of the competitive firm, since the monopolist cannot escape the law of diminishing returns.

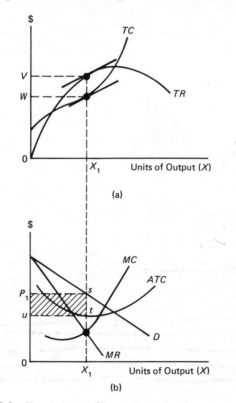

Figure 8-3. Short-run profit maximization by a monopolist.

Finally, we assume that he must buy his inputs in a competitive market.

Figure 8-3(a) shows the monopolist's TR curve along with his TC curve. TR exceeds TC by a maximum amount at output X_1, where tangents to the curves have the same slope. One more unit of output beyond this point (X_1) will add more to TC than to TR and will reduce total profits; if the monopolist stops short of output X_1, TR is increasing faster than TC and it would add to profits if he produced more. Hence, as in the competitive case, profits are maximized where the slopes of the two curves are equal, where $MR = MC$. Figure 8-3(b) shows the solution in terms of MR and MC, where the profit-maximizing price (P_1) charged by the monopolist is indicated by the point on the demand curve vertically above the point where $MR = MC$. Total profit in graph (a) is the distance VW, which must be equal to the area of the rectangle $P_1 stu$ in graph (b) (or profit per unit st times the number of units ut). Therefore, for the profit-maximizing monopolist, P_1 and X_1 represent short-run equilibrium price and output.

Figure 8-4 illustrates the case in which the monopolist is suffering losses. Graph (a) shows that there is no possible output for which

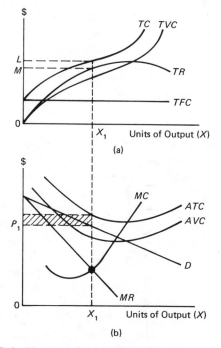

Figure 8-4. Short-run loss minimization by a monopolist.

TR exceeds TC. Under these circumstances, the monopolist cannot maximize profits, but he can and does minimize his losses. To do this, he will again follow the rule of producing where $MR = MC$, thus setting a price P_1 for output X_1, as indicated in graph (b). His loss is equal to the hatched area in the graph, or the loss per unit times the number of units, which is equal to the distance LM in graph (a). As long as TR exceeds total variable cost (TVC), the monopolist will continue to operate in the short run: he not only covers all variable costs but he can also repay part of his fixed costs, whereas if he shut down he would lose all of the fixed costs. But if TR falls below TVC he will stop production in the short run. He would also not produce in the long run; he would go out of business, unless he could cover all costs by altering the size of his plant. Being a monopolist does not guarantee profits.

LONG-RUN EQUILIBRIUM

If the monopolist constructs a plant that maximizes his long-run profits, it will also maximize his short-run profits. Figure 8-5(a) illustrates long-run and short-run profit maximization by a monopolist. The monopolist will produce output X_1 that he will sell at price P_1, since at this price and output $LMC = MR$ and $SMC_1 = MR$. If, on the other hand, the monopolist constructs a plant with an average cost curve of SAC_2, he would sell output X_2 at price P_2 in order to maximize his profits, since $SMC_2 = MR$; but only short-run profits would be maximized because $LMC \neq MR$. In the long run he could increase his profits by increasing his scale of plant to SAC_1. Therefore, the monopolist's long-run equilibrium price and output are found where $SMC = LMC = MR$.

We are assuming, of course, that the demand curve for the good does not change its shape or position, if the monopolist is to have a stable long-run equilibrium position. If demand increases (curve shifts to the right) or becomes more elastic, then the monopolist will increase the scale of his plant, as shown in Figure 8-5 (b). Here the monopolist employs plant SAC_3 and produces output X_3, where once again the condition of long-run equilibrium, $SMC_3 = LMC = MR$, is satisfied. Notice that the long-run profit maximization position in Figure 8-5(a) involves using a smaller-than-optimum-size plant (to the left of the minimum point on the LAC curve) at less than maximum efficiency (to the left of the minimum point on the SAC_1 curve). In Figure 8-5(b), long-run equilibrium is achieved with a plant scale larger than optimum, which operates at greater than maximum efficiency.

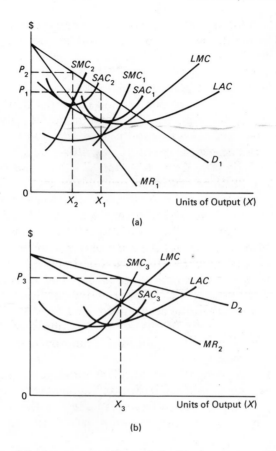

Figure 8-5. Long-run profit maximization by a monopolist.

We are also assuming that the cost curves do not shift because of changes either in input prices or in technology. Further, entry of additional firms is ruled out in our model by definition; if another firm became part of the industry, we would no longer have a monopoly. At the beginning of this chapter, we discussed the possible barriers to entry that would enable a firm to maintain a monopoly position in the real world.

MULTIPLANT MONOPOLY

Suppose that a monopolist is operating two different plants in the short run. How would he go about maximizing profit, if the two plants do not have similar cost curves? The answer is that he would produce each additional unit of the good in the plant having the lowest MC for that unit, until MC for the last unit produced equaled MR. If the units of the good were infinitely divisible, then profit maximization would be achieved when $MC_1 = MC_2 = MR$. This is illustrated in Figure 8-6. Graphs (a) and (b) show the MC curves for plant I and Plant II, respectively. By summing MC_I and MC_{II} horizontally, we get each level of total output that has the same MC in each plant; this is shown in graph (c) by $MC_T = MC_I + MC_{II}$. Therefore, when $MC_T = MR$, then $MC_I = MC_{II} = MR$, and the condition for profit maximization is satisfied.

Consider a numerical example. Suppose that the monopolist could produce another unit of the good for $1 in plant I and for $1.25 in plant II. If this additional unit could be sold for a price that added $1.50 to total revenue then the monopolist would produce this unit, and he would produce it in plant I and add only $1 to total cost. In this fashion he would always produce in the plant where the addition to total cost is the smallest, as long as this addition to total cost continues to be less than the addition to total revenue brought about by selling the added unit of the good. By following this rule, the rising MC in each plant would continue to approach MR, until finally each MC equaled MR.

In the long run, when the multiplant monopolist has the opportunity to plan the number and size of his plants, it would be most profitable for him to produce from plants having the lowest possible long-run average cost. In other words, the short-run average cost

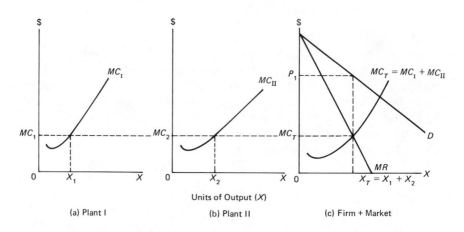

(a) Plant I   (b) Plant II   (c) Firm + Market

Figure 8-6. Multiplant monopolist in the short run.

curve for each plant should be tangent to the LAC at the minimum point of the LAC. This is illustrated in Figure 8-7(a), where the monopolist's initial plant would be SAC_1, which is tangent to LAC_1 at the minimum point of LAC_1, and output is X_1. Suppose the monopolist plans to build two plants? In this case, the long-run average cost curve would shift up to LAC_2, and the lowest-cost plant would be SAC_2. This would occur if problems of management were associated with an expanding enterprise, as assumed in Chapter 6. In addition, there would be increasing costs attributable to the expansion of the industry, assuming that the monopoly is an increasing-cost industry, as covered in Chapter 7. The monopolist would continue to add plants until the long-run marginal cost of output from the last plant equaled MR. This is shown in Figure 8-7(b), where LMC_M represents the incremental rise in total cost stemming from the increase in output due to the additional plants. The graph indicates that the monopolist would build two plants and produce $2X_1$ units of output, since at this output $LMC_M = MR$. This would be the equilibrium output, and P_1 would be the equilibrium price in the long run. In general, the number of plants (N) would be equal to the total monopoly output divided by the output per plant. In terms of Figure 8-7, $N = 2X_1/X_1 = 2$.

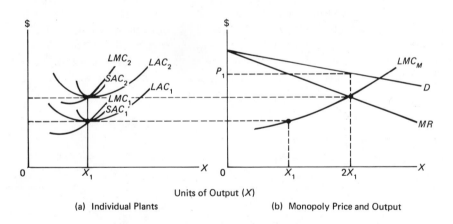

Units of Output (X)

(a) Individual Plants   (b) Monopoly Price and Output

Figure 8-7. Multiplant monopolist in the long run.

PRICE DISCRIMINATION

So far we have assumed that the monopolist charges the same price to all buyers of this good. This price is the one that will maximize his profits. We shall now see that the monopolist can make even greater profits if he is able to sell his good to different consumers or groups of consumers at different prices, or if he charges the same price when the cost is different for sales to different buyers or group of buyers. These practices are called **price discrimination**. There are three types of price discrimination that are called first-degree, second-degree, and third-degree price discrimination. We shall discuss them in turn, starting with the last type.

Third-Degree Price Discrimination

In the case of **third-degree** price discrimination the monopolist finds that he can add to his profits by separating his market into submarkets. He sets a different price in each submarket, although within each submarket the cost is the same. For this course of action to enlarge the monopolist's profits, the different submarkets must be separated geographically or in some other way. Otherwise, buyers in the low-priced submarket could make themselves a profit by reselling the good in the high-priced submarket and thereby undermine the monopolist. Another requisite for third-degree price discrimination is that there be different elasticities of demand in the various submarkets; otherwise, there would be no advantage in discrimination, as demand would then be identical in all submarkets.

These conditions for discrimination, separated markets, and different price elasticities can be clarified by means of Figure 8-8. We assume that the monopolist can separate his total market—graph (c)—into two parts, as shown in graphs (a) and (b), with different demand

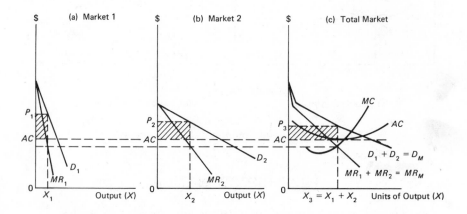

Figure 8-8. Third-degree price discrimination by a monopolist.

elasticities. The total market demand (D_M) and MR curves (MR_M) are the horizontal summation of the respective curves of submarket 1 [graph (a)] and submarket 2 [graph (b)] as indicated in graph (c). As usual, the profit-maximizing monopolist equates MR and MC for his total market, and the appropriate output is X_3. But instead of charging the corresponding total market price P_3, he will divide the output X_3 into X_1, to be sold in submarket 1 at price P_1, and X_2, which he will sell in submarket 2 at P_2.

He determines the quantity and price for each submarket by setting the MR for each submarket equal to the level determined by the intersection of MR_M and MC. By applying the $MR = MC$ rule to each submarket, it can be seen that any other distribution of sales would result in a reduction of profit in both submarkets. The total profit in each submarket is equal to the difference between the price and average cost (AC) multiplied by the output, as shown by the hatched areas in the graphs. The sum of the profit in submarket 1 and that of submarket 2 exceeds the total market profit that would have been possible without price discrimination. But if the elasticity of demand is the same in both submarkets 1 and 2, then the price would necessarily be the same and discrimination would not yield greater profits. That is, since the relationship between MR and P is $MR = P - P/e$, then if MR and e are the same in both submarkets, P must also be the same.

Second-Degree Price Discrimination

Second-degree price discrimination occurs when a monopolist charges the consumer a lower price when the consumer purchases a larger quantity of the good, assuming that the lower price is not wholly a consequence of lower costs. Examples of this kind of price discrimination can be found in the pricing policies of electric and gas companies. Suppose that a representative consumer of an electric company has a demand curve as shown in Figure 8-9. The electric company engages in second-degree price discrimination and charges the consumer price P_1 for quantities purchased up to an amount X_1, P_2 for amounts taken from X_1 to X_2, and P_3 for any purchases exceeding X_2. Suppose that the consumer wishes to buy X_3 units of electricity. Without discrimination, the price for the entire quantity would be P_3, and the monopolist's total revenue would be equal to $P_3 \cdot X_3$, or the area of the rectangle OP_3AX_3. With second-degree price discrimination, the monopolist is able to enlarge his revenue rectangle OP_3AX_3 by an amount equal to the striped areas in Figure 8-9.

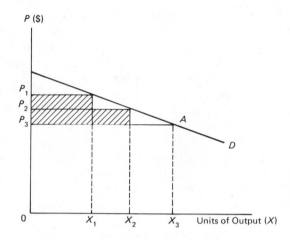

Figure 8-9. Second-degree price discrimination.

First-Degree Price Discrimination

First-degree price discrimination, or perfect price discrimination, as it is also called, exists if the monopolist is able to charge each buyer of his good the maximum price that the buyer would be willing to pay rather than go without the good. In other words, the monopolist is able to sell each unit of his good for the maximum price for that unit. This is illustrated in Figure 8-10. The demand curve shows that there are consumers willing to buy the good once the price goes below P_3. For example, at P_2 the monopolist will sell X_1 units, and so forth. Suppose that the monopolist decides to sell X_n units. Ordinarily, his total revenue would equal $P \cdot X_n$, or the area OP_1AX_n. By practicing first-degree price discrimination, he is able to increase his total revenue by an amount equal to the striped triangle, or P_1P_3A, yielding him a total revenue of OP_3AX_n. This added revenue (P_1P_3A) garnered by the monopolist is called **consumer surplus.**

The concept of consumer surplus refers to the advantage to the consumer of being able to purchase a good for a price that is less than the price that the consumer would have been willing to pay rather than go without the good. Suppose that a consumer would be willing to pay up to $0.50 for a cup of coffee rather than do without, but the restaurant charges only $0.30 a cup; the consumer surplus would be $0.20 in this case. Referring to Figure 8-10, we see that a nondiscriminating monopolist would sell all X_n units at the single price P_1. Therefore, all consumers willing to pay the higher

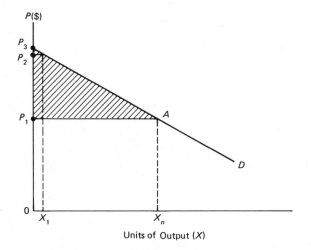

Figure 8-10. First-degree price discrimination.

prices represented by the stretch of the demand curve P_3A would be able to buy the good for P_1 per unit. Hence, the total consumer surplus would be P_1P_3A. By practicing first-degree price discrimination, the monopolist is able to convert all of this consumer surplus into his own additional revenue. An example of this kind of price discrimination would be the pricing of the only doctor in a remote village, who is able to charge each patient a different fee for the same treatment, depending on the patient's ability and willingness to pay rather than go without the treatment.

MONOPOLY COMPARED WITH PERFECT COMPETITION

Of importance to consumers of a good and to the welfare of the economy in general is the difference between the equilibrium price and quantity of the good produced by a monopoly and those of the same good produced by a perfectly competitive industry. To make both types of industry comparable, we assume constant returns to scale for all firms; we also assume constant cost industries where the costs are the same for both industries. Given these assumptions, the results of the comparison are shown in Figure 8-11. The long-run supply curve (LRS) of the competitive industry would be horizontal, and it would be equal to the LAC of the monopoly. If the market demand curve is D in the graph, then the competitive industry would be in equilibrium when $LRS = D$; the equilibrium price

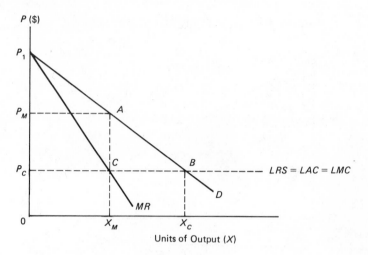

Figure 8-11. Long-run price and output for monopoly and perfect competition.

and output would be P_c and X_c, respectively. Assuming no price discrimination, the monopolist would maximize profits by deriving the MR curve and equating it to the LMC (= LRS), and his price and output would be P_M and X_M, respectively. Hence, the monopoly would lead to higher prices and less output as compared with perfect competition. As a consequence, consumer surplus would be smaller under monopoly: $P_1 A P_M$ as against $P_1 B P_c$ in perfect competition.

The foregoing comparison does not necessarily imply that consumers and the economy in general would always benefit if all monopolistic or oligopolistic industries were forced into the perfectly competitive mold. Suppose, for example, that the U.S. automobile industry was made to conform to the requirements of a competitive industry. If it were, there would be a large number of small firms, each producing an identical car. Any technological or other efficiencies of large-scale production would be lost, as each artificially small firm would be stuck by legislation on the upper reaches near the beginning of its LAC curve. Consumers would have fewer cars at higher prices, and there would be no variety. On the other hand, suppose that it was decided that the society should retain the advantages of large-scale production, and the number of big low-cost auto firms was increased to provide a competitive atmosphere. In this case, the ensuing large increase in the supply of cars would drive the price below cost; all but a few firms would have to leave the industry, thereby returning the industry to the original situation.

THE REGULATION OF MONOPOLIES

Although dissolution or divestiture may be called for, as in the well-known cases of Standard Oil of New Jersey (1911) and American Tobacco Company (1911), there are methods by which the government can deal with the undesirable social consequences of monopoly power, other than by transforming the structure of the industry. We shall consider two approaches to monopoly regulation. One type of governmental intervention is the regulation of the monopolist's price. Another way of approaching the problem is by means of a tax levied against the monopolist.

Governmental monopoly price regulation is illustrated by Figure 8-12(a). Without governmental interference, the monopolist would

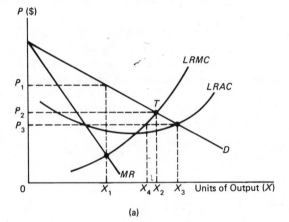

(a)

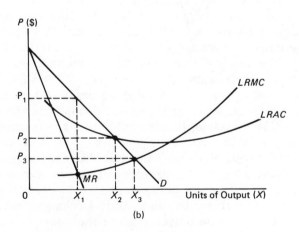

(b)

Figure 8-12. Regulation of monopoly price.

maximize profits when $MC = MR$; the price and output would be P_1 and X_1, respectively; and profits would be substantial. Suppose the price is regulated so that P_2 is the maximum price that the monopolist can charge his customers; then his demand curve becomes P_2TD. The price P_2 is selected because the LMC crosses the demand curve at this level. Since MR equals P_2 up to the demand curve, the monopolist will now maximize profit by producing X_2 where $P_2 = MR = LMC$, a result similar to competitive equilibrium. From the viewpoint of society, the price is now lower and output is greater than before regulation. If the price is lowered to P_3, which is equal to LAC, output would not be increased by the monopolist to X_3. MR and P_3 are equal up to the demand curve; the monopolist would maximize profit where $P_3 = LMC$, which indicates an output of X_4. But demand would equal X_3, and there would be a shortage amounting to $X_3 - X_4$.

On the other hand, if the demand curve and the cost curves happened to be like those shown in Figure 8-12(b), the monopolist would go out of business if the price were regulated at P_3, where the LMC curve crosses the demand curve. At the P_3 price level, the monopolist cannot cover LAC, and the ensuing losses would force him to discontinue operations. In this case, a regulated price of P_2 would enable the monopolist to cover LAC by producing X_2, and all excess profits would be eliminated.

Monopoly Taxes

The other method of regulating monopolies is by means of taxation. We shall consider two different kinds of monopoly taxes: a lump-sum tax and a per-unit tax. A **lump-sum tax** means that the monopolist must pay a fixed amount of money per time period to the government, regardless of how much of the good is produced. In effect, the tax is a fixed cost to the monopolist and it can be analyzed as such. Figure 8-13(a) shows that the fixed tax simply raises the level of the firm's total fixed cost by an amount equal to the tax. The total cost curve also moves up, but the shape of the curve remains the same, which implies that the marginal cost curve is unchanged by the tax. Figure 8-13(b) indicates that in terms of average and marginal curves, the tax shifts the average total cost curve upward along the stationary MC curve. Confronted by the same MC and MR curves before and after the tax, the monopolist can do no better under the circumstances than to continue to produce and sell the same output (X_3) at the same price (P), as determined by the $MC = MR$ profit-maximization rule. The consumer is unaffected by the tax, but the monopolist finds that his profits are lower because the tax has shifted his average cost curve upward.

The other method of taxing a monopoly is by means of a <u>per-unit tax, or a tax per unit of output</u>. In this case the total tax increases with output, so that it would be zero when nothing is produced and would get larger as output grows. This kind of tax causes the total cost curve to swivel upward from its starting point at the beginning of the total fixed cost curve, as shown in Figure 8-14(a), where the two total cost curves diverge as output increases. Since the TC curve including the tax is steeper than the original TC curve at any given output, the MC curve of the former must be above the MC

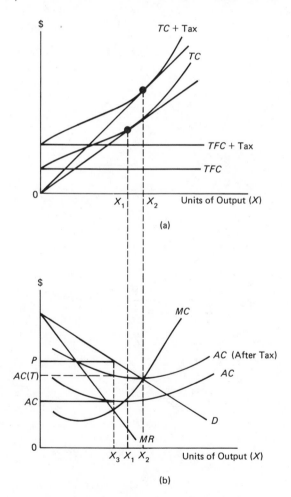

(a)

(b)

Figure 8-13. Fixed or lump sum tax.

curve of the latter. These MC curves are illustrated in Figure 8-14(b), in which the AC curve including the tax is shown to be a uniform distance (equal to the unit tax) above the original AC curve.

The profit-maximizing monopolist will react by equating his unchanged MR curve with the shifted MC curve, and he will produce a smaller output (X_2) and charge a higher price (P_2). Inevitably the monopolist has lower profits after the tax is imposed. This can best be seen by considering that his total revenue curve would remain the same while his total cost curve is higher, as shown in graph (a), and so his total profit must be smaller. Nevertheless, the consumer must pay a higher price as a result of the tax, and in this sense part of the

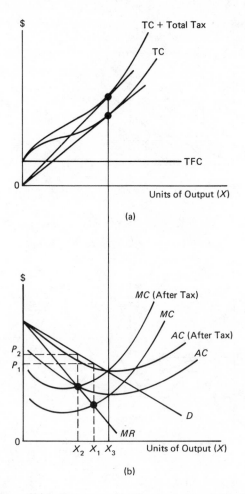

Figure 8-14. Tax per unit of output or variable tax.

tax on every unit still sold has been shifted to the consumer. Recall that in the case of a lump-sum tax the consumer is unaffected by the tax.

APPLICATION: POLAROID CORPORATION

Polaroid Corporation provides an excellent example of the power of monopoly. The Polaroid monopoly has its roots in the U.S. patent system, which grants an inventor of a product or process the exclusive right to exploit the product or process for a period of 17 years. As such, a monopolistic position based on a patent does not violate the antitrust laws. Nevertheless, the patent system has not been an important factor in the development of industrial concentration in the United States. Generally, it is possible for other companies to circumvent a patent by developing different products or processes that serve the same purpose. But in the case of the Polaroid so-called instant camera, many years would pass before another company would be able to offer a similar camera. Consequently, Polaroid Corporation had a monopoly in instant photography from 1947 to 1976, the year Eastman Kodak Company finally introduced its version of the instant camera. It might be argued that a conventional camera is a good substitute for the Polaroid camera, and hence Polaroid did not have a real monopoly. To say this is to say that the horse and buggy is a good substitute for the automobile as a means of transportation. For some purposes they may be good substitutes, but not when it is important to you to reach your destination in less time. In like manner, the Polaroid camera allows photographers to reach their destination in a matter of minutes rather than days.

One need only consider the first ten years of the Polaroid camera as a commercial product to realize the vast potential inherent in the monopolization of a good with broad public appeal. The Polaroid camera was first offered for sale to the public in 1948, and sales for that year were $1 million.[1] Ten years later, in 1958, Polaroid's sales were $65 million, second only to Eastman Kodak's in photographic products. By 1958, Polaroid Corporation held 238 patents, which covered not only the basic processes of its instant photography but other possible alternative processes as well. In addition, the company spent and still spends considerable sums on research, always searching for refinements and new methods of instant photography; of course, all discoveries are patented, which serves to extend the period of patent protection. For this reason, Kodak could

not offer a competitive camera until 1976, even though Polaroid's
initial patents expired in 1965.

By 1968, Polaroid's sales had grown to $402 million, and by 1978,
sales approximated $1.33 billion. Currently, the company holds
over 1900 U.S. patents, most of which pertain to instant photography. The Polaroid monopoly was well entrenched when Eastman
Kodak entered the instant photography market in 1976. Still, Kodak,
with its enormous resources and prestige, was able to capture 40% of
this market; apparently the market share going to Kodak has stabil-
ized at approximately 40%, with Polaroid still the dominant company in instant photography.

The profitability of a successful monopoly is also well illustrated
by Polaroid Corporation. The founder of Polaroid Corporation is
Edwin H. Land, the inventor of instant photography. His family
fortune, based solely on family holdings of Polaroid stock, currently
exceeds $200 million.

INNOVATION: THE CONCEPT OF MONOPOLY POWER

At the beginning of this chapter, we defined a monopoly as an
industry with only one firm producing a good for which there are no
close substitutes. That is the standard concept of monopoly. This
concept implies that the element of monopoly grows weaker as the
number of firms in the industry gets larger, and it also implies that
it is possible to determine when there are no "close" substitutes for
the good in question. Perhaps the best discussion of the concept of
monopoly is still to be found in a well-known article by the noted
economist Abba P. Lerner: "The Concept of Monopoly and the
Measurement of Monopoly Power."[2]

Lerner rejects the idea that the degree of monopoly necessarily
diminishes as the number of sellers grows. He points out that there
may be many sellers, but if one seller controls a large proportion of
the total supply then the monopoly element may be very strong.
On the other hand, a firm may control a small proportion of the
total supply but still possess a considerable degree of monopoly if
the firm's market is located at a distance from the other suppliers.
In this case, the cost of transporting the good into his market may
give the isolated firm an exclusive market. This leads Lerner to conclude that physically identical goods at different locations are really
different goods. By identifying location as a characteristic of a good,
Lerner has rejected the idea of classifying goods strictly on the basis
of their physical characteristics. Instead, he chooses "substitut-

ability at the margin" as the criterion for determining the similarity of different goods, regardless of their physical appearance. Goods are substitutable at the margin if they serve the same purpose for the consumer; and if they serve the same purpose then they are the same good. To use Lerner's example, if one pound of coal and four pounds of wood yield the same heat when burned, and if they cost the same, then a pound of coal and four pounds of wood represent the same good.

Lerner's concept of substitutability greatly weakens the approach to monopoly power based on the proportion of the supply of a good under the control of a single seller. Indeed, a firm may control the entire supply of a good for which there are no physically similar goods, and yet not be a monopolist in Lerner's sense of the word; there may be physically dissimilar goods that serve the same purpose for the buyer as the good in question. These considerations lead Lerner to a new approach to the problem of monopoly and monopoly power.

In the case of the perfectly competitive firm, output is always adjusted to the point where marginal cost is equal to price. In the absence of competitive markets, when the firm's demand curve slopes downward $P \neq MC$, since the firm now maximizes profit where $MR = MC$, and MR is always less than P. Therefore, when the firm is maximizing profit, MC is less than P, and Lerner focuses on this divergence of P from MC. Accordingly, he puts forth his **index of the degree of monopoly power** as

$$\frac{P - MC}{P}$$

Using this index, we see that in the case of a competitive firm, the index would be zero, and there would be no monopoly power. For example, suppose $P = MC = 10$, then

$$\frac{P - MC}{P} = \frac{10 - 10}{10} = \frac{0}{10} = 0$$

But suppose that $P = 10$ and $MC = 8$, then

$$\frac{P - MC}{P} = \frac{10 - 8}{10} = \frac{2}{10} = 0.20$$

And if $P = 10$, and $MC = 2$, then

$$\frac{P - MC}{P} = \frac{10 - 2}{10} = \frac{8}{10} = 0.80$$

Therefore, the degree of monopoly power increases as the index approaches 1.0. In this way, Lerner has produced a measure of monopoly power that avoids the conceptual problem discussed earlier. Notice, however, that Lerner's measure is accurate only insofar as the firm actually maximizes profit. In other words, it is a measure of the exercise of market power, not a measure of the possession of market power.

SUMMARY

A monopoly is an industry consisting of only one firm, and the good produced by the monopolist does not have any satisfactory substitutes. In the long run it is not possible for new firms to enter the industry; otherwise the monopoly would be destroyed. A monopoly may come about through the discovery of a new product, process, or device; or through the control of essential raw materials. Accordingly, monopoly is the extreme opposite of perfect competition.

To maximize short-run profit, the monopolist follows the same basic rule adhered to by the perfectly competitive firm: it produces that output at which marginal revenue equals marginal cost, which also represents the greatest obtainable difference between total revenue and total cost. Note that in the case of a monopolist, the demand curve slopes downward since it is also the market demand curve, and hence the marginal revenue curve is always below the demand curve; therefore, marginal revenue is always less than the price of the good. Like the perfectly competitive firm, the monopolist will not produce in the short run if total revenue is below total variable cost, which is the same as saying that price is less than average variable cost.

In the long run, the monopolist will maximize profit at that price and output where short-run marginal cost is equal to long-run marginal cost and both are equal to marginal revenue. If the price exceeds long-run average cost at this output, then the monopolist will be making an abnormal profit in the long run. If the price is less than long-run average cost, then the monopolist will suffer losses and the monopoly will cease to exist. Being a monopolist is no guarantee of abnormal profits.

The multiplant monopolist will maximize short-run profits by producing each additional unit of the good in the plant having the lowest marginal cost for that unit, until the marginal cost of the last unit produced equals the marginal revenue for that unit. In the long run, the multiplant monopolist will continue to add plants until the long-run marginal cost of output from the last additional plant equals marginal revenue.

A monopolist may be able to increase profits by engaging in price discrimination—by not selling his good for the same price to all consumers. There are three types of price discrimination. First-degree price discrimination means that the monopolist is able to charge each buyer of his good the maximum price that the buyer would be willing to pay rather than go without the good. Second-degree price discrimination occurs when the monopolist charges a consumer lower prices as the consumer purchases larger quantities of the good, provided that the lower prices are not entirely due to lower costs. With third-degree price discrimination, the monopolist is able to separate his market into submarkets, and he is able to charge a different price in each submarket. For third-degree price discrimination to be effective, the monopolist must be able to keep the submarkets segregated, and the elasticity of demand must be different in each submarket.

A comparison of monopoly with perfect competition shows that monopoly results in higher prices and less output. The government can deal with the undesirable social consequences of monopoly power by regulating the monopolist's price, and also by means of taxation. We discuss two types of monopoly taxes. A lump-sum tax means that the monopolist must pay a fixed sum of money per time period to the government. The price that the consumer must pay for the good is not affected by a lump-sum tax, but the profits of the monopolist are lower because the tax causes his average cost curve to shift upward. A per-unit tax means that the monopolist must pay a tax on each unit of the good that he produces; therefore, as output increases, the total tax gets larger. In the case of a per-unit tax, the consumer ends up paying a higher price for the good, and the monopolist has smaller profits.

A good example of the results of monopoly power is the Polaroid Corporation. On the basis of exclusive patents on its instant cameras, Polaroid has become an industrial giant with sales exceeding $1 billion a year. The profitability of a successful monopoly can also be illustrated by Polaroid Corporation. The inventor of instant photography and the founder of Polaroid Corporation, Edwin H. Land, has a family fortune in excess of $200 million.

The concepts of monopoly and monopoly power have been greatly clarified by A. P. Lerner. Since a monopoly is defined as an industry with only one firm producing a good with no close substitutes, it is important to determine what is meant by "close" substitutes. According to Lerner, goods should not be classified on the basis of their physical characteristics, but rather in terms of the purposes they serve. That is, goods that do not appear to be alike would be substitute goods if they served the same purpose for the consumer. Therefore, a firm may control the entire supply of a good for which there are no physically similar goods, but still not be a monopolist if there are other goods that serve the same purpose as the good in question. Lerner has also proposed an index of the degree of monopoly power based on the difference between price and marginal cost. The index is

$$\frac{P - MC}{P}$$

For example, we know that a competitive firm maximizes profit when $P = MC$. Therefore, in the case of perfect competition, monopoly power is zero. As the divergence between the price and marginal cost increases, the degree of monopoly power increases.

Notes

1. For a discussion of Polaroid's early years, see Francis Bello, "The Magic That Made Polaroid," *Fortune* (April, 1959), p. 124.
2. *The Review of Economic Studies*, Vol. 1 (June 1934), pp. 157-175; reprinted in W. Breit & H. M. Hochman, eds., *Readings in Microeconomics*, 2d ed. (New York: Holt, Rinehart and Winston, Inc., 1971), pp. 207-234.

Problems and Questions

1. What are the circumstances that give rise to monopoly?
2. Suppose there is only one electric power company serving a community. Why might this company not be a monopoly in the sense in which we have been using this term?
3. Is there any difference in the short-run equilibrium position and the long-run equilibrium position of a monopolist?
4. Distinguish between first-degree, second-degree, and third-degree price discrimination.
5. a. Define "consumer surplus."
   b. How does first-degree price discrimination affect consumer surplus?
6. Suppose that the government decides to use taxation as a means of regulating monopolies. What kind of tax would be most beneficial to consumers? Why?

7. Would you agree that the degree of monopoly diminishes as the number of sellers grows?
8. Suppose that Firm A sells its good for $12 per unit and its marginal cost is $7, while Firm B sells its good for $6 per unit and its marginal cost is $1. According to Lerner, which firm has a greater degree of monopoly power?
9. Why is the monopolist's marginal revenue from selling one more unit of output always less than the price of the additional unit?
10. What is the relationship between price elasticity of demand and total revenue in the case of a monopolist?

Recommended Reading

Cohen, K. J., and R. M. Cyert. *Theory of the Firm*, Chap. 10. Englewood Cliffs, N.J.: Prentice-Hall, Inc., 1965.

Hicks, J. R. "Annual Survey of Economic Theory: The Theory of Monopoly," *Econometrica*, Vol. III (Jan. 1935), pp. 1–20.

Lerner, A. P. "The Concept of Monopoly and the Measurement of Monopoly Power," *The Review of Economic Studies*, Vol. 1 (June 1934), pp. 157–175; reprinted in W. Breit and H. M. Hochman, eds., *Readings in Microeconomics*, 2d. ed., pp. 207–234. New York: Holt, Rinehart and Winston, Inc., 1971.

Machlup, F. *The Political Economy of Monopoly*. Baltimore: The Johns Hopkins University Press, 1952.

Robinson, Joan. *The Theory of Imperfect Competition*. London: Macmillan & Company, Ltd., 1933.

Zeuthen, F. *Economic Theory and Method*. Cambridge, Mass.: Harvard University Press, 1955.

9

The Theory of
Monopolistic Competition

Suppose that we start with a perfectly competitive industry and allow each firm to distinguish its good from that of every other. The difference need not be very great; perhaps it is only a slightly different package, or a minor change in ingredients, or even the promotion of a belief in the minds of some consumers that the product of one seller is somehow superior to that of all the others. This industry structure is called **monopolistic competition**. It is competitive in the sense that there are a large number of sellers in the industry, so that the decisions and actions of any single seller do not influence the behavior of any other seller. Also, it is usually assumed that there are no significant barriers to entry, so that new firms may easily enter the industry—although this assumption could be modified.

On the other hand, since each seller differentiates his good from that of the others, there is an element of monopoly. But it is a very weak monopoly element because all the products are good substitutes. For example, there are many different kinds of candy bars, one with nuts, another with raisins, another with caramel, and so forth, and each consumer may have his favorite; but if his favorite bar is not available or if it gets too expensive, the average consumer is willing to try another kind. In general there are many good substitutes for each product in monopolistic competition, unlike a monopoly in which there are only extremely poor substitutes. As a result of these conditions the demand curve for each seller is very elastic, but not perfectly elastic, as in the case of perfect competition. Since the demand curve is not perfectly elastic (not a horizontal line on a graph), each seller is able to set his own selling price, and he finds that sales increase as he lowers the price.

The firm in monopolistic competition is able to influence its sales not only by changing the price, but also by changing the good, as well as through advertising and other forms of selling activity. Sellers are constantly looking for ways to alter their goods profitably. By the same token, they are always ready to undertake advertising, or to hire additional salesmen, if the result will be greater profits.

The basic theory of monopolistic competition was developed by Edward H. Chamberlin, who was a Harvard University economist, in his book *The Theory of Monopolistic Competition*, published in 1933.[1] The theory grew out of a widespread feeling among economists that a need existed for a theory capable of analyzing the large number of real-word industries operating somewhere between perfect competition and monopoly. In this chapter, we discuss short-run and long-run equilibrium conditions in general in a monopolistically competitive industry, and then we examine the firm's adjustment process as conceived by Chamberlin.

SHORT-RUN EQUILIBRIUM

Figure 9-1 shows the profit-maximizing equilibrium position of the monopolistically competitive firm in the short run, disregarding selling costs. The demand curve has very little downward slope, which indicates that close substitutes are available: if the price is increased slightly, sales fall off greatly, indicating that buyers can easily find substitutes for the good. The cost curves are governed by the same kind of considerations as in the perfectly competitive case. As usual, we assume that the firm wants to maximize profits, and in accordance with our rule, profits are maximized when $MR = MC$, at output x_1 and price P_1 in Figure 9-1. Total profit is equal to the average profit per unit, or P_1 minus ATC (average total cost), times the number of units produced, x_1.

This is the adjustment of the typical firm. Since the good of each producer is very similar to that of every other producer, there is no

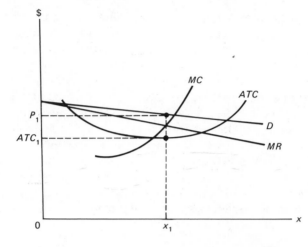

Figure 9-1. Short-run profit maximization by a firm in monopolistic competition.

reason to expect great differences in their cost curves or in the position and shape of their demand curves. Therefore, differences in output and price among the firms in the industry will not be great, although some differences may well occur. Indeed, some firms may be suffering losses in the short run while others are making profits, since monopolistic competition does not imply that all firms will be profitable in the short run. In the event that a firm is faced with a loss, it will minimize the loss by operating where $MR = MC$ as long as the price exceeds average variable cost. If the price is less than average variable cost, the firm will minimize the loss by not operating, although it cannot leave the industry in the short run. This conclusion holds for firms in any type of industry, and was explained in detail in connection with our discussion of perfect competition. Of course, in the long run, when entry and exit are possible, the firm will leave the industry if the price should fall below average total cost.

The basic rule of profit maximization can be applied to the analysis of selling costs and product variation. If the firm finds that it can increase total revenue more than total costs by incurring an additional unit of selling costs or by a small variation of the good, then expenditures for these purposes are worth undertaking. An illustration of a profitable selling expenditure is shown in Figure 9-2. The initial profit-maximizing output is x_1 at price P_1, as determined by $MR_1 = MC$ at point 1, and total profit is the corresponding hatched area. Now assume that the firm spends a lump sum, say one thousand dollars, on advertising. This will have the effect of shifting

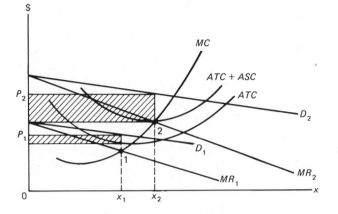

Figure 9-2. Profit maximization with selling costs.

the ATC curve upward, but will not change the MC curve, since in effect the advertising expenditure is equivalent to an increase in fixed costs; the firm has added a fixed amount to costs regardless of output. By adding the average selling cost (ASC) to the ATC curve we derive the $ATC + ASC$ curve, in the same way as we added average fixed cost to average variable cost to get ATC. But advertising expenditures would not only shift the ATC curve upward, they would also be expected to increase the demand for the product as indicated by the higher demand curve D_2, and perhaps also make the demand curve less elastic. Profits would now be maximized by equating the new marginal revenue curve (MR_2 corresponding to D_2) with MC at point 2, and by producing x_2 at price P_2. The graph shows a greater profit now, and therefore the advertising expenditure is worth undertaking. In general, the firm should adjust its advertising expenditures to the point where profits are the greatest.

If demand had shifted less, the outcome could have been smaller profits, in which case no advertising expenditure would have been advisable. Such may be the outcome if all sellers decide simultaneously to advertise; and it would result in only a small increase in demand for each seller, since each would merely retain his old customers and perhaps attract a few new buyers from outside the industry. But with costs rising sharply due to advertising and little consequent increase in demand, each seller would reason that advertising is not profitable and would discontinue these expenditures. He would not give thought to what the other sellers are planning or doing because this kind of rivalry is not a characteristic of monopolistic competition, although it is extremely important in the case of oligopoly, which is the subject of the next chapter.

We may therefore conclude that advertising will gain in profitability as the proportion of firms engaging in advertising declines. This proportion will vary if we drop the static type of analysis in which all sellers reason in the same manner simultaneously. Given a dynamic analysis with the existence of uncertainty, we can enumerate several reasons why different sellers might undertake varying amounts of advertising at different times. For example, differences may arise because of variations in the evaluation of consumer responses, in advertising campaign timing, and in problems internal to each firm.

Product variation may be analyzed similarly to variation in selling costs. If the product change adds more to total revenue than to total cost, then it is profitable to change the product. Unlike the case of selling costs, it may be possible to alter the good and add to demand without increasing unit cost, or perhaps even to decrease cost per unit. For example, a shampoo may be placed in unbreakable plastic containers instead of glass bottles, possibly leading to greater sales at less cost per fluid ounce. Of course, since we are now assuming that the firm is producing in the short run, all product changes must be feasible in terms of the existing plant. In the long run the plant can be adapted to a new product, and this may lower unit costs even more.

LONG-RUN EQUILIBRIUM

The monopolistically competitive firm will maximize long-run profits at that output where $MR = SMC = LMC$, which is the same rule followed by the monopolistic firm and the competitive firm; however, as we have seen, in the case of the competitive firm $MR = P$ since its demand curve is a horizontal line, and therefore long-run equilibrium for the competitive firm consists of $MR = P = SMC = LMC = SAC = LAC$. Suppose that the firm adjusts to the demand curve D_1 shown in Figure 9-3. By following the long-run profit-maximization rule as indicated by point 1, it will produce output x_1 and set the price at P_1. Profit per unit is the difference between P_1 and LAC (= SAC_1), and total profit is this unit profit multiplied by the number of units, x_1.

If we assume that entry into the industry is easy, then the foregoing profit-maximization position will not also be a long-run equilibrium position, for it will change as new firms enter the industry

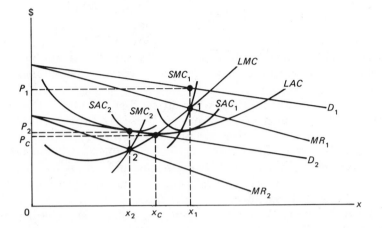

Figure 9-3. Long-run profit maximization by a firm in monopolistic competition.

to share in the abnormal profits. As these new firms produce additional amounts of goods similar to those of the old firms, the old
firms find that some of their customers are attracted to the goods
of the new firms, and the demand curves of the old firms shift downward. In other words, at any given price the total demand must be
shared by a larger number of firms, and so each firm finds that it is
able to sell a progressively smaller amount at any given price. As long
as abnormal profits exist this process continues. If we simplify the
analysis by assuming that all firms have identical demand and LAC
curves, then new firms will enter until the demand curve of each firm
becomes tangent to its LAC curve. This long-run equilibrium position
is shown in Figure 9-3 at output x_2 and price P_2, where D_2 is tangent to LAC, and $MR_2 = SMC_2 = LMC$ at point 2. Entry will cease
because there are no longer any abnormal profits to attract new
firms. Therefore, unlike the competitive firm, the monopolistically
competitive firm is in long-run equilibrium when $MR_2 = SMC_2 = LMC \neq P_2 = SAC_2 = LAC$, at price P_2 instead of P_c.

Notice that we have tacitly assumed that the entry of new firms
leaves the LAC curve unaffected, implying that the industry is one of
constant costs. But we could have assumed an increasing-cost industry, in which case the LAC curve would gradually move upward as
new firms entered the industry and bid up the cost of resources. The
rising LAC curve would then lead to the equilibrium-tangency position of the LAC curve with the falling demand curve at a higher price
than P_2 in the graph. On the other hand, a decreasing-cost industry

would be one in which the entry of new firms would lead to economies for all firms and the *LAC* curve of each would decline, leading to a final equilibrium position at a price lower than P_2. For a more detailed analysis of the shifts in the *LAC* curve, see our previous discussion of long-run adjustments in a competitive industry in Chapter 7.

If we relax our assumptions of identical demand and cost curves, there may exist islands of abnormal profit where firms enjoy exceptional consumer loyalty. For example, even though there are now many different kinds of candy bars, a Hershey bar is still considered almost synonymous with a chocolate bar and seems to enjoy an added measure of consumer preference. Abnormal profits may be more widespread if various systematic devices are employed for the purpose of blocking the entry of new firms, or at least making entry more difficult. For example, if a license is required to engage in a particular business in a city or state, the number of new firms may be limited by the difficulty of acquiring the necessary license.

The basic analysis of selling costs and product variation applies in the long run in much the same way as in the short run. Increases in selling costs raise the *LAC* curve and tend also to shift the demand curve upward. As in the short run, the key consideration is whether or not total revenue increases more than total cost as selling expenditures are incurred; if so, the additional selling expense will be undertaken and profit will be increased. In the long run, selling efforts may be intensified because of the entry of new firms. The firm now engages in advertising—not to stop the entry of new firms, since the average firm is relatively so small that by itself it is helpless in this regard, but in response to the gradual decline in demand for its product brought about by the entry of new firms. In the same way, product variations may be employed to increase or protect profits.

CHAMBERLIN'S THEORY OF MONOPOLISTIC COMPETITION

Chamberlin assumes that all firms have identical cost and demand curves, and that the behavior of the "representative" firm is the same as that of all firms in the industry. Figure 9-4 shows the two demand curves pertaining to the representative firm that are basic to Chamberlin's analysis. The demand curve d_1 is perceived by the representative firm as its demand curve, given that a price change by the representative firm will not cause any other firm to change its price. The demand curve D indicates how the quantity demanded of the repre-

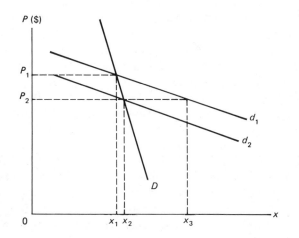

Figure 9-4. Chamberlin's two demand curves for the representative firm.

sentative firm varies with price when all firms, including the representative firm, change their prices simultaneously. Since Chamberlin assumes that what the representative firm does, all firms do, the demand curve D reflects what actually happens to the quantity demanded from the representative firm when the representative firm changes its price. For example, Figure 9-4 shows that the representative firm's demand will be x_1 at price P_1. If this firm now lowers its price to P_2, while all other firms maintain their prices, its demand will increase greatly to x_3, as shown by d_1, since this firm now attracts buyers away from the other firms. But when all firms lower their prices to P_2, as assumed by Chamberlin, the representative firm experiences a much smaller increase in the demand for its good, from x_1 to x_2, as shown by D. When all firms match the representative firm's price cut, this firm is unable to gain buyers at the expense of the other firms. This increase from x_1 to x_2 is the representative firm's share of the overall increase in demand brought about by the general price cut. Since the representative firm finds that the demand for its good is really x_2 at price P_2, it now perceives its demand curve as d_2. In this fashion, the d curve will continue to move down the D curve, if the representative firm continues to lower its price.

Short-Run Equilibrium

Let us consider the behavior of the representative firm in the short-run. Since Chamberlin adheres to the profit maximization assumption, the firm is in equilibrium when $mc = mr$. To see how Chamberlin's adjustment process works, suppose that the price is P_1 in Figure 9-5(a). At this price the firm is not maximizing profit, since $mc \neq mr$; the profit-maximizing price and output are P_2 and x_3, respectively, where $mc = mr$. Accordingly, the firm reduces its price to P_2 in order to sell x_3, as indicated by demand curve d. But, as explained above, all firms will do what the representative firm does, and when the price is lowered to P_2, the quantity demanded increases only to x_2, as indicated by demand curve D. With a demand of x_2 at price P_2, the firm is still not maximizing profit. The firm interprets its failure to sell x_3 at P_2 as the result of a downward shift in its d curve to the dashed d' curve. Therefore, the firm concludes that another price reduction is required in order to maximize profit, now indicated where $mc = mr'$. This process repeats itself as the firm continues

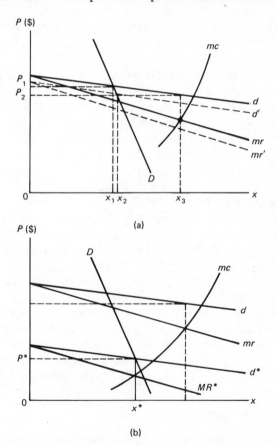

(a)

(b)

Figure 9-5. Short-run equilibrium of the representative firm.

to be thwarted in its effort to maximize profit, but it does not go on indefinitely. Eventually, the price will decline to the point where $mc = mr$, as shown in Figure 9-5(b); P^* and x^* are the profit-maximizing levels of price and output. The firm now has no further incentive to alter the price, and it is therefore in short-run equilibrium.

Long-Run Equilibrium

If the representative firm is making abnormal profits, new firms will be attracted to the industry in the long run. We assume that there are no obstacles preventing firms from entering or leaving the industry and that existing firms can expand or contract in the long run. Figure 9-6(a) shows a representative firm making abnormal profit in both the short run and the long run at price P^* and output

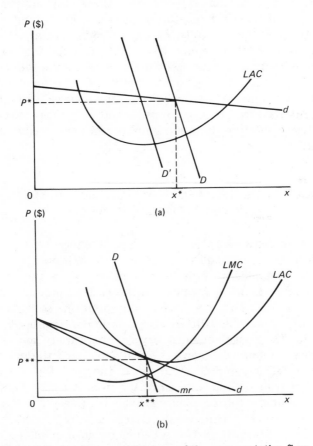

Figure 9-6. Long-run equilibrium of the representative firm.

$x^*.^2$ The entry of new firms causes the D curve to shift to the left because a relatively constant total market demand must be shared by a larger number of firms, and so each firm finds that it is able to sell less at every price. This is shown in the graph by the shift from D to D'. Of course, if firms got out of the industry, the movement of D would be in the opposite direction.

The representative firm responds to this shrinking demand by reducing its price, hoping to recoup lost sales by moving out along the d curve. It is doomed to disappointment as sales increase by a much smaller amount along the D curve. The firm again assumes that the d curve is moving downward. Therefore, two changes are now occurring in the graph: the D curve is shifting to the left, and the d curve is moving downward.

Equilibrium will be restored when abnormal profits have been eliminated, and, as a consequence, new firms stop entering the industry. This will occur when the d curve reaches a tangency point on the LAC curve, as shown by P^{**} and x^{**} in Figure 9-6(b); at this point the price P^{**} is equal to LAC. Through the adjustment process, the D curve will intersect the d curve at the same tangency point. At this point, the representative firm has no further incentive to cut its price, since any other price on the d curve would be below LAC. Profits have returned to normal, and new firms stop entering the industry. Therefore, long-run equilibrium is reached at price P^{**} and output x^{**}.

MONOPOLISTIC COMPETITION AND PERFECT COMPETITION COMPARED

We have already noted the major differences between perfect competition and monopolistic competition. We now consider the economic consequences of these differences. Since the assumption of homogeneous goods is dropped in the case of monopolistic competition, as compared with perfect competition, consumers enjoy a variety of similar but different goods under monopolistic competition. But the consumer must pay for this variety in the form of higher prices. A look at Figure 9-7 will show that the price for the good of a perfectly competitive firm with the same LAC curve would be P_c in long-run equilibrium, since the price must be equal to the minimum point on the LAC curve. Even with easy entry a monopolistically competitive firm would charge a higher price P_m in the long run. In addition, if costs are higher because of selling expenses and product variation costs, then the price would be even higher than

P_m. Note that these costs may not benefit the consumer, since he may merely become bewildered by misleading advertising or superficial product changes, which contribute little to his satisfaction.

Turning from the consumer to the economy as a whole, we find that in monopolistic competition the firm in long-run equilibrium will operate a plant that is smaller than the optimum size. Since the demand curve has a negative slope, it must be tangent to the LAC curve before the minimum point on the LAC curve is reached, and the firm is led to operate a smaller, less efficient plant than would be the case in perfect competition (see SAC_m Figure 9-7). Even this smaller plant is operated at less than its minimum cost, because the tangency occurs before this minimum is reached.

This difference between the long-run equilibrium output of the monopolistically competitive firm and that of the competitive firm is called **excess capacity**. In Figure 9-7, excess capacity is shown by the difference between x_c and x_m. This situation accounts for the higher price that must be paid for the good by the consumer. According to Chamberlin, this higher price is justified by the variety of goods that a monopolistically competitive industry offers to the consumer, as compared with a perfectly competitive industry. Nevertheless, if unnecessary advertising and product variation costs are incurred by monopolistically competitive firms, then prices may be unjustifiably higher.

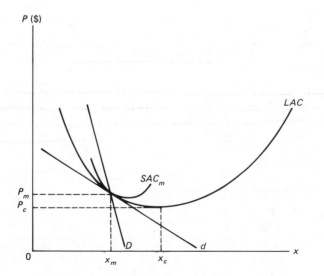

Figure 9-7. Monopolistic competition and perfect competition compared.

APPLICATION: THE NEW YORK CITY
RESTAURANT INDUSTRY

The New York City restaurant industry is a regional industry that provides an excellent example of monopolistic competition. This industry has all the earmarks of monopolistic competition. A monopolistically competitive industry must contain a large number of small firms. There are literally thousands of restaurants in New York City. Each firm must produce a good that is similar to, but different from, that produced by the other firms in the industry. All New York City restaurants provide prepared food for the public, but there are many variations from one restaurant to the next. These differences may be based on the national origin of the food, such as France or Italy; differences may stem from the type of service and degree of elegance provided; and, of course, variations arise simply because of differences in location—a restaurant may be preferred because of its convenient location. Finally, there are no barriers or obstacles to entry into this industry: while it may seem an expensive proposition to open a New York City restaurant, the cost is modest compared to that of entering most manufacturing industries.

Firms in monopolistically competitive industries employ advertising and product variations as means of attracting additional buyers. New York City restaurants engage in either or both of these practices. Many restaurants advertise simply to inform the public of their existence, location, and menu; while many others advertise to create an impression of unrivalled excellence, or to suggest that they serve a very exclusive clientele, implying that the reader of the ad can experience social distinction merely by dining in their establishment. Product variation is easily achieved in the restaurant business. Most restaurants vary their menus periodically. In many restaurants, the chef may offer a special creation from time to time, or he may produce his own version of a well-known dish. Since part of the enjoyment of dining out comes from the restaurant's atmosphere and service, product variation also includes interior decoration and the proper training of employees.[3]

Although the New York City restaurant industry is considered here, the same analysis would apply to the restaurant industry in any large city. It would not be appropriate to discuss the restaurant industry of the entire nation in terms of monopolistic competition, since location is such an important characteristic in determining the degree of substitution among restaurants. For example, restaurants in Chicago are very poor substitutes for those in New York City: people in New York City would not travel to Chicago for the purpose of dining out, even if Chicago restaurant prices were substantially below those in New York City.

THE THEORY OF MONOPOLISTIC COMPETITION EVALUATED

Chamberlin's theory of monopolistic competition has been severely criticized as well as warmly praised. Many critics have challenged Chamberlin's simplifying assumptions of identical cost and demand curves for all firms in an industry. They point out that these assumptions are inconsistent with the idea of differentiated goods. If there are differences, even small ones, in the goods of different sellers, then costs should vary from one seller to another; on the other hand, if cost and demand curves are identical, this implies identical goods, in which case the industry can be analyzed in terms of perfect competition.

Another problem arises in the definition of the industry itself. If the goods in a monopolistically competitive industry are similar but different, it may be difficult to determine where to draw the line in the array of substitute goods making up the industry. For example, can we refer to the "baking industry," and consider oyster crackers as good substitutes for cupcakes, and these as good substitutes for pumpernickel bread? In terms of our discussion of the New York City restaurant industry, is a Pizza Hut a good enough substitute for a fancy French restaurant to be regarded as part of the same industry? Chamberlin sought to deal with this problem by replacing the industry concept with what he called the **product group**. In a product group, each firm is a monopolist in the sense of having a distinctive good, but its market is somehow connected with that of the other firms in the group. Unfortunately, the product group approach does not provide any precise way of determining which firms should be included in the group.

Chamberlin's theory has been criticized because of its behavioral assumption, which states that the representative firm believes that if it reduces its price the other firms will not reduce their prices as we saw in the analysis associated with Figure 9-5, when the representative firm lowers its price, all firms do the same, and the representative firm always sells less than it anticipated. The critics ask why the representative firm never learns that whatever it does, all other firms will also do. In other words, the representative firm never adjusts to the realities of its market. Critics also assert that there are few, if any, real-world markets that can be analyzed in terms of Chamberlin's theoretical model. They say that markets that seem to conform to Chamberlin's theory turn out upon closer examination to be oligopolies.

As we saw earlier in this chapter, the downward-sloping demand curve of the representative firm leads in the long run to a higher price and a smaller output than would have been the case had the firm been in a perfectly competitive industry. This difference is what we called excess capacity, and the existence of excess capacity in monopolistic competition has generated another controversy. Recall that Chamberlin claimed that the higher price due to monopolistic competition is justified because the consumer has a greater product choice in a monopolistically competitive industry than he would have in a competitive industry. But critics have questioned whether the higher price is indeed justified by greater product choice. On the other hand, it is argued that since the long-run average cost curve is used in the analysis of excess capacity, it follows that a long-run demand curve should also be employed. Long-run demand curves are generally more elastic than short-run demand curves, and hence the tangency point would be closer to the minimum point on the long-run average cost curve, in which case the price would be closer to the competitive price.

Chamberlin's theory of monopolistic competition has also elicited great praise.[4] His book greatly stimulated microeconomic theory in general and the field of industrial organization in particular—a major accomplishment. It provided the framework for theories of oligopoly, as well as for the other market structures. It stimulated empirical research on the behavior of actual industries and markets, and was therefore largely responsible for promoting the combination of theoretical analysis and empirical research, so characteristic of modern economic theory, in the field of microeconomic theory. Chamberlin also formally recognized the existence and importance of selling costs, product differentiation, and product variations. We can conclude that while Chamberlin's theory is not without shortcomings, his theoretical innovations contributed greatly to the progress of microeconomic theory.

SUMMARY

A monopolistically competitive industry has all the characteristics of a perfectly competitive industry, except that the product of each firm is slightly different from that of every other firm. Since there is no great difference from one good to another, they are all excellent substitutes. As a result, each firm's demand curve is very elastic, but not perfectly elastic as is the case with the perfectly competitive firm. Product differences create the opportunity of using advertising and selling techniques to increase sales.

In general, the firm will maximize profit in the short run by equating short-run marginal cost and marginal revenue. If the firm is faced with a loss, it will minimize the loss by equating short-run marginal cost and marginal revenue. If the price is less than average variable cost, the firm will minimize the loss by not operating, although it cannot leave the industry in the short run. In addition, expenditures on selling and advertising are determined by the marginal approach. If greater expenditures on advertising enlarge total revenue by more than the increase in total cost, then these expenditures will be profitable for the firm. The same reasoning also applies to expenditures on product variation.

In the long run the monopolistically competitive firm will maximize profit by equating marginal revenue to both short-run and long-run marginal cost. If this yields abnormal profits, new firms will enter the industry. The entry of new firms is reflected by the downward shift of the demand curves of the existing firms. This will continue until the firm's demand curves become tangent to their long-run average cost curves, at which point abnormal profits will be eliminated and entry will cease. The industry will then be in long-run equilibrium. The same basic analysis of selling costs and product variation discussed in connection with the short run applies in the long run.

Edward H. Chamberlin, who developed the theory of monopolistic competition, produced a detailed analysis of the adjustment processes within the firm and the industry in both the short run and the long run. Basic to Chamberlin's analysis are two demand curves pertaining to the firm. One demand curve is perceived by the firm as the demand curve for its good, given that a price change by that firm will not be followed by the other firms. The other demand curve shows how much of the firm's good will be demanded if all firms change their prices simultaneously. Chamberlin ingeniously employs his dual demand curve approach to determine how price and output adjustments occur within the firm and the industry in both the short run and the long run. The final short-run and long-run equilibrium positions are the same as those described above.

When we compare monopolistic competition with perfect competition, we find that under monopolistic competition the consumer has a variety of similar but different goods to choose from, while all firms in a perfectly competitive industry produce identical goods.

But the consumer must pay for this variety in the form of higher prices. In addition, in long-run equilibrium the monopolistically competitive firm utilizes a plant that is smaller than the optimum size, and this plant is operated at an output that is less than the minimum cost output for this plant. Therefore, a monopolistically competitive industry is always less efficient and has higher prices than a perfectly competitive industry.

The New York City restaurant industry is a good example of monopolistic competition. There is a large number of restaurants in New York City. Each restaurant produces prepared food for the public, but there are variations from one restaurant to another. There are no barriers to entry in this industry. Finally, New York City restaurants engage in advertising and product variation in order to attract customers. Therefore, this industry possesses all the characteristics of a monopolistically competitive industry.

Chamberlin's theory of monopolistic competition has been both criticized and praised. Critics have objected to Chamberlin's simplifying assumptions of identical cost and demand curves for all the firms in an industry. They say that if there are differences in the products of each firm, then this should result in differences in cost and demand. The theory is also criticized on the grounds that it is extremely difficult, if not impossible, to define an industry since this depends on how one determines whether a good is a substitute for another good. The behavioral assumption that each firm believes it can cut its price unilaterally has also been attacked, since this implies that firms never learn from experience. Objections have also been leveled against Chamberlin's position that product variety fully justifies the higher price for the good in a monopolistically competitive industry, as compared with a competitive industry. On the other hand Chamberlin's theory has been praised because his book stimulated both theoretical and empirical research in microeconomic theory. It promoted work on theories of oligopoly and other market structures, and it led to empirical research on the behavior of actual industries and markets. Chamberlin also formally incorporated selling costs and the role of product variation into theoretical analysis.

Problems and Questions

1. What is the major difference between monopolistic competition and perfect competition in terms of industry structures?
2. Why is it so difficult to define an industry in monopolistic competition?

3. How does the firm determine whether or not to spend additional money on advertising?
4. Distinguish between Chamberlin's two demand curves.
5. According to Chamberlin's analysis, how does long-run equilibrium differ from short-run equilibrium?
6. In what way is the consumer better off given a monopolistically competitive industry rather than a perfectly competitive industry? How is the consumer worse off?
7. What were the main contributions of Chamberlin's theory to economic theory?
8. Why is product variation important in monopolistic competition? How would the firm decide whether or not a change in its product would be profitable?
9. What does "excess capacity" refer to in a monopolistically competitive firm?
10. Why is the New York City restaurant industry an example of monopolistic competition?

Notes

1. Cambridge, Mass.: Harvard University Press, 1933.
2. To simplify the graph, the short-run cost curves have been omitted.
3. Note that in our discussion of the restaurant industry we have dropped Chamberlin's simplifying assumptions of identical cost and demand curves. Therefore, we would expect restaurant prices to vary as a result of such differences as cost, service, interior decor, reputation, and so forth.
4. Characteristic of the positive view of Chamberlin's theory is the paper by Joe S. Bain in "The Theory of Monopolistic Competition After Thirty Years," *American Economic Review*, Vol. LIV (May, 1964), pp. 28–32. The paper by Bain was presented at the 1963 annual meeting of the American Economic Association, along with other interesting papers on monopolistic competition by R. L. Bishop and W. J. Baumol; also included are discussions of these papers by J. W. Markham and P. O. Steiner. Our discussion draws mainly on Bain's paper.

Recommended Reading

Chamberlin, Edward H. *The Theory of Monopolistic Competition*, 6th ed. Cambridge, Mass.: Harvard University Press, 1948.

Cohen, K. J., and R. M. Cyert. *Theory of the Firm: Research Allocation in a Market Economy*. Englewood Cliffs, N.J.: Prentice-Hall, Inc., 1965.

Demsetz, Harold. "The Nature of Equilibrium in Monopolistic Competition," *Journal of Political Economy*, Vol. LXVII (February, 1959), pp. 21-30.

Stigler, George J. *Five Lectures on Economic Problems*. London: Longmans, Green & Co., 1949.

"The Theory of Monopolistic Competition After Thirty Years," *American Economic Review*, Vol. LIV (May, 1964), pp. 28-57. Contains several papers presented at the 1963 annual meeting of the American Economic Association.

Triffin, Robert. *Monopolistic Competition and General Equilibrium Theory*. Cambridge, Mass.: Harvard University Press, 1949.

10

Oligopoly Theory

A monopoly consists of only one firm, whereas pure competition and monopolistic competition represent the opposite market extremes of firms so numerous that each seller does not find it necessary to give any attention to the actions of the others. Therefore, in each of these three market forms the seller does not concern himself about other sellers. In the case of oligopoly, however, the outstanding distinguishing characteristic is a keen awareness by each seller in the industry of the actions and reactions of the other sellers. This situation of recognized interdependence exists because of the relatively small number of firms in the industry and the significant share of the market controlled by each. This is the case because of various kinds of barriers to entry, for example, because efficient operation in a given industry requires a very large firm and so only a few firms are needed to satisfy the market demand. The many different types of barriers to entry into an industry are discussed here in connection with our analysis of long-run equilibrium.

Unlike the case of pure competition, where products are homogeneous, or of monopolistic competition, in which products are differentiated, there may be pure oligopolies, consisting of firms making homogeneous products like cement, or differentiated oligopolies like the automobile industry. Undoubtedly, oligopoly is very prevalent market form in the United States, represented not only by cement and automobiles, but also by cigarettes, tires, cans, aluminum, airplanes, sulfur, drugs, and other industries.

Because there are few sellers and an acute awareness of interdependence on the part of each seller, the members of the industry may find it expedient to engage in some form of collusion or cooperation as a means of protecting or increasing profits. Collusion may be beneficial to the firms in the industry because it reduces rivalry and uncertainty, and it may also be geared to preventing new firms from entering the industry. Collusion may be formal or informal. **Formal collusion** consists of a definite, explicit agreement governing the behavior of the firms in the industry. This is also known as a **cartel**, and although cartels are illegal in the United States they sometimes occur. **Informal collusion** refers to looser forms of cooperation, which may not be as effective or enduring as formal collusion but which are less susceptible to government detection, investigation, or regulation. This cooperation may take the form of unwritten, tacit agreements or may occur through the gradual establishment of beneficial behavior patterns among the firms in the industry.

Therefore, our analysis of oligopoly will take into account each of three cases of oligopolistic behavior: no collusion (but instead independent, noncooperative behavior); informal collusion; and formal collusion. Each of these cases is analyzed in terms of the short run and the long run. To simplify the analysis without doing violence to the result we shall assume homogeneous products in each case, i.e., a pure oligopoly. Some of the effects of product differentiation are considered toward the end of the chapter. We shall also assume that the cost curves of an oligopolist are similar to those of firms in the other market structures already considered. But before proceeding with our analysis of oligopoly models, some attention must be given to duopoly theory.

DUOPOLY THEORY

The Cournot Model

Duopoly refers to the case of a market in which there are two sellers only. Therefore, it is really a special case of oligopoly. In modern economic theory, duopoly has been largely replaced by the more general approach consisting of oligopoly theory. Still, duopoly theory incorporates the idea of mutual interdependence, the basic concept of oligopoly, in its purest form: There are only two sellers and each must take into account the behavior of the other. This is brought out clearly in the earliest and best-known duopoly model, which was put forth in 1838 by the famous French economist, Antoine Augustin Cournot (1801–1877).[1] We shall limit our discussion of duopoly to this so-called Cournot model.

We follow Cournot's example and suppose that each of two sellers called S_1 and S_2 owns a spring that produces a desirable mineral water. We also assume that the cost of production is zero, that each seller wishes to maximize his profit, that the demand curve is linear,

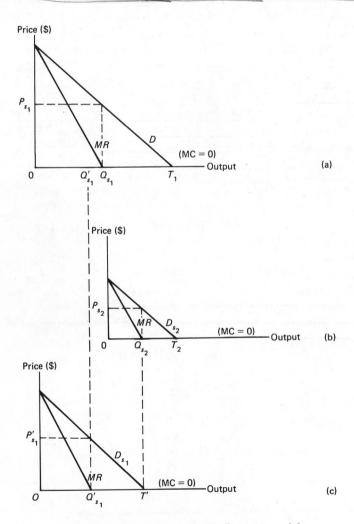

Figure 10-1. Adjustments in the Cournot model.

and that each seller takes the output of the other as given. Will this situation result in a stable equilibrium, and if so, how?

Figure 10-1(a) shows the market demand curve D. Notice that with a zero production cost, marginal cost is zero and the MC curve coincides with the horizontal axis. Suppose that S_1 starts his business first. He will maximize his profit at that output where $MC = MR$, which is Qs_1 at price Ps_1 in graph (a), or one-half of OT_1. Recall that the MR curve always bisects the distance between any point on a linear demand curve and the vertical axis, and MR is therefore equal to MC at $\frac{1}{2}OT_1$. S_2 now starts his business. He views the situation and takes S_1's output as given. Since S_1 is supplying Qs_1 of the total demand, S_2 is left with the remainder, or $T_1 - Qs_1$. This quantity is shown in graph (b) as $OT_2(= T_1 - Qs_1)$. To maximize his profits S_2 sells Qs_2 at price Ps_2, where his $MR = MC$. With the entry of S_2 into the market and the consequent decline in price, S_1 must re-adjust his position. S_1 now considers his maximum market to consist of OT_1 minus the amount supplied by S_2, which is $Qs_2(= T_2 - Qs_2)$, or OT'_1, as depicted in graph (c). S_1 maximizes his profit under these circumstances by selling $Q's_1$, i.e., he is forced to cut his output from Qs_1 to $Q's_1$. This gives S_2 the opportunity to secure a larger share of the total market. The nature of the adjustments and readjustments by the two sellers in the Cournot model should now be clear, but when will they stop and where will equilibrium occur? A further example should answer these questions.

Suppose that the maximum demand in the market is 100 gallons, that is, in terms of Figure 10-1(a) $OT_1 = 100$. Let us trace the pattern of output adjustments by the two sellers.

Seller	Output
S_1	$Qs_1 = \frac{1}{2}(100) = 50$
S_2	$Qs_2 = \frac{1}{2}(100 - 50) = 25$
S'_1	$Q's_1 = \frac{1}{2}(100 - 25) = 37.5$
S'_2	$Q's_2 = \frac{1}{2}(100 - 37.5) = 31.25$
S''_1	$Q''s_1 = \frac{1}{2}(100 - 31.25) = 34.375$
S''_2	$Q''s_2 = \frac{1}{2}(100 - 34.375) = 32.8125$
$\vdots$	$\vdots$

Even this simple example seems to indicate that each of the two sellers will end up selling the same quantity, since in the few adjustments shown, S_1 adjusts from 50 to 34.375 and S_2 goes from 25 to 32.8125. By means of a simple formula we can determine exactly how much will be produced by the whole industry and by each seller after all adjustments have been made. For the industry, we have

$$Q = T\left(\frac{n}{n+1}\right)$$

where Q is industry output, T is maximum demand, and n is the number of sellers. For our example,

$$Q = 100\left(\frac{2}{2+1}\right) = 100\left(\frac{2}{3}\right) = 66\frac{2}{3}$$

To find the amount produced by each seller the formula becomes

$$Q = \frac{T}{n+1}$$

For our example,

$$Q = \frac{100}{3} = 33\frac{1}{3}$$

Therefore, in equilibrium each seller will supply one-third of the market.

We can now compare the duopoly outcome with what we could expect in a monopoly and in a competitive market. In a monopoly,

$$Q = T\left(\frac{1}{1+1}\right) = T\frac{1}{2}$$

In our example,

$$Q = 100\left(\frac{1}{2}\right) = 50$$

That is, total industry output would be less in a monopoly, 50 as compared with $66\frac{2}{3}$. In a competitive industry of 10,000 firms,

$$Q = T\left(\frac{10,000}{10,000+1}\right) = T(\text{approx. } 1)$$

that is,

$$\frac{n}{n+1} \to 1, \text{ as } n \to \infty$$

In our example,

$$Q = 100(1) = 100$$

Total competitive output would be 100, as compared with $66\frac{2}{3}$ in duopoly and 50 in monopoly. In general, we can conclude that as the number of firms in the industry increases, total output will increase. Given a downward sloping industry demand, the market price will decline as output rises.

The most persistent criticism of the Cournot model has concerned its lack of realism: not only does the model depict a highly simplified industrial situation, but each seller always behaves as though the other's output is fixed, in spite of his experience of continuous adjustments and readjustments. But in spite of its shortcomings, this model still stands as a pathbreaking first step in the analysis of oligopoly.

The Theory of Games

About a hundred years after Cournot developed his duopoly model, a new and novel approach to the problem of interdependence and conflict was advanced by the famous mathematician, J. von Neumann, working in collaboration with a noted economist, O. Morgenstern. The new theory is contained in their book *Theory of Games and Economic Behavior.*[2] The essence of **game theory** is that such diverse situations as military battles, poker or chess, and certain types of markets are alike in that they all involve a conflict of interest. One side wishes to defeat or outdo the other side. At the same time, the behavior of each antagonist is conditioned by that of the other. Given this kind of situation, Von Neumann and Morgenstern sought to determine how a rational person ought to behave. Although game theory can be employed to analyze oligopolistic situations, the results are generally less conclusive and definite than in cases where there are only two adversaries, such as duopoly. We therefore limit our discussion to duopoly. We further restrict our analysis to constant-sum games, meaning that total winnings or profits are the same regardless of the outcome of the game, that is, the more one player or duopolist obtains, the less the other gets. The following example shows the outcome of the simple, but determinate, two-person constant-sum game.

The actions open to the duopolists are called **strategies**, and the winnings of each duopolist resulting from any combination of strategies can be displayed in a table called a pay-off matrix. Table 10-1 is such a matrix, in which the entries represent duopolist 1's winnings for each of three strategies, shown in the first column as 1a, 1b, and 1c. We suppose that duopolist 2 also has three possible strategies for each strategy of duopolist 1, and these are given in the top row as 2a, 2b, and 2c. Suppose that the constant sum of the game is 100. If duopolist 1 selects strategy 1a and duopolist 2 chooses strategy 2a, the table shows that duopolist 1 will make 20 and duopolist 2 will end up with 80; i.e., duopolist 2's winnings equal the constant sum minus the winnings of duopolist 1, or the constant sum of 100 minus the 20 going to duopolist 1. Each duopolist is aware that whatever strategy he selects, the other duopolist will adopt the strategy that will yield him the greatest return. For example, if duopolist 1 takes strategy 1a, then duopolist 2 will prefer 2a since he will gain 80, as compared with 65 or 70 if he had selected strategy 2b or 2c, respectively. But, given these circumstances, duopolist 1 can do better than this. By selecting strategy 1c, duopolist 1 is assured of getting 40 no matter what duopolist 2 may do. In fact, strategy 1c is the best that duopolist 1 can do, since 1c is the maximum of the row minima, that is, the highest minimum value of the three rows. Since duopolist 2 will always select his strategy so as to minimize duopolist 1's gain, it makes sense for duopolist 1 to take as his strategy the greatest of the row minima, called the "maximin." In our example this is strategy 1c. By similar reasoning, duopolist 2 maximizes his return by selecting the strategy that gives the minimum of the column maxima, or the lowest maximum value of the three columns, that is, the "minimaxes." In our example, this means that he selects strategy 2b, since he knows that he

Table 10-1. Pay-Off Matrix: Duopoly, Constant-Sum Game

Strategy of Duopolist 1	Strategy of Duopolist 2			Row Min.
	2a	2b	2c	
1a	20	35	30	20
1b	30	25	40	25
1c	50	40	70	40
Column Max.	50	40	70	

will receive 60 in this case, for duopolist 1 will respond by choosing 1c. Had duopolist 2 selected strategy 2a or 2c, he would have had to settle for less, 50 or 30, respectively. The outcome of this game is determinate: duopolist 1 takes strategy 1c and gains 40, and duopolist 2 chooses strategy 2b and nets 60.

Our example illustrates a **strictly determined game**, which is the name given to the case where the "maximin" and "minimax" overlap. Game theory is most effective in solving such two-person constant-sum cases. The conclusions reached through game theory are much less definite when there are more than two players, when the value of the game is not constant, and when players have varying degrees of information. Unfortunately, economists are usually confronted with situations possessing these characteristics, and this has limited the application of game theory in economic analysis.

OLIGOPOLY THEORY: NO COLLUSION

The Short Run: No Collusion

Given the basic assumption of profit maximization, we would expect an oligopolist to change his price and output frequently in response to any changes in costs or demand, so that the profit maximization rule, $MC = MR$, is always satisfied. But observation of the actual behavior of oligopolists reveals that their prices tend to be rather inflexible or rigid. This rigidity could possibly be explained by replacing the profit maximization assumption with other behavioral assumptions, or at least by modifying the profit maximization assumption. The search for better assumptions is being actively pursued in economic research. However, an explanation of rigid oligopoly prices consistent with the profit maximization assumption has been developed by economists. This explanation involves what is called a **kinked demand curve**.[3]

Figure 10-2 illustrates the construction and shows the consequences of the kinked demand curve. We assume that the prevailing price is P and output is x. At this price and output we construct two demand curves for the oligopolist. One demand curve $A\text{-}C\text{-}D_2$ is based on the assumption that any price change by the oligopolist will be followed by all the other members of the industry. Another demand curve $B\text{-}C\text{-}D_1$ follows the assumption that a change in price will not be met by the rest of the firms in the industry. This second demand curve is much more elastic than the first, indicating that a reduction in price by the oligopolist increases sales much more than would be the case if the other firms also reduced their prices; that is, the price-cutter is taking customers away from the other firms. This

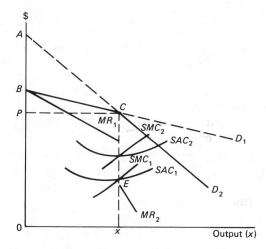

Figure 10-2. The kinked oligopoly demand curve.

demand curve (B-C-D_1) also indicates that sales would fall off rapidly if the oligopolist is the only one raising his price, since customers would now buy more from his rivals.

The kinked demand curve is derived from the assumption that a decrease in price by an oligopolist will be followed by the others in order to retain their customers (the relevant demand curve being C-D_2). But a price increase will not be followed (the relevant demand curve being B-C), since the rest of the firms are now content to maintain their relatively lower prices and thereby attract the customers of the firm that raised its price. Given this behavior pattern, the relevant demand curve for each firm would be B-C-D_2, with a sharp change in slope or a kink at C. The existence of the kink produces a discontinuous MR curve. The first part of the MR curve, B-MR_1, is derived from the BC portion of the demand curve, and the second part of the MR curve, E-MR_2, is associated with the C-D_2 stretch of the demand curve. As a result there arises a gap or discontinuity, MR_1-E, in the MR curve at the output corresponding to the kink.

We can now use this theory to explain the maintenance of rigid prices even though oligopolists strive to maximize profits, and even if there is a certain amount of shifting of the cost curves and demand curves. Suppose that the oligopolist's SAC and SMC were as shown in Figure 10-2 by SAC_1 and SMC_1. Profit would be maximized by producing output x since SMC_1 falls in the MR gap. To produce more than x would mean that $SMC_1 > MR_2$, or that more was being added to total cost than to total revenue, and total profit would decline. If less than x were to be produced, $MR_1 > SMC_1$, indicating that additional output would increase total profits by adding more to total revenue than to total costs. Therefore, profits are maximized at output x and price P. But if cost now rises to SAC_2 and SMC_2, the firm would not respond, since the profit-maximizing output and price would have to be the same because the same reasoning applies to the new set of cost curves. In general, the cost curves could move anywhere within the MR gap without necessitating a change in output or price.

In addition, it is easy, by looking at the graph, to visualize a movement of the demand curve B-C-D_2 to the right or left such that the price remains at P and a fixed set of cost curves, say SAC_2 and SMC_2, remain in the shifted MR gap. In this case output would increase or decrease, depending on whether the demand curve shifted to the right or to the left, but the price would remain rigid. Thus, if we accept the assumptions of the kinked demand curve, the analysis explains how price rigidities can be consistent with the profit maximization assumption under conditions of flexible demand and cost curves.

The Long Run: No Collusion

The nature of the long-run equilibrium position of an oligopolistic firm or industry depends on the conditions governing entry or exit of firms, and on the adjustment of the existing firms as they respond to changes in demand and cost. Exit from the industry is easily accomplished by the firm simply by not replacing productive facilities as they wear out. Entry into the industry by new firms may be easy, moderately difficult, very difficult, or blocked, depending on the circumstances.

If entry is easy, new firms will continue to enter the industry as long as they can share in any abnormal profits being made by the firms already in the industry. Upon the elimination of profitable entry by new firms and the completion of profit maximization adjustments of old firms, long-run equilibrium will prevail. Nevertheless, a situation may exist such that new firms will not enter even though excess profits are being made by the firms already in the industry. Assume an industry with n firms and also assume that the typical firm has a LAC curve and a demand curve D_1, as shown in Figure 10-3. The firm makes a profit per unit of AB on x units in the long run by equating MR_1 and LMC (and also SMC, which is omitted to simplify the graph). Now we suppose that if one more firm enters the industry and the total market is now divided among the $n + 1$ firms, each firm will have a smaller share of the market, as repre-

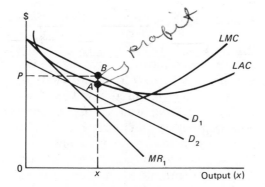

Figure 10-3. Long-run entry leads to losses.

sented by the demand curve D_2 in the graph. Given D_2 as the typical firm's demand curve, we can see that profitable production is impossible because the LAC curve is above D_2 at every possible output. Therefore, a new firm aware of this situation will not enter in the first place because entry would result in losses even though profits exist in the industry before entry. This situation may be compared with the long-run tangency-equilibrium position in monopolistic competition, where additional firms can easily enter the industry, but refrain from doing so because entry will not be profitable for them. In the case of oligopoly a tangency solution is unlikely because each firm accounts for a relatively large share of the market and the entry of just one more firm causes a significant shift to the left of the demand curve of each existing firm.

Entry conditions may be classified as moderately difficult where the firms in the industry possess well-established trademarks or brand names, or where they have developed special skills or knowhow in the production or distribution of the product. If the profit potential seems great enough to a new firm, these entry obstacles can be overcome. Modern advertising and selling techniques coupled with mass communications media make it possible for a new product to become widely known in a relatively short time, provided a large enough expenditure is warranted by the profit potential. Of course, this is not always a major problem in the case of an undifferentiated product like cement, but even here a new firm must establish a "good name" for itself and this is usually a selling job that may be expensive. Where special skills or knowhow exist, the newcomer may be able to attract specialists away from existing firms through various devices: higher pay, attractive retirement and stock option plans, a desirable location, promises of rapid advancement, etc.

Very difficult entry conditions exist where economies of scale are so important that only a very large undertaking can possibly hope to succeed, or where the established firms have in the past forced new firms out of business by means of prolonged price wars. Where a huge enterprise is necessary for efficient operation, at least three major obstacles exist for the potential new firm. These are the large initial money outlay, the long waiting period for profits even if successful, and the possibility of failure. In order to construct the necessary plant and equipment, hire personnel, accumulate initial inventories, and build a distribution organization, the new firm would require very large amounts of money and credit, which may be very difficult to acquire. It may take a relatively long time to complete this initial program and an even longer time to achieve profitable operations in the face of well-established opposition; in the meantime losses may be very heavy. But worst of all, success is not guaranteed, and the new firm may finally be forced out of business, inflicting extreme losses on all concerned. The outstanding example of this situation is the automobile industry, where entry is expensive and hazardous.

Finally, entry may be completely blocked. Some industries are effectively blockaded from new firms by the laws and regulations of local, state, or federal government. The U.S. patent laws give patent holders exclusive rights to products or processes for a period of years, during which time the patent holder often develops related products and processes, which he also patents, thereby effectively barring new firms from the industry. Other established firms in the industry may gain access to these patents by offering the patent holders rights to their own exclusive patents in exchange. On the state or local level, various laws may exist that make it necessary to secure a license or franchise before going into business. If the number of licenses or franchises is limited, perhaps through the political machinations of existing firms, then newcomers are kept out of the industry. Then too, entry may be impossible if certain essential raw materials are owned or controlled by the firms in the industry. If the natural resource required is limited in supply or is concentrated geographically, it may be easily swallowed up by a few firms.

Given these various obstacles to entry, which range from those that make entry only moderately difficult to those that make it impossible, it is little wonder that the long-run equilibrium position in an oligopolistic industry is not as clear-cut as in a competitive industry (easy entry), a monopolistically competitive industry (generally easy entry), or a monopoly (no entry). In an oligopolistic industry where no collusion exists, the existence of long-run abnormal profits will

depend on entry conditions. If entry barriers are impossible to overcome, the existence of short-run excess profits would continue in
the long run. If entry is very difficult, a firm would enter in the face
of such formidable obstacles only if the potential profits were large
enough to warrant undertaking the great risks involved. Once
prospective profits are considered insufficient relative to this risk
level, i.e., relative to the potential losses, entry would not be worth
attempting even though anticipated profits are still large. By the
same reasoning, even if entry were only moderately difficult, a residue of excess profits would remain in the long run, because these
profits are not great enough relative to the risk level to attract new
firms. In the case of easy entry and relatively few firms (fewness being a leading feature of oligopoly), an additional firm would have a
noticeable influence on the demand enjoyed by each firm, shifting
each firm's demand curve to the left. Therefore, only by coincidence
would a tangency solution occur. More likely the entry of one more
firm, after a certain point, would shift the demand curves of all firms
from a profitable position to one of losses, as illustrated in Figure
10-3. Hence the firm would be deterred from entering. So in an oligopoly easy entry does not assure the elimination of excess profits
even in the long run.

The long-run easy-entry solution assuming the kinked demand
curve situation is depicted in Figure 10-4. Suppose the short-run
equilibrium position is output x_1 and price P_1, as indicated by demand curve D_1. In the long run firms enter the industry and sell
their outputs at the prevailing price P_1. As additional firms enter, the
demand curve of each firm shifts to the left. When the typical firm's

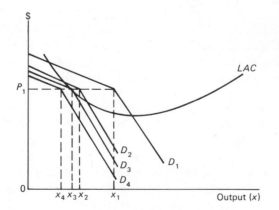

Figure 10-4. The kinked demand curve in the long run.

demand curve has reached D_2, one more firm may cause the demand curve for each firm to move to D_4, where losses are unavoidable. Even if all demand curves move exactly to D_3, which is the tangency solution, the last firm would be making only normal profits along with all other firms. But since there are fairly large discontinuities in the shifts of each firm's demand curve when an additional large firm enters an oligopolistic industry, a tangency solution would be a coincidence.

OLIGOPOLY THEORY: INFORMAL COLLUSION

The Short Run: Informal Collusion

As we pointed out earlier in this chapter, informal collusion is designed to reduce the degree of rivalry and uncertainty that prevails if oligopolists act independently. In addition, informal collusion is not as susceptible to government detection and investigation as formal collusion. Lacking a formal, written agreement, informal collusion takes place by means of a tacit agreement or "understanding" among the members of the industry. Perhaps the most common type of informal collusion is price leadership. Among the various methods by which price leadership can be established, the best known are leadership by a barometric firm, by a dominant firm, or by a low-cost firm.

As the name implies, price leadership means that one of the firms in the industry sets or changes the price of its product with the understanding that the other members of the industry will alter their prices to conform to the change. Sometimes this leadership is practiced by a firm which is influential in the industry because of the quality of its management or its demonstrated capability of "reading the market," even though it may not be the largest or most efficient firm in the industry. Just as the little state of Maine has long served as a political barometer, so the barometric firm serves its industry by indicating through its price changes how the economic pressures are changing. Of course, the barometric firm itself may be influenced in its pricing decisions by pressures from other firms in the industry. These pressures do not take a formal or written form, but may be exerted in a casual manner at social functions or club meetings.

A natural setting for price leadership is found in some industries where there is one very large firm and a number of small firms. In this case the price is set by the dominant firm at such a level that the small firms can sell all they desire at that price; the dominant firm will then maximize its profit on whatever amount of the product remains to be sold at the set price. Figure 10-5 illustrates this situation. The market demand curve is D_M and the marginal cost curve of the dominant firm is MC_D. By summing the MC curves of the small firms horizontally, we find the supply curve of the small firms S_s. If the dominant firm were to set the price at P_1, then the entire market demand would be supplied by the small firms, as indicated by the intersection of S_s and D_M at P_1, and the dominant firm would sell nothing. If the price were fixed at P_2 the small firms would supply P_2A, leaving an amount of the total demand equal to AB for the dominant firm to supply.

We can now construct a demand curve for the dominant firm. At P_1 the dominant firm's demand is zero, and at P_2 it is $P_2C = AB$. By connecting these points, or others derived in a similar manner, we obtain D_D, which is the dominant firm's demand curve; and the corresponding marginal revenue curve MR_D is easily added. Given this demand curve D_D, the dominant firm will maximize its profits by equating its marginal cost and marginal revenue ($MC_D = MR_D$) and setting the price at P_2. The dominant firm will sell x_D at this price and the small firms will sell x_s, where $x_D + x_s = x_M$, the total market demand.

Price leadership may be undertaken by the industry's **low-cost firm**. This case is shown in Figure 10-6. Assume that there are three firms in the industry, each with a different cost level. Also assume

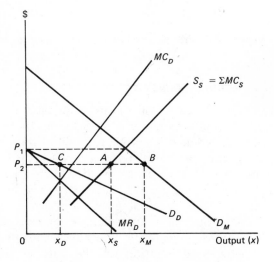

Figure 10-5. Price leadership by a dominant firm.

that they have a tacit understanding that the market will be equally divided, so that $D_L = D_2 = D_3$. The low-cost firm will maximize profits by equating its MC_L and MR_L and selling x_L at price P_L. Firm 2 would also like to maximize its profits at P_2 and x'_2, where $MC_2 = MR_2$, and so would firm 3 at P_3 and x'_3, where $MC_3 = MR_3$. But, especially since we have been assuming homogeneous products (i.e., pure oligopoly), firm 2 and firm 3 fear that they will lose their markets to the low-cost firm if they set their prices at P_2 and P_3, respectively, since the price of the low-cost firm is P_L. Therefore, they follow the price (P_L) set by the low-cost firm and each retains a share of the market, x_2 and x_3, respectively, but each makes less than maximum profits.

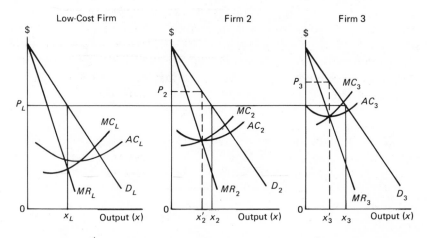

Figure 10-6. Price leadership by a low-cost firm.

The Long Run: Informal Collusion

The long-run behavior of an oligopolistic industry in which informal collusion exists is determined to a great extent by the conditions of entry. If entry is blocked, the long-run equilibrium position will be the same as in the short run, barring any disruptive influences within the industry. These might be alterations in the informal arrangements as a consequence of such things as long-run scale changes of existing firms, technological innovations, new management, and so forth. Such long-run changes may disturb the price leadership agreement or may result in a new leader or no leader at all, but rather independent action on the part of the individual oligopolists.

But the breakdown of these forms of oligopolistic collusion is more likely to occur in a situation where entry into the industry is easy. The entry of new firms breeds uncertainty among the old firms regarding the policies and programs of the new firms, and this may lead to instability. The outcome of easy entry in the case of price leadership by a dominant firm is illustrated in Figure 10-7, which reproduces the relevant parts of Figure 10-5 plus the LAC curve of the dominant firm. As entry of additional small firms occurs, the supply curve of the small firms shifts to the right, as shown by S'_s, and this means that the demand curve of the dominant firm will shift to the left as indicated by D'_D. If the long-run average cost curve of the dominant firm is LAC_D, then the dominant firm cannot avoid losses no matter what output it produces, since there is no possible output which will yield a price equal to or in excess of average cost. Therefore, the dominant firm will be forced to change its market strategy. This may involve a protracted price war, which the dominant firm could afford to conduct with its superior financial strength, and which would lead to the exit of many small firms. The dominant firm may also adopt a strategy of creating an image for the industry as one characterized by price wars and chaotic market conditions, in order to discourage future entry.

If entry were either moderately difficult or very difficult, collusive agreements would be more secure. The existence of obstacles to entry implies that entry tends to be more costly than would be the case in the absence of these obstacles, and hence new firms would

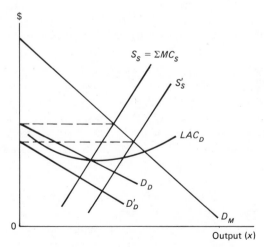

Figure 10-7. Price leadership by a dominant firm with easy entry.

not be attracted unless excess profits were large enough to warrant these additional costs. If profits were below this level new firms would be discouraged and this would create a profit cushion for the established firms, which would give more security to their agreements. Indeed, the price leader may regard as at least part of his leadership function the establishment of a price somewhat lower than the one that might attract newcomers. In other words, some industry profits would be sacrificed for security and stability.

OLIGOPOLY THEORY: FORMAL COLLUSION

The Short Run: Formal Collusion

Even though not legal in the United States, collusive agreements which are clear and explicit are sometimes reached by firms in an industry. These agreements are usually formed for the purpose of eliminating the uncertainties of oligopoly, or to put into effect policies leading to larger or more stable profits, or both. The resulting organization, called a **cartel**, determines industry and firm actions with respect to prices, output, profit-sharing, and so forth. The price and output effects may be much the same as if the industry were a single-firm monopoly.

Figure 10-8 shows a case of a cartel arrangement in which price and output are identical to those of a monopoly. In this example, we assume that three firms with different costs form a cartel. The total market demand for the industry's homogeneous product is given in the graph, and a corresponding MR curve is derived. The marginal costs curves of the three firms are summed horizontally to get an industry MC_M curve. Profits for the industry are maximized by equating MR_M and MC_M, indicating a total industry output of X_M at price P_M, the same as a monopoly. Each firm's share of the total output is determined by equating MR_M with its own MC, and we find that x_1, x_2, and x_3 are produced by firms 1, 2, and 3, respectively. The profit or loss of each firm is of course the difference between the market price P_M and its average cost times its output, which is shown by the hatched areas in the graphs.

The amount of profit actually retained by each firm may or may not be related to this initial profit distribution. It depends on the prearranged cartel profit formula, which is often determined by the bargaining strength of the participating firms, tempered by any concessions and compromises necessary to assure everyone's adherence to the agreement. Concessions must be made, since a recalcitrant firm or firms could undermine the entire cartel. Indeed, there is usually considerable enticement for a cartel member to strike out on his own, since he could undercut the cartel price and thereby generate substantial additional sales. If the cartel maintains its set price, the price-cutting recalcitrant firm reaps additional profits; but if the cartel engages in a price war, this can create further problems for the cartel, since falling prices cause profits to dwindle. Other cartel members may then decide that they could do better on their own, and the cartel may soon dissolve.

In the example of Figure 10-8, let us assume that firm 1 is now making more profits as a result of a cartel arrangement, whereas firm 2 is making about the same profit as it made before the agreement, and firm 3 is suffering losses, as shown in Figure 10-8. Under these assumed circumstances, firm 1 may divide part of its additional profits between firms 2 and 3 so that both would be better off than they were before the agreement. Even if firm 1 finds it necessary to give all of its cartel profits to firms 2 and 3, it may do so and still support the cartel because of other advantages. With the cartel in force there is bound to be greater stability in the industry, and the danger of destructive price wars is limited to occasions when firms break away, and even then a price war may be averted by negotiation. Firm 1, as the efficient low-cost firm, may be able to exert its influence over the cartel and guide the long-run development of the industry in such a way that its future profits are much enlarged. Another advantage of the cartel for its members is the long-run manipulation of industry prices and markets by the cartel for the purpose of discouraging entry into the industry.

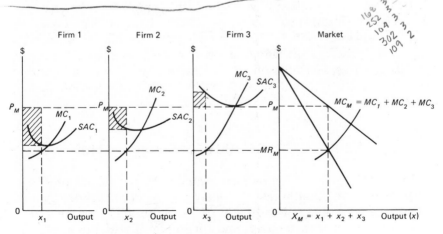

Figure 10-8. Profit maximization by a cartel.

The Long Run: Formal Collusion

The long-run advantages of cartels to member firms cited in the last two sentences, namely industry-wide planning and restriction of entry, are not always attained. If the industry is successful and growing, large and efficient corporations in other industries may be tempted to diversify into the cartelized industry. Such an outside corporation might be so sophisticated and financially powerful that the cartel would balk at engaging this newcomer in a protracted and costly power struggle. In this case, either the new firm would enter into the cartel agreement or it would try to garner larger profits outside the cartel by not having to share its profits with the cartel members. In the latter event, a larger part of the cartel's profits would go to the new firm than would have been the case had the newcomer joined the cartel. In addition, the cartel agreement would probably have to be renegotiated on the basis of the new market conditions, which might lead to disgruntled firms striking out on their own in the manner of the interloper. These difficulties for the cartel would be compounded as the number of new firms entering the industry increased, and the breakdown of the cartel and industry-wide planning would follow. Even if the entering firms joined the cartel, it would just be a matter of time until profits per firm would grow very thin, as the number of firms increased and caused the cartel's MC curve (MC_M in Figure 10-8) to shift to the right, bringing about a corresponding decline in price.

To protect itself against the intrusion of outsiders, the cartel finds it expedient to erect barriers to entry—to make entry costly and difficult or even to attempt to block entry completely—for example, by trying to set up such barriers as patents and cross-licensing agreements, franchises, and control over essential raw materials. In addition, the cartel might adopt a price system that would prevent profits from getting high enough to attract large corporations, and at the same time would be sufficiently flexible to undercut smaller firms attempting to get a foothold in the industry.

THE ROLE OF PRODUCT DIFFERENTIATION

Up to this point we have been assuming homogeneous products, or pure oligopoly. Although the analysis is somewhat more complicated when product differentiation is introduced, the same framework of analysis can be used, and for the most part the results are very similar. Instead of going through all of the cases discussed here we shall simply indicate some of the major considerations to be taken into account when product differentiation exists.

There are numerous ways whereby a seller's product can be differentiated from those of his rivals. First and foremost, a product distinction must exist in the mind of the consumer, whether or not there is a material difference in fact. Therefore, brand names and extensive advertising are favorite methods of convincing the consumer that a particular easily identified product is superior to all other similar products. Indeed, advertisers direct the consumer to "accept no substitutes" or to use only "Super White" laundry detergent for a "really white wash." Whether or not the ingredients of "Super White" *are* significantly different from any of the other detergents is not vital, as long as the consumer believes that a significant difference exists. In many cases this appeal to the consumer may be enhanced by the use of packaging techniques. By putting a product which is in fact very similar to other available products in an attractive container or package, the seller may lead the consumer to feel that he is getting a better product or that other people will be impressed by his purchase. In some cases, of course, the consumer may be aware that the product itself is no different from others, but he cannot resist the package.

In many cases the product may vary in actual design, or in its inherent quality. Automobile tires are sold mainly on the basis of quality and to a lesser extent design (tread), whereas in the sale of automobiles both quality and design are stressed. There are many products which can be designed to meet different taste patterns, and oligopolists are keenly aware of the sales advantages inherent in a popular design. The differences in the quality of various products may or may not warrant the existing price differential. Here advertising again comes into play as a means of supporting a price, often by claiming an inherent quality that is more than the product possesses. On the other hand, quality differences are often real and substantial, and represent an effort to give the consumer a better product for the same price as a rival product; this is equivalent to selling the same product at a lower price, since in both cases a real advantage is offered to the consumer.

It should be stressed that all of these activities directed toward changing the product or its image in the mind of the consumer are forms of **nonprice competition**, in the sense that they are substitutes for price cutting. (They may well not only avert price wars but, instead, bring about price increases.) The major purpose of nonprice competition is to attempt to shift the demand curve to the right and to make it less elastic.

Figure 10-9 illustrates how profits can be sharply increased by shifting the demand curve to the right from D_1 to D_2, assuming that average costs are AC_1 before and after the shift. On the other hand, if the oligopolist spends a large sum of money on advertising in order to shift his demand curve from D_1 to D_2, then the outcome can be radically different. Recall that a lump sum spent on advertising would have the same effect on the cost curves as an increase in fixed costs, so that the average total cost curve would rise while the MC curve would be unchanged. Suppose that the AC_1 curve rose to AC_2 in the graph. In this case the oligopolist would now have a loss instead of a profit, even though the demand curve is now D_2. These considerations lead to the basic rule governing advertising and other selling expenditures, as well as spending on product variation: these expenditures should be increased only as long as they increase total revenue more than total cost, or as long as the MR exceeds the MC. This is the fundamental rule of profit maximization and it applies to all types of business outlays. Looking at Figure 10-9, it should be clear that the oligopolist would avoid the situation depicted by D_2 and AC_2.

In the long run, expenditures on advertising and product differentiation can be employed by the industry members either collusively or independently to discourage entry into the industry. Heavy advertising and intensive product development over a long period may establish a strongly entrenched market position for existing industry members. Potential newcomers are then faced with added dimensions of uncertainty as they must face the risks involved in product design and selling and the sometimes extended time period necessary to de-

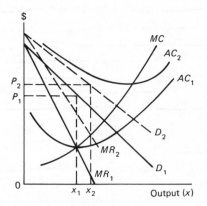

Figure 10-9. Effects of selling expenditures in oligopoly.

velop their share of the market; too, there is always the gnawing possibility of direct warfare with industry leaders and the associated possibility of ultimate failure.

Differentiated products also give producers wider access to patent protection as a means of preventing or discouraging entry. Not only may a process be patented, but different approaches to the performance of the product may be patentable. For example, the Polaroid Corporation has captured and retains a significant portion of the photography market through its unique patented cameras. Even a particular part of the product may be patented and will help discourage entry, if this part makes the product especially desirable to consumers.

Furthermore, the firms in the industry may get so large and efficient as a result of patent protection (or established brands) that even after the patent expires, potential newcomers may find it very risky to challenge the entrenched giants of the industry.

APPLICATION: OLIGOPOLY AND THE REAL WORLD

There is no doubt that oligopoly is the major market structure in U.S. manufacturing industry. It permeates almost all sectors and industries, as Table 10-2 reflects. The table shows some, but by no means all, of the industries in which the four largest companies accounted for at least 70% of the value of shipments in 1967. The degree of concentration in the motor vehicle industry is no surprise, but we generally think of food products as being far less concentrated. That this is not always the case is shown by the concentration ratios of the four largest firms in cereals, chocolate products, and chewing gum, which are 88%, 77%, and 86%, respectively. If we consider the eight largest firms in these industries we find that the concentration ratios approach 100%. In addition, cereals and chocolate products became increasingly more concentrated during the period from 1958 to 1967. We know that heavy advertising expenditures are characteristic of these oligopolistic industries, as each seller endeavors to convince consumers that his product is superior to that of his rivals. In food products, who has not heard of Wheaties, Milky Way, or Wrigley's gum?

There seems to be an endless variety of soaps and detergents, but the fact is that four companies controlled 70% of the market in 1967, and eight companies accounted for nearly four-fifths of this market. If we look at both man-made and organic fibers, we find that four companies swallow up about 85% of the total market. Now con-

Table 10-2. Concentration Ratios for Manufacturing, 1967 and 1958

Industry and Year		Number of Companies	Value of Shipments (million $)	Percent Accounted for by		
				4 largest	8 largest	20 largest
FOOD PRODUCTS						
Cereals	1967	30	793.0	88	97	99+
	1958	34	433.0	83	95	99+
Chocolate products	1967	27	520.5	77	89	99+
	1958	26	446.8	71	84	98
Chewing gum	1967	19	303.7	86	96	100
	1958	24	184.3	89	96	99+
TOBACCO						
Cigarettes	1967	8	3,044.6	81	100	100
	1958	12	2,159.1	79	99+	100
CHEMICALS						
Man-made fibers	1967	13	902.8	86	99+	100
(1958 N.A.)	1963	8	731.8	82	100	100
Organic fibers	1967	22	2,033.2	84	94	(N.A.)
(1958 N.A.)	1963	14	1,403.2	94	99	100
Soaps and detergents	1967	599	2,593.4	70	78	86
(1958 N.A.)	1963	641	2,127.8	72	80	88
STONE, CLAY, AND GLASS						
Flat glass	1967	39	611.3	94	98	99
	1958	13	382.7	92	99	100
PRIMARY METAL						
Primary copper	1967	15	262.6	77	98	100
	1958	11	161.7	87	99	100
Primary aluminum	1967	10	1,608.7	N.A.	100	100
	1958	6	801.7	N.A.	100	100
MACHINERY, EXCL. ELECT.						
Typewriters	1967	20	595.5	81	99	100
	1958	15	230.1	79	99	100
ELECTRICAL EQUIP. AND SUPPLIES						
Telephone and telegraph equip.	1967	82	1,536.7	92	96	99
	1958	44	749.7	92	97	99+
Electron tubes (receiving)	1967	28	300.6	94	99	99+
(1958 N.A.)	1963	30	321.1	87	99	99+
TRANSPORTATION						
Motor vehicles (1958 N.A.)	1967	107	27,296.0	92	98	99+

SOURCE: U.S. Bureau of the Census, *Census of Manufactures, 1967*, Vol. 1 (Washington, D.C.: U.S. Government Printing Office, 1971).

sider such resources as copper and aluminum. In these days of short-ages and rising prices, one may well speculate about whether these are related to the fact that virtually 100% of the shipments of primary copper and primary aluminum are accounted for by only eight companies.

Although it is not shown in the table, if the consumer goes shopping for refrigerators, vacuum cleaners, laundry equipment, sewing machines, photographic equipment, or greeting cards, he will be buying items for which at least 70% of the market is controlled by the four largest companies. How this situation bears on the welfare of the consumer depends upon the nature of each of these oligopolistic markets. We will consider such matters as consumer welfare and economic efficiency in Chapter 14, which is devoted to welfare economics.

INNOVATION: ENTRY-PREVENTION THEORY

As we know, conventional oligopoly theory assumes a recognized interdependence among the firms in the industry; each firm is keenly aware of the actions of every other firm. The major emphasis is on the relationships among the firms already in the industry, with little or no attention given to the threat of potential entry into the industry. In recent years, economists have been analyzing the effect of potential entry on the behavior of existing firms in the industry.[4] This represents an innovation in oligopoly theory because the profit maximization decisions of firms must be based not only on the possible reactions of their actual rivals in the industry, but also on the threat posed by potential rivals who may be attracted to the industry.

Although a number of economists have developed entry-prevention models of oligopoly, we shall confine our discussion mainly to the so-called **Sylos Postulate** approach, which forms the foundation for much of the theory in this area. This postulate holds that potential entrants expect established firms to maintain their output at the pre-entry level even after the new firms enter the industry. Therefore, potential entrants will make their entry decisions on the basis of their cost conditions and postentry demand outlook, given the output levels of the firms in the industry. If the potential entrant's anticipated cost and demand curves do not indicate an abovenormal postentry profit, then the potential entrant will not enter.

On the other hand, established firms are assumed to recognize the problem of setting a price and output that will deter entry. Established firms are able to set a higher price and make a greater abnormal profit to the extent that there are barriers to entry. For example, if firms within the industry are able to buy some essential inputs at a cost advantage as compared with potential entrants, or if they have created strong consumer preferences for their goods, it might be possible for established firms to make some abnormal profits without attracting new firms. But existing firms must be careful because if abnormal profits are great enough, some potential entrants may be prepared to enter the industry, and even absorb some initial losses, if they feel that they may be able to drive some of the existing firms out of the industry and reap the large profits. This would occur if the potential entrant were a financially strong multiproduct firm able to offset losses in a new market with profits from other markets where it is already firmly entrenched.[5] Of course, if the old firms have exclusive patents or own certain inputs available only in limited quantities, potential entrants may be effectively barred from the industry for a long time.

Underlying the present discussion are the assumptions that the total market demand is constant and that the technology of the industry remains the same. If industry demand is growing, this opens up the possibility of a market share for a new entrant, and therefore encourages potential entrants. The existing firms are faced with the problem of how to absorb the increases in market demand before new entry occurs. Under these conditions, the old firms would be forced to reexamine their entry-prevention strategy, giving special attention to the factors that determine market shares in the first place. Given changing technology, it might be possible for a potential entrant to discover a new technology that can give it a cost advantage over the established firms, or that can lead to a good with greater consumer appeal than the goods of the firms already in the industry. For example, the computer industry provides many cases of new firms able to survive and prosper because of the opportunities created by both growing demand and rapidly changing technology.

SUMMARY

The distinguishing characteristic of oligopoly is the awareness by each firm in the industry of the actions of the other firms. This situation of recognized interdependence exists because of the relatively small number of firms in the industry. The nature of the good is not critical, since oligopolies may produce homogeneous or differentiated goods. As a consequence of the small number of firms, the possibility of collusion exists. Two types of collusion can be identified. Formal collusion (also called a cartel) consists of a definite, explicit agreement governing the behavior of the firms in the industry. Informal collusion refers to looser forms of cooperation, such as price leadership. Duopoly is a form of oligopoly in which there are two sellers only. The best-known and earliest (1838) duopoly model, the Cournot model, is presented in this chapter.

Another, and much later, approach to duopoly and oligopoly is the theory of games, which appeared in 1944. The essential idea behind game theory is that business, like such games as poker or chess, involves a conflict of interest. Although game theory can be employed to analyze oligopolistic situations consisting of several firms, the results are generally less conclusive and definite than in cases where there are only two adversaries, such as duopoly. Therefore, in this chapter the presentation is limited to duopoly.

The actions open to the duopolists are called strategies. The winnings of each duopolist stemming from any combination of strategies are displayed in a table called a pay-off matrix. Since duopolist 2 will always select his strategy so as to minimize duopolist 1's gain, it is rational for duopolist 1 to take as his strategy the greatest of the row minima, called the maximin; and, by similar reasoning, duopolist 2 maximizes his return by selecting the strategy that gives the minimum of the column maxima, called the minimax. The example in this chapter illustrates a strictly determined game, in which the maximin and minimax are equal.

The analysis of oligopoly in this chapter is approached in terms of three general types of oligopolistic behavior: no collusion, informal collusion, and formal collusion. Each of these three types is analyzed in terms of the short run and the long run. The case of no collusion in the short run is discussed in terms of the kinked demand curve, which explains the existence of rigid oligopoly prices while retaining the basic assumption of profit maximization. The kinked demand curve is derived from the assumption that a decrease in price by an oligopolist will be matched by the other oligopolists, but a price increase will not be followed by the others. The existence of the kink in the demand curve produces a discontinuous marginal revenue curve. In general, the firm's cost curves can move anywhere within the marginal revenue gap without calling forth a change in output or price.

The long-run equilibrium position of an oligopolistic firm and industry depends on the conditions governing entry into the industry. Entry by new firms may be easy, moderately difficult, very difficult, or blocked. If entry is blocked, short-run abnormal profit will continue in the long run. If entry is very difficult, a firm will enter in the face of formidable obstacles only if the potential profits were large enough to warrant assuming the great risks involved. Even if entry is only moderately difficult, a residue of excess profits will remain in the long run, because once profits contract to a certain level they will not he great enough relative to the degree of risk to attract new firms. Even when entry is easy, in the sense of no obstacles preventing entry, abnormal profit may continue to exist, if the entry of a new firm produces losses for all firms; this will deter new firms from entering. Therefore, in the long run the final equilibrium

depends on the specific assumptions concerning entry conditions.

Informal collusion takes the form of a tacit agreement among the members of the industry, and it is less susceptible to detection. Price leadership is the most common type of informal collusion, and the price leader may be a barometric firm, a dominant firm, or a low-cost firm. As the name implies, price leadership means that one of the firms in the industry sets or changes the price of his product, with the understanding that the other members of the industry will alter their prices to conform to the change. In the case of the barometric firm, leadership is provided by a firm that is influential in the industry for one reason or another. Price leadership by a dominant firm occurs where there is one very large firm and many small firms. The dominant firm sets the price in such a way that the small firms can sell all they desire at that price, and the dominant firm will then be able to maximize its profit by satisfying the rest of the market demand at the price. A low-cost firm will practice price leadership by establishing a price that will allow it to maximize its profit. The higher-cost firms would like to charge a higher price in order to maximize their profit, but if they did then their buyers would buy from the low-cost firm. Therefore, these firms make less than maximum profits. In the long run, these forms of informal collusion will tend to break down to the extent that entry into the industry is easy.

Formal collusion, called a cartel, takes the form of an explicit agreement among the members of the industry concerning prices, output, and so forth. Generally, the cartel sets the price and output so as to maximize industry profit, in which case the results are the same as in a monopoly. The distribution of the profit among the cartel member firms usually depends on a prearranged cartel profit formula. In the long run, the existence of the cartel may be threatened or terminated by the entry of new firms. To discourage entry, the cartel might use such devices as cross-licensing agreements, pricing policies, and control over essential raw materials.

Although our analysis of oligopoly has been conducted in terms of homogeneous products, the results are very similar when product differentiation is introduced. But there are some important differences. Heavy advertising and intensive product development may establish a strongly entrenched market position for existing firms in industry. Differentiated products also give wider access to patent protection as a means of preventing or discouraging entry.

Oligopoly is the major type of market structure in U.S. manufacturing industry. Numerous large U.S. industries are dominated by relatively few firms. Industries in which the four largest firms account for at least 70% of industry shipments include motor vehicles, cereals, chocolate products, chewing gum, typewriters, and cigarettes.

Entry-prevention theory represents an innovation in oligopoly theory. In recent years, economists have been analyzing the effect of potential entry on the behavior of existing firms in the industry. The analysis has been based to a large extent on the Sylos Postulate, which holds that potential entrants expect established firms to maintain their output at the pre-entry level even after the new firms enter the industry. On the other hand, established firms are assumed to recognize the problem of setting a price and output that will deter entry. To the extent that existing firms have cost or other advantages as compared with potential entrants, it might be possible for them to make abnormal profits without attracting new firms. It becomes more difficult for established firms to deter entry when the demand for the good is growing rapidly or when technology is changing, thereby creating opportunities for new firms.

Notes

1. *Recherches sur les principes mathématiques de la théorie des richesses* (Paris, 1838). English translation by N. T. Bacon, *Researches into the Mathematical Principles of the Theory of Wealth* (New York: Macmillan Publishing Co., Inc., 1897).
2. 2d ed. (Princeton, N.J.: Princeton University Press, 1947).
3. First proposed by P. M. Sweezy, "Demand Under Conditions of Oligopoly," *Journal of Political Economy*, Vol. 47 (Aug., 1939), pp. 568–573.
4. This section is based on J. N. Bhagwati, "Oligopoly Theory, Entry-Prevention, and Growth," *Oxford Economic Papers*, N.S., Vol. XXII (Nov., 1970), pp. 297–310. Reprinted in R. E. Neel, *Readings in Price Theory*. (Cincinnati: South-Western Publishing Co., 1973).
5. See Bhagwati, in ibid.

Problems and Questions

1. What is a cartel, how does it function, and what may lead to its breakdown?
2. How do you explain the existence of inflexible oligopoly prices, while assuming that oligopolists wish to maximize profit and that costs are changing?
3. Why are the conditions of entry into the industry especially

important in oligopoly, as compared with perfect competition, monopoly, and monopolistic competition?

4. Why is price leadership important in oligopoly, and how are price leaders determined?

5. Is product differentiation of critical importance in oligopoly? Assuming that it exists, what role does it play?

6. What is entry-prevention theory?

7. Would easy entry into an oligopolistic industry guarantee the elimination of abnormal profits?

8. What is the Sylos postulate?

9. What contribution does the theory of games make to the analysis of oligopoly? What are the limitations of this approach?

10. Is oligopoly an important market structure in the United States economy?

11. Suppose that there is price leadership by a dominant firm in the short run. Why might the dominant firm change its market strategy in the long run?

Recommended Reading

Bain, Joe S. *Barriers to New Competition*. Cambridge, Mass.: Harvard University Press, 1956.

Bhagwati, Jagdish N. "Oligopoly Theory, Entry-Prevention, and Growth," *Oxford Economic Papers*, N.S., Vol. XXII (Nov., 1970), pp. 297–310.

Fellner, William J. *Competition Among the Few*. New York: Alfred A. Knopf, Inc., 1949.

Modigliani, Franco. "New Developments on the Oligopoly Front," *Journal of Political Economy*, Vol. LXVI (June, 1958), pp. 215–232.

Rothschild, K. W. "Price Theory and Oligopoly," *The Economic Journal*, Vol. LVII (1947), pp. 299–320. Reprinted in G. J. Stigler and K. E. Boulding, eds., *Readings in Price Theory*. Chicago: Richard D. Irwin, Inc., 1952, pp. 440–464.

Stigler, George J. "The Kinky Oligopoly Demand Curve and Rigid Prices," *Journal of Political Economy*, Vol. LV (1947). Reprinted in G. J. Stigler and K. E. Boulding, eds., *Readings in Price Theory*. Chicago: Richard D. Irwin, Inc., 1952, pp. 410–439.

Von Neumann, John, and Oskar Morgenstern. *Theory of Games and Economic Behavior*, 2d ed. Princeton, N.J.: Princeton University Press, 1947.

11

Input Price Determination in Perfectly Competitive Markets

We now turn our attention from the production and price of goods and services to the employment and price of the inputs used to produce these goods and services. Clearly, the more goods produced, the more inputs required. From another point of view, the payments received for the inputs constitute income for their owners and this income in turn enables the owners of the inputs to buy the goods—the output—produced by firms.

In economic theory, the determination of the extent to which the various kinds of inputs share in the output is called distribution theory. Distribution theory may be pursued on the micro level, where we determine how the different inputs divide the sales dollar of the firm, or on the macro level, where we try to account for the share of the nation's income going to the major input categories. For the latter purpose, inputs are usually classified into four groups: labor, capital, land, and entrepreneurship.

The pricing and employment of inputs, or to use the broader term, distribution theory, is best understood in the context of the overall, interrelated economic system; that is, in terms of general equilibrium theory. The concept and analysis of general equilibrium is taken up in Chapter 13. Our purpose in this chapter is more modest. Instead of seeking out the mutual interdependence of the entire system, including input prices, we focus out attention in this chapter on how a firm determines the employment and the price to be paid to a single, variable input, as well as to each of several variable inputs. We also determine the role of the market in the establishment of the prices of inputs. This, then, is a first approach to the problems of distribution theory.

Although we know that the price of the input, which is an element of cost to the firm, constitutes income for the input, we cannot assume that this is the entire income of the input. If the input is an individual, he may derive income from more than one source; for example, he may work for wages, he may receive interest from bonds, and he may collect some rent. In this chapter we ignore these other sources of income and concentrate on how the price to be paid to an input is determined under various circumstances. The **marginal productivity theory**, which is set forth below, is the basic theory used in microeconomics to explain the demand for an input.

THE DEMAND FOR A SINGLE VARIABLE INPUT BY THE FIRM

A firm demands the services of an input because the input adds to the firm's output of the good, and hence adds to the revenue of the firm. But the purchase of the services of the input also increases the firm's costs. We have already seen that a profit-maximizing firm will produce another unit of output if this unit results in an addition to total revenue that exceeds the corresponding addition to total cost, if $MR > MC$. This principle can be expressed in terms of units of input rather than of output. The firm would also add to its profit if the sale of the output produced by an additional unit of input adds more to total revenue than the purchase of the unit of input adds to total cost.

Figure 11-1 illustrates this relationship. Let W equal the cost of a unit of input to the firm. We are here assuming that the firm can purchase as many units of the input as it requires at a cost of W_1, which is the case when perfect competition exists in the input market. The **value of the marginal product** (VMP) is equal to the marginal product of the input multiplied by the selling price of a unit of this product, or $MP_L \cdot P_x = VMP$, where the subscript L stands for input and the subscript x is output. For example: if $MP_L = 5$ and $P_x = \$2$, then $VMP = \$10$. We assume that all units of input are identical, and that perfect competition exists in the product market. Given these assumptions, the negative slope of the *VMP* curve in Figure 11-1 is a reflection of the law of diminishing returns: the marginal product and hence the *VMP* must continuously decline beyond a certain point as additional units of input are added. The profit-maximizing firm will hire additional units of input until the cost of a unit of input equals the value of the marginal product of the input, or until W_1 = *VMP* in Figure 11-1, which shows that L_1 units are hired. If the cost of a unit of input declined to W_2, and if the firm were using only L_1 units, then *VMP* > W_2. It would then be profitable for the firm to hire L_2 units of the input, where W_2 = *VMP*. Therefore, the *VMP* curve is in effect the firm's demand curve for the input.

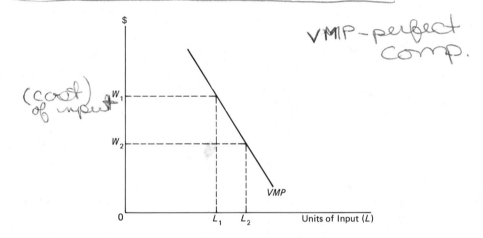

Figure 11-1. Profit-maximizing employment of a single-variable input.

If we assume that fixed costs do not exist, profit maximization in terms of inputs can be easily compared with the corresponding output solution. Figure 11-2(a) shows the profit-maximizing output x_1 and price P_1, along with the profit area A. This is simply the short-run profit maximization position of the competitive firm, which we examined in Chapter 7. Graph (b) indicates the same maximum profit area A in terms of input L_1, as explained in connection with Figure 11-1, but with a value of average product curve added. Finally, graph (c) shows that input L_1 does indeed yield an output x_1, which is the production function relating physical inputs to physical outputs. Fixed costs have been excluded here for the sake of simplicity, but the graphs could be adjusted to include these costs and the resulting profit areas would again be the same in both graphs.

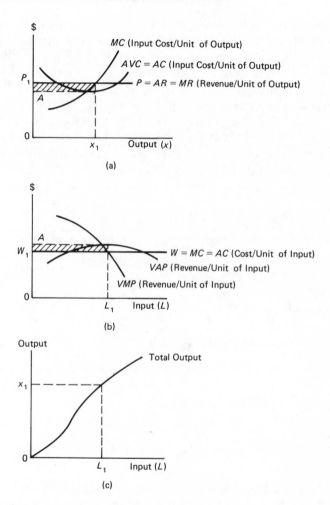

Figure 11-2. Comparison of output and input profit maximization solutions.

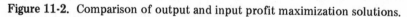

THE FIRM'S DEMAND FOR A SPECIFIC VARIABLE INPUT WHEN SEVERAL VARIABLE INPUTS ARE EMPLOYED

We now assume that the firm employs more than one variable input, and we want to determine how this situation affects the demand for a specific variable input. In the case of a single input, the VMP curve is the demand curve for the input. With more than one variable input, there is the possibility of changing the quantities employed of the other inputs in response to a change in the price of the specific input. This kind of response would have the effect of shifting the *VMP* curve of the specific input. For example, suppose that there are two variable inputs, K and L, and suppose that the firm employs L_1 units of input L at the input price W_1, as shown in Figure 11-3. If the input price falls to W_2 the firm would expand employment to L_2 on the basis of the lower price of L alone. But now that there is another variable input with a constant price, the demand for the specific input (L) would be affected in three ways. First, there is the **substitution effect**: the firm substitutes the relatively cheaper L for K. In the process, the *VMP* curve for L would tend to shift to the left, as shown by VMP_1' in Figure 11-3, because the marginal product of L would decline as more L and less K are employed. Next, there is the **output effect**: the lower price of L enables the firm to buy both more L and more K with the same dollar outlay, and hence increase its output of goods. This effect tends to shift the *VMP* curve for L to the right. Finally, there is a **profit-maximizing** effect; the lower cost of L means that the firm's marginal cost curve shifts downward (to the right), and this will stimulate an expansion of output and a corresponding increase in the use of L and K. This effect will lead to a shift to the right of the *VMP* curve for L.

   The net result of the operation of the substitution, output, and profit-maximizing effects is to shift the *VMP* curve for L to the right, as shown by VMP_2 in Figure 11-3. The firm's demand curve for input L, given these three effects, is no longer the original VMP_1

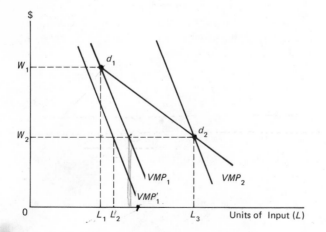

Figure 11-3. Demand for an input when several inputs are employed.

curve, nor is it the shifted curve VMP_2. To derive the effective demand curve for L, we must plot the points showing the quantity of L employed at various input prices after all effects and adjustments have occurred. Two such points, d_1 and d_2, have been found in Figure 11-3; by connecting these points, the demand curve $d_1 d_2$ for the input is derived.[1]

We have derived the firm's demand curve for a specific variable input when several variable inputs are employed. Now we want to determine how the firm would combine several variable inputs in order to maximize profit. Assuming three inputs (A, B, and C), the firm must employ these inputs in such a way that the following set of equalities is satisfied:

$$\frac{W_A}{MP_A} = \frac{W_B}{MP_B} = \frac{W_C}{MP_C} = MC_x = P_x$$

By dividing the marginal product (MP) of the input into its price (W), we get the marginal cost (MC) of a unit of output; and for each input the MC must equal P_x, the price of a unit of output. This is simply an application of our profit maximization rule for firms in competitive markets. Consider the following example:

$$\frac{\$4}{2} = \frac{\$6}{3} = \frac{\$8}{4} = \$2 = \$2$$

If a unit of input A costs the firm \$4 per hour, and if this unit of input A adds 2 units of output, then each additional unit of output will cost the firm \$2; this is the marginal cost of a unit of output. If this MC_x is less than the selling price per unit of output (P_x), then an additional unit of A would be employed by the firm. Suppose that W_A declines from \$4 to \$3, so that

$$\frac{W_A}{MP_A} = MC_x < P_x, \quad \text{or} \quad \frac{\$3}{2} = \$1.50 < \$2.00$$

Since the cost of an additional unit of output is now less than its selling price, the firm would increase its profit by employing more of input A, until

$$\frac{W_A}{MP_A} = MC_x = P_x$$

THE MARKET DEMAND FOR A VARIABLE INPUT

We have derived the firm's demand curve for a specific variable input when several variable inputs are employed, as shown in Figure 11-3. If we know this demand curve for each firm in the market, we will know the amount of the variable input demanded at a given price by each firm in the market. To find the total market demand at the given price, we need only add up the quantities of the input demanded by all firms at this price. This is illustrated in Figure 11-4, where the amount of the variable input employed by the typical firm at input price W_1 is L_1, and the relevant demand curve of the firm is dd. By adding all such L_1's for all firms we find the point R on the market demand curve D_M. Note that the scale on the horizontal axis of the market graph would have much larger numbers as compared with the scale on the horizontal axis for the firm.

Suppose that the input price declines to W_2 in the graph. Can we simply repeat this process of summation in order to discover another point on the market demand curve? If we did, we would be guilty of ignoring the decline in the price of the good resulting from the increase in output by *all* the firms in the industry. Since we are assuming competitive markets, a single firm can change its output without influencing the market price; but when all firms increase their output simultaneously, the market supply curve shifts to the right and the price of the good falls. This means that we must adjust the *dd* curve by shifting it to the left, since the *VMP* declines as the price of

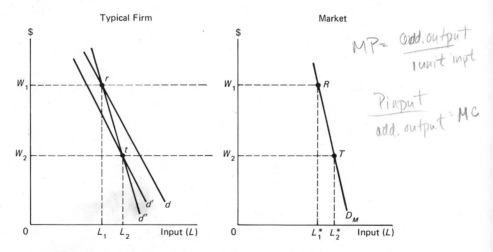

Figure 11-4. The market demand for a variable input.

the good declines (recall that $VMP = MP_A \cdot P_x$). Suppose that dd shifts to $d'd'$, then at input price W_2 the firm will demand L_2. The market demand consists of the sum of each and every firm's demand for L, as shown by point T on the market demand curve. All points such as R and T trace out the market demand curve for the input (D_M). The shifting demand curve of the firm can be eliminated by constructing an input demand curve which already incorporates these shifts. For example, such points as r and t yield the input demand curve $d''d''$ for the firm, which takes all shifts into account.

THE MARKET SUPPLY OF A VARIABLE INPUT

Nonhuman variable inputs, such as fertilizer for agriculture or various kinds of equipment for industry, depend on price increases to stimulate the production of additional supplies. This is because each firm that produces these inputs regards the rising portion of its marginal cost curve as its supply curve, as we concluded in Chapter 7. Therefore, the market supply curve for a nonhuman variable input will have a positive slope.

When we turn to human variable inputs, or labor, we have to recognize that individuals have the option of choosing between work and leisure. In Chapter 3, indifference curve theory was used to show how an individual's preferences for work and leisure can be analyzed. We found that an individual will maximize his satisfaction when he is on the highest attainable indifference curve representing his trade-off between work and leisure. This same analysis can be employed to derive the supply curve of labor. Figure 11-5(a) duplicates the analysis of Chapter 3. The indifference curves I_1, I_2, and I_3 show how much leisure (R) an individual would sacrifice in order to earn additional income (N), where R^* represents the maximum amount of leisure possible, and the slope of such straight lines as R^*N^* represents the hourly wage rate. Figure 11-5(a) shows that if the wage rate line is R^*N^*, the individual will maximize his satisfaction at point 1, where R^*N^* is tangent to indifference curve I_1; he will be working R^*R_1 hours (i.e., giving up R^*R_1 hours of leisure), and receiving income N_1.

Point 1 can now be plotted on a graph showing the relationship between the wage rate and the hours worked. This is done in Figure 11-5(b), where the wage rate W_1 is the slope of R^*N^* and the hours worked, L_1, is equal to R^*R_1. We now have a point on the individual's supply-of-labor curve. Suppose that the wage rate increases.

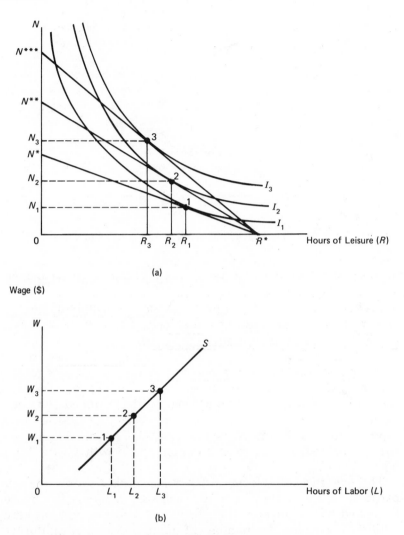

Figure 11-5. The supply of labor by an individual.

This is shown by the steeper wage rate line R^*N^{**}. The higher wage rate makes it possible for the individual to reach a higher indifference curve I_2, where his satisfaction is maximized at point 2. Hours worked, $R^*R_2 = L_2$, are plotted with the higher wage rate W_2 in Figure 11-5(b), and we now have another point on the individ-

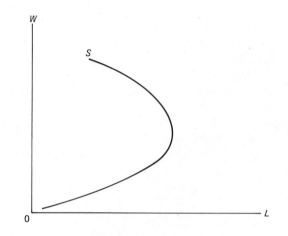

Figure 11-6. Backward-bending supply-of-labor curve.

ual's supply-of-labor curve. Point 3 is found in a similar manner. If we connect all points such as 1, 2, and 3 in graph (b), we have the individual's supply-of-labor curve. The **market supply-of-labor** curve consists of the summation of the individual supply curves for all individuals, and it slopes upward to the right.

There is the possibility that an individual's preference for leisure versus work, as expressed in his indifference curves, will result in a negatively sloped individual supply-of-labor curve; or perhaps a portion of the individual's curve will be positively sloped and part will be negatively sloped. The latter case, called a **backward-bending supply curve**, is illustrated in Figure 11-6. The rationale for such a curve is discussed in Chapter 3 in connection with Figure 3-3, page 53.

The existence of a backward-bending market supply curve for a particular type of labor in an industrialized economy is a matter to be settled by empirical testing.[2] Still, most workers do not have the option of selecting the number of hours they will work during the week—it is usually 40 hours or nothing; and a higher overtime wage usually must be paid in order to bring forth additional hours of work. Also, as wages rise more, labor becomes available as housewives, students, and the semiretired are attracted to the market. If we consider the long run, we find that higher pay usually induces more people to acquire the requisite knowledge and skills for an occupation. For the preceding reasons, we shall assume that the typical market supply curve of labor has a positive slope.

THE MARKET PRICE AND EMPLOYMENT
OF A VARIABLE INPUT

Figure 11-7 shows how the market price and total employment of the variable input are determined by the intersection of the market demand and the market supply curves. The analysis behind this equilibrium position of supply and demand of inputs is the same as that underlying the supply-demand equilibrium of goods and services. If the price of the input falls below W_M in the graph, then demand for the input will exceed the supply, and employers will bid the price back up to W_M. On the other hand, if the input's price rises above W_M, then supply will be excessive relative to demand, and as workers compete for scarce jobs the price will sink back to W_M. This is how the price of the input (W_M) is set by the market; the competitive firm, in turn, determines its employment of the input so that the adjusted $VMP = W_M$.

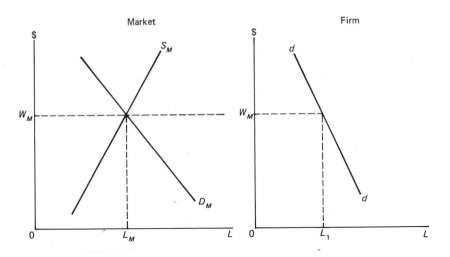

Figure 11-7. The market price and employment of a variable input.

APPLICATION: MINIMUM WAGE LAWS

With the passage of the Fair Labor Standards Act of 1938, those workers who were covered by the Act could not be paid less than $0.25 per hour. Since then, the coverage has been broadened, and the level of the minimum wage rose to $2.90 an hour in 1979, $3.10 in 1980, and is scheduled to increase to $3.35 in 1981. The **mini-**

mum wage is an example of a price floor, a form of governmental interference with the pricing mechanism which is given some consideration in Chapter 7. Here we wish to discuss more specifically the employment effects of the minimum wage law.

Figure 11-8 duplicates Figure 11-7, which shows the market equilibrium price (W_M) and employment (L_M) of a variable input such as labor. Suppose now that a minimum wage is established at W'_M. The market demand curve tells us that at W'_M the demand for labor is L_1, so that employment will decline by an amount equal to the difference between L_M and L_1; this is the drop in employment as compared with the equilibrium situation before the minimum wage was established. But given a minimum wage of W'_M, the supply of labor will increase to L_2. Therefore, taking into account the increase in supply, as well as the decrease in demand, unemployment will be equal to the difference between L_2 and L_1.

In practice, the unemployment generated by the minimum wage is found mainly amoung unskilled workers—teenagers in particular, especially black teenagers.[3] Ironically, the law is supposed to help these workers. A good example of how teenage workers are affected by minimum wages is provided by the multibillion-dollar fast-food industry, which employs large numbers of unskilled teenage workers.[4] To companies like McDonald's and Burger King, a rise in the minimum wage means higher costs, and, if everything else stays the same, lower profits. Firms in the fast-food industry are very

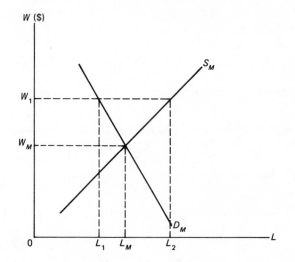

Figure 11-8. The minimum wage and employment.

aggressive and they respond quickly to changing conditions. Some, like Steak-n-Shake and Red Lobster Inns, responded to the 1978 jump in the minimum wage by cutting their daily pre-opening preparation time; opening waitresses now arrive 30 minutes to an hour later, and hence they receive pay for fewer hours. Steak-n-Shake is replacing teenagers by fewer, older workers. The latter, since they tend to be more productive, are easier to train, and there is less turnover. Some fast-food restaurants have cut their work force by combining jobs or by reducing their supervisory staff. Others are moving in the direction of self-service restaurants, as represented by the Hanahan's and York Steak House restaurants of General Mills.

INNOVATIONS: INTEREST, RENT, AND PROFIT

As we noted in the beginning of this chapter, distribution theory is concerned with the determination of the payments to the various inputs. Traditionally, economists have analyzed input payments in terms of four categories: wages to labor, rent to land, interest to capital, and profit to entrepreneurs. In the foregoing analysis of input pricing and employment we used a generalized input instead of the four categories, although we did distinguish between nonhuman and human (labor) inputs in our treatment of supply. Generally, it is the supply side that causes special problems. We shall concentrate in this section mainly on the problems associated with the analysis of rent and profit. Innovations in these areas have been in the direction of disassociating rent with land, and profit with entrepreneurship, and treating both as a generalized return capable of accruing to any input.

Interest

As to the other two categories in the traditional classification, labor and capital, we have covered some of the peculiarities of labor in this chapter, and additional topics are considered in the next one. Capital and interest is a broad topic that has been treated in recent years in connection with macroeconomics and monetary theory. For our purposes, we shall very briefly define the interest rate in terms of both the classical theory and the liquidity preference theory of the famous English economist, J. M. Keynes.

The classical theory states that individuals prefer current consumption to future consumption, and therefore they must be paid interest to induce them to forego current consumption, that is, to save. This notion is called **time-preference**. On the other hand, capital goods (factories, machines, etc.) are productive, and they will be demanded up to the point where their marginal productivity or marginal efficiency equals the interest rate. The equilibrium interest rate is established where the supply of saving, as determined by time-preference, equals investment demand (the demand for capital goods). In other words, the interest rate is determined by the supply of saving and the demand for investment, as shown in Figure 11-9, where $S^* = I^*$ at r^*.

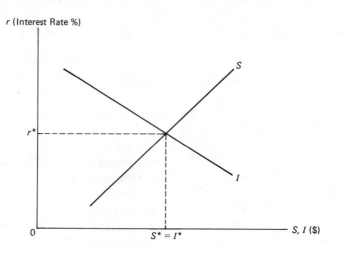

Figure 11-9. Neoclassical interest rate determination.

The **liquidity preference theory** holds that the interest rate is determined by the supply of and the demand for money. We will not go into the forces behind this supply and demand, as explained by J. M. Keynes, because this would take us out of microeconomics, since a full explanation involves a considerable amount of macroeconomic theory. Figure 11-10 illustrates how the interest rate is determined by the liquidity preference theory. The equilibrium interest rate is r^*, where the supply of money equals the demand for money.

Rent

In economic theory, the term **rent**, usually called **economic rent**, refers to that part of the payment to an input in excess of the amount necessary to retain the services of the input in its current

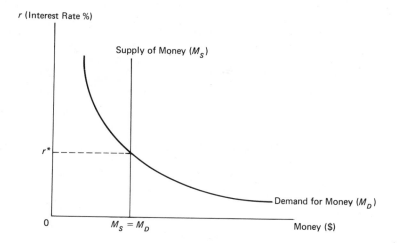

Figure 11-10. The liquidity preference theory of interest.

employment. This surplus return to the input is determined by the difference between the input's payment in its present employment and the payment it would receive in its next-best employment opportunity (its opportunity cost).

Unlike the traditional concept of rent as a return to land, the contemporary concept can be applied to any input. For example, suppose a baseball player earns $100,000 a year playing baseball, but the most he can earn outside of baseball is $20,000. Assuming that he would quit playing baseball and take the $20,000 job if his baseball earnings fell below $20,000, then he will be receiving an economic rent of $80,000. If we suppose that this baseball player can do nothing other than play baseball, then the entire $100,000 will be considered rent; the *demand* for his services would determine the amount of rent he would receive. By the same token, suppose there is a piece of city land zoned for a particular use. Here too the entire payment to the owner of the land will consist of economic rent, and the demand for the land will determine the amount of rent. In general, to the extent that the supply of the input is inelastic, whether the input is land or superior athletic ability, the amount of rent depends on the level of demand. This is illustrated in Figure 11-11, where the supply of the input is perfectly inelastic, and the entire payment (the striped area) consists of rent. This is called **pure economic rent**, and it depends entirely on the level of demand.

In the case of a firm, the supply of the fixed inputs is perfectly inelastic in the short run, but not in the long run. The rent attribut-

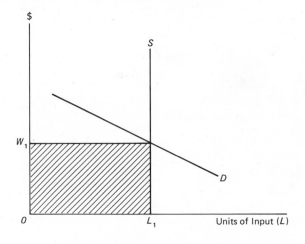

Figure 11-11. Pure economic rent.

able to the short-run fixed inputs is called **quasi-rent**, not economic rent, because in the long run all inputs are variable. Figure 11-12 employs the firm's short-run cost curves to determine the level of quasi-rent. Assuming a price of P_1, the firm will maximize profit, as usual, when $P_1 = MC$ at point A, and produce x_1. The total revenue is equal to OP_1Ax_1. The total payment to the variable input (total variable cost) equals $ODCx_1$. The difference between total revenue and total variable cost, or DP_1AC, is attributable to the fixed input, and this difference is the total quasi-rent. A part of this quasi-rent, equal to EP_1AB, is called **economic profit** or **abnormal profit**, and this is due to employing the fixed input in the industry in question. The other part of quasi-rent, equivalent to $DEBC$, is the opportunity cost of the fixed input relative to the rest of the economy. Nevertheless, in the short run, the fixed input cannot be used elsewhere in the economy, and therefore the total return attributable to the fixed input is quasi-rent.

Our discussion of rent would be incomplete if we ignored the original concept of **land rent** as developed by the great British economist David Ricardo (1772–1823) early in the nineteenth century. For Ricardo, rent arose because of differences in land fertility; the more fertile the land, the higher the rent. As land of declining fertility is brought into production, the cost of a bushel of corn (or wheat or oats) goes up. Naturally, the most fertile land available will be used first; but as the price of corn goes up, the use of less fertile land becomes economically feasible because the higher price will

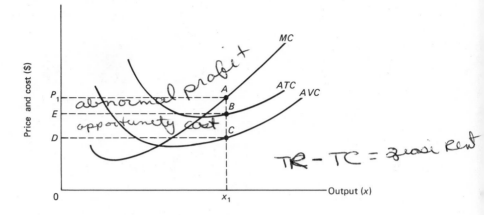

Figure 11-12. Quasi-rent.

cover the higher cost of production. Under these conditions land of greater fertility and a lower cost of production will command rent. This can be illustrated by Figure 11-13. Farm 1 has more fertile land and hence lower costs than Farm 2. The market price P_1 is high enough so that Farm 2 can operate at a normal profit. Farm 1 earns rent equal to the striped area because of its lower cost of production. Unlike abnormal profit, this rent will persist in the long run because it is based on the inelastic supply of superior land. New farms can be brought into production in the long run, but they must resort to less fertile, higher-cost land. Anyone desiring the more fertile land must be prepared to pay the rent. Notice that rent is not a determinant of price, but that rent increases as the price goes higher. Therefore, rent is price determined, not price determining. Finally, Ricardo's concept of rent can be applied to any industry where costs vary from firm to firm because of differences in the productivity of an input, even if the input is not land.

Profit

In Chapter 7 we defined profit as the difference between total revenue and total cost. We also distinguished between normal profit and abnormal profit (or economic profit). **Normal profit** is the return to the entrepreneur for performing the managerial function, and it is determined by the market for managerial services in accordance with the opportunity cost doctrine. In this sense, normal profit is included in total cost; and if the firm is producing an output such

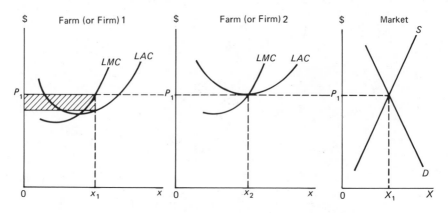

Figure 11-13. Ricardian rent.

that total cost equals total revenue, the entrepreneur is receiving a normal profit. This is always the case in a competitive industry in long-run equilibrium. In the short run, or in a long-run disequilibrium situation, it is possible for the firm to earn an abnormal profit (or economic profit). This profit can persist in the short run, although not in the long run.

Normal profit should be distinguished from **economic profit**.[5] Numerous theories have been advanced to explain the emergence of economic profit. We shall concentrate on some contemporary developments in the area of profit theory.[6] First of all, the entrepreneur who starts a firm exposes himself to the risk of loss, to failure of the firm. Therefore, there must also exist the possibility of an economic profit, in order to motivate potential entrepreneurs to assume the risk of failure. But the entrepreneur does not know in advance whether his enterprise will suffer losses or make economic profits. It all depends on unpredictable changes in the industry and in the economy, which lead to unanticipated shifts in supply and demand. In other words, the future is uncertain, and it is this uncertainty that gives rise to the possibility of economic profits (and losses). The firm cannot avoid this uncertainty by buying insurance, since insurance only covers types of uncertainty for which probabilities can be calculated, as in life insurance or fire insurance. These insurable uncertainties are usually referred to as **risk** to distinguish them from the uninsurable uncertainties that give rise to economic profit.[7]

We can now clearly see the difference between economic profit and economic rent. Economic profit is an unpredictable windfall that disappears in the long run in a competitive industry, whereas economic rent stems from input supply inelasticities and can persist in the long run. Therefore, if a competitive firm has costs that are lower than those of the other firms in its industry because of an especially skillful and talented entrepreneur, the firm will receive economic rent, not economic profit.

SUMMARY

In this chapter and the next one, we are concerned with the determination of the prices of the inputs used to produce goods and services; this is usually referred to as distribution theory. This chapter explains input price determination in perfectly competitive markets, while in Chapter 12 we turn to the behavior of input prices in imperfectly competitive markets.

Starting with the demand for a single variable input by the firm, we find that the firm will maximize profit by employing the input up to the point where the cost of a unit of the input equals the value of the marginal product (*VMP*) of the input, where *VMP* is equal to the marginal product of the input multiplied by the selling price of the good produced by the input. The *VMP* curve is the firm's demand curve for the input.

The firm's demand for a specific varible input when several variable inputs are employed is affected by a substitution effect, an output effect, and a profit-maximizing effect. The net result of these three effects is to shift the *VMP* curve for the input in question to the right. To derive the effective demand curve for the input, it is necessary to plot the points showing the quantity of the input employed at various input prices after all effects and adjustments have occurred. The market demand for this variable input is found by adding the quantities of the input demanded by all firms at each price, after taking into account changes in the price of the product resulting from the increase in output by all firms in the industry. Note that a single competitive firm can change its output of the good without influencing the good's price, but when all firms increase their output simultaneously the price of the good will decline. The market demand curve derived in this manner is found to have a negative slope.

The market supply curve for a variable input will have a positive slope. In the case of a nonhuman variable input the positive slope occurs because each firm that produces this input regards the rising portion of its marginal cost curve as its supply curve. In addition, for several reasons explained in the chapter, we can assume that the typical market supply curve for human variable inputs also has a positive slope. We may conclude that the market price and total employment of a variable input are determined by the intersection of the market demand and the market supply curves.

Minimum wage laws provide an interesting example of governmental interference with the input pricing mechanism. A minimum wage is an example of a price floor, a price set above the equilibrium price. As such, a minimum wage results in a decrease in the demand for labor, and an increase in the supply of labor. Therefore, minimum wages lead to unemployment. The unemployment generated by the minimum wage is found mainly among unskilled workers, teenagers in particular, and more specifically black teenagers. A good example of how teenage workers are affected by minimum wages is provided by the fast-food industry. Companies like McDonald's and Burger King respond to increases in the minimum wage by cutting back on employing teenage workers in order to reduce costs.

Our analysis of input price determination was conducted in terms of a generalized input, instead of using the traditional input categories of labor, capital, land, and entrepreneurship. Innovations in this area have been in the direction of disassociating rent from land and profit from entrepreneurship, and treating both as a generalized return to any input.

Capital and interest is a broad topic, which now receives most attention in connection with macroeconomics and monetary theory. Economic rent refers to that part of the payment to an input in excess of the amount necessary to retain the services of the input in its current employment. This surplus return to the input is determined by the difference between the input's payment in its present employment and the payment it would receive in its next-best employment opportunity. Unlike the traditional concept of rent as a return to land, the contemporary concept can be applied to any input. The rent attributable to the short-run fixed inputs of the firm is called quasi-rent. Normal profit is the return to the entrepreneur for performing the managerial function, and it is determined by the market for managerial services in accordance with the opportunity cost doctrine. In the short run, it is possible for the firm to earn an abnormal profit (also called economic profit), but not in the long run in a competitive industry. The entrepreneur does not know in advance whether he will make economic profits or losses; it depends on unpredictable changes in the industry and in the economy. In other words, the future is uncertain, and it is this uncertainty that gives rise to the possibility of economic profits (and losses).

Notes

1. C. E. Ferguson has proved that the operation of the three effects will lead to a negatively sloped demand curve (such as d_1d_2) for the input. See "Production, Prices, and the Theory of Jointly Derived Input Demand Functions," *Economica*, N.S., Vol. 33 (1966), pp. 454–461.

2. Backward-bending supply curves are more likely to be associated with high-income recipients, such as lawyers, entertainers, and physicians. The higher an individual's income, the greater the temptation to enjoy the fruits of that income in the form of more hours devoted to such activities as golf, travel, or even lunch.

3. See T. G. Moore, "The Effect of Minimum Wages on Teenage Unemployment Rates," *Journal of Political Economy* (July/August, 1971), pp. 897–902.

4. The examples from the fast-food industry are from Paul Ingrassia, "Rise in Minimum Wage Spurs Some Firms to Cut Work Hours and Hiring of Youths," *The Wall Street Journal* (August 15, 1978), p. 48.

5. For an excellent discussion of profit theory see J. Fred Weston, "The Profit Concept and Theory: A Restatement," *The Journal of Political Economy*, Vol. XLIV (April, 1954), pp. 152–170.

6. See Martin Bronfenbrenner, *Income Distribution Theory* (Chicago: Aldine-Atherton, Inc., 1971), Chap. 15.

7. This distinction was first made by Frank H. Knight in his well-known book *Risk, Uncertainty, and Profit* (Boston: Houghton Mifflin, 1921).

Problems and Questions

1. How would you distinguish between the concepts of rent and profit?
2. What is a backward-bending supply curve, and how do you explain it?
3. Would you advocate minimum wage laws? Explain why or why not.
4. What is the relationship between the demand for a single-variable input by the firm and the law of diminishing returns?
5. How would a firm combine several variable inputs in order to maximize profit?
6. Employ indifference curves to derive an individual's supply of labor curve.
7. In the derivation of the firm's demand for a specific variable input when several variable inputs are employed, what are the

roles of the substitution effect, the output effect, and the profit-maximizing effect?
8. What determines the market price of a variable input?
9. What is the difference between quasi-rent and economic rent?
10. How do we account for the emergence of economic (or abnormal) profit?

Recommended Reading

Bronfenbrenner, Martin. *Income Distribution Theory*. Chicago: Aldine-Atherton, Inc., 1971.

Ferguson, C. E. *The Neoclassical Theory of Production and Distribution*, Chaps. 6 and 7. London: Cambridge University Press, 1969.

Hicks, J. R. *The Theory of Wages*. London: Macmillan & Company, Ltd., 1932.

Hicks, J. R. *Value and Capital*, 2d ed. New York: Oxford University Press, 1946.

Robinson, Joan. *The Economics of Imperfect Competition*. London: Macmillan & Company, Ltd., 1933.

Input Price Determination in Imperfectly Competitive Markets

The purpose of this chapter is to determine how departures from perfect competition affect the pricing and employment of inputs. We start by assuming imperfect competition in the goods market, and perfect competition in the input market. We then consider the results of imperfect competition in both the goods market and the input market. This takes us into a discussion of labor union activity.

IMPERFECT COMPETITION IN THE GOODS MARKET AND PERFECT COMPETITION IN THE INPUT MARKET

The Demand for a Single Variable Input by the Firm

We have seen that the demand curve for a single variable input of a firm selling its product in a competitive market is the value of marginal product or VMP curve, where $VMP = MP \cdot P_x$. If the firm does not sell its output in a competitive market, the price of the product (P_x) no longer denotes the addition to total revenue attributable to the sale of an additional unit of output. In an imperfectly competitive market, whether it be monopoly, monopolistic competition, or oligopoly, the firm's product demand curve is negatively sloped and the MR curve lies below the D curve. Therefore, the addition to total revenue resulting from the sale of an additional unit of output is less than P_x; it is MR_x. So if we want to calculate the value of the additional output resulting from the addition of a unit of variable input, we must multiply the marginal product of the unit of input by the corresponding marginal revenue, i.e., $MP \cdot MR_x = MRP$. To distinguish the result from the competitive VMP, **marginal revenue product** or MRP is the name attached to the imperfectly competitive counterpart of VMP. The firm's demand curve for the input is now the MRP curve instead of the VMP curve.

The difference between the competitive seller's VMP curve and the MRP curve of the imperfectly competitive seller is demonstrated in Figure 12–1. Assume that both types of sellers have the same production function, or physical input-output relationship, and hence the same marginal physical product curve (MP), as shown in graph (b). Graph (a) shows the price P_{xC} at which the competitive seller can sell any quantity of product x. Now suppose that product x is slightly differentiated so that additional units can be sold only at reduced prices, as shown by the demand curve P_{xI}. The addition to total revenue from selling another unit of output is no longer P_{xC} but MR_{xI}, which is smaller than P_{xI} and smaller yet than P_{xC}. Therefore, the value of an identical amount of output, by an additional unit of input L, must be less in imperfectly competitive markets than in competitive markets for the good. This is shown in Figure 12–1(c), where the MRP curve lies below the VMP curve, i.e., $MRP = MP \cdot MR_{xI} < VMP = MP \cdot P_{xC}$, since $MR_{xI} < P_{xC}$.

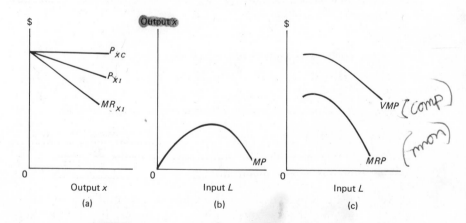

Figure 12-1. Comparison of VMP and MRP.

Suppose the prevailing input price is W_1, as in Figure 12-2. Then, given an input demand curve for the imperfectly competitive firm of MRP, profits are maximized when L_1 units of L are employed or where $W_1 = MRP$. If this is compared with the behavior of the competitive firm, we find that employment by the competitive firm would be larger at all input prices. For example, with an input price of W_1, the competitive firm employs L_2 instead of L_1; or, alternatively, for a given volume of employment such as L_1, the competitive firm pays a higher price for the input, W_2 instead of W_1. Paying an input less than its VMP, or W_1 at employment L_1, is called **monopolistic exploitation** of the input.

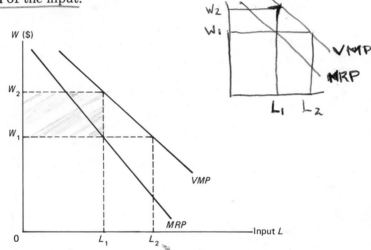

Figure 12-2. Comparison of input pricing and employment under competitive and noncompetitive conditions.

The Firm's Demand for a Specific Variable Input When Several Variable Inputs Are Employed

As in Chapter 11, we now assume that the firm employs several variable inputs, and we wish to determine how this affects the demand for a specific variable input. We shall apply the same reasoning employed in Chapter 11 to derive the adjusted demand curve for the input under competitive conditions in order to arrive at the adjusted demand curve given imperfect competition in the goods market.

In the present case, MRP curves are applicable rather than VMP curves. Assume that the firm is a monopolistic seller of the good. We have seen that the MRP curve is the firm's demand curve for a single variable input. With more than one variable input, there is the possibility of changing the quantities of the other inputs in response to a change in the price of the specific input. If the quantities of the other inputs are changed, this would have the effect of shifting the MRP curve of the specific input.

For example, suppose that the firm is in an equilibrium position, as shown in Figure 12-3, where it employs L_1 units of variable input L at input price W_1. Assuming that the price of input L falls to W_2, the firm would expand employment along MRP_1 to L_2 on the bais of the lower price of L alone. But given other variable inputs with constant prices, the demand curve for the specific variable input would shift because of substitution, output, and profit-maximizing effects, as explained in Chapter 11. The net result of these effects is to shift MRP_1 to the right, as shown by MRP_2 in Figure 12-3, and the demand for the input would now be L_3 at input price W_2. The effective demand curve for L must reflect the combined impact of the substitution, output, and profit-maximizing effect. Starting with point D_1 in the graph, we find point D_2, which takes the three effects into account. By connecting D_1 and D_2, we derive the downward-sloping adjusted demand curve for the input.

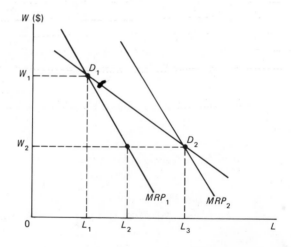

Figure 12-3. Demand for a variable input when several variable inputs are employed.

How would the firm combine several variable inputs so that profits are maximized? Assuming three variable inputs—A, B, and C—the profit-maximizing combination would have to satisfy the following condition:

$$\frac{W_A}{MP_A} = \frac{W_B}{MP_B} = \frac{W_C}{MP_C} = MC_x = MR_x$$

The only difference, as compared with the competitive firm discussed in Chapter 11, is that MR_x is applicable rather than P_x. The reasoning is otherwise the same.

The Market Demand for a Variable Input

The total demand for a variable input in a world of monopolies is simply the summation of the demands of each monopolist at every possible input price, that is, the horizontal summation. There is no need to adjust for product price changes as in the competitive case, since now each monopolist using the input has a product demand curve that is the market demand curve, and so the *MRP* curve does not shift with price changes.

In the cases of oligopoly and monopolistic competition, a reduction in the price of the input would lead to an increase in output by all firms. The larger output of each firm is associated with a product price lower than would be the case if any single firm acted alone, so that each firm's product demand curve and *MRP* curve would shift to the left. Therefore, the market demand for the input by the industry would be derived in the manner explained in Chapter 11.

The Market Supply and Market Price of a Variable Input

Given the same supply conditions of the input as are assumed in competitive product markets, namely a positively sloped supply curve, the total employment and price of the input are determined by the intersection of this curve and the market demand curve for the input. The equilibrium price and employment are illustrated in Figure 12–4.

MONOPOLY IN THE GOODS MARKET AND MONOPSONY IN THE INPUT MARKET

The Demand for a Single Variable Input by the Firm

The major change in this section is the introduction of imperfectly competitive conditions in the buying of inputs by firms. To simplify

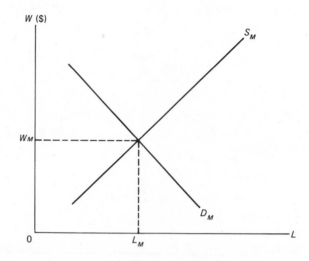

Figure 12-4. Market equilibrium price and employment of a variable input.

the analysis we shall present only the case where there is just one buyer of the input, which is called **monopsony**. We could also distinguish two other cases: **oligopsony**, where each of a few input buyers is capable of influencing the input price by his market actions, and **monopsonistic competition**, in which many input buyers compete for differences in input services, whether real or imagined.

Since a monopsonist is the only buyer of the input, the input supply curve facing the monopsonist is the positively sloped market supply curve of the input. It follows that the **marginal input cost** (*MIC*), or the addition to the monopsonist's total cost caused by adding one more unit of input, will always exceed the price of that unit of input; and the *MIC* curve will have a steeper positive slope than the supply curve of the input.

Figure 12–5 shows the S curve and the *MIC* curve for a variable input A. Suppose that the firm can purchase four units of A for $1 per unit, giving a total cost of $4, as shown in the graph. The rising S_A curve indicates that five units of A would cost $1.20 per unit, and the total cost is $6.00. Therefore, the addition to total cost resulting from the purchase of one more unit, from four units to five units, is $6 — $4 = $2; that is, the *MIC* is $2 even though the actual price of the fifth unit is $1.20. This relationship between the S and *MIC* curves can also be explained as follows. The firm must pay $1.20 not only for the fifth unit but for all units, including the

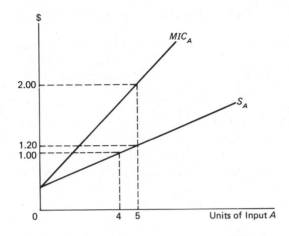

Figure 12-5. The supply curve and the marginal input cost curve of a monopsony.

first four units. That is, the cost of the first four units goes up from $1 per unit to $1.20 per unit when the fifth unit is purchased, so that the firm must now pay an additional $0.80 (4 · $0.20) for the first four units. Since the fifth unit adds $1.20 to total cost and the first four units now cost $0.80 more, the total addition to cost due to adding the fifth unit is $1.20 plus $0.80, or $2.

Figure 12-6 illustrates how the firm determines the quantity of input A to employ and the price to be paid. As usual, the profit-maximizing firm will continue to add units of input A as long as the

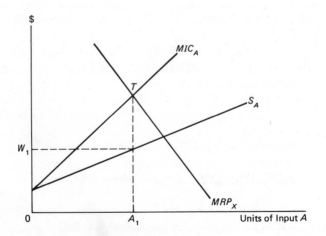

Figure 12-6. Input pricing and employment under monopsony and monopoly.

resulting addition to total revenue exceeds the addition to total cost; that is, as long as $MRP_x > MIC_A$, which means that as more of the input is employed there will be a corresponding addition to total profits. If $MIC_A > MRP_x$, the firm must reduce inputs; this will reduce total cost more than total revenue, and profits will then improve. Therefore, total profit must be at a maximum when $MRP_x = MIC_A$, or at point T in the graph, when A_1 units of input A are employed. The price that the firm must pay to secure A_1 units of A is shown by the supply curve S_A. The supply curve indicates that A_1 units of A are available to the firm at price W_1 per unit. The difference between what the monopsonist receives for the output of the additional input, point T on the MRP curve, and what he pays for the input, W_1, is referred to as **monopsonistic exploitation** of the input.

The Optimum Combination of Several Variable Inputs

To find the profit-maximizing combination of several inputs, say three, we follow the procedure already explained in this chapter and in Chapter 11. The main difference in the case of monopsony is the use of the MIC values instead of the W values. Therefore, the firm would maximize profits when the following condition is satisfied:

$$\frac{MIC_A}{MP_A} = \frac{MIC_B}{MP_B} = \frac{MIC_C}{MP_C} = MR_x = MC_x$$

SUMMARY OF INPUT PRICING AND EMPLOYMENT

Figure 12–7 presents an overall view of the firm's profit-maximizing employment of a variable input under the different types of product and input markets assumed in this chapter and in Chapter 11. Where imperfect competition is assumed, the specific case covered in the graph for the goods market is monopoly, and for the input market it is monopsony.

APPLICATION: LABOR UNION ACTIVITY

First, let us examine the impact of a wage increase brought about by labor union activity. Assume that the specific labor market is competitive, and that the goods market is also competitive. Without union action, the wage rate and employment will be determined by the intersection of the supply and demand curves for labor, as illustrated by wage rate W_M and employment L_M in Figure 12-8.

Now assume that a labor union exists and that it is able to increase the wage rate to W_1. At this higher wage rate the demand for the labor in question will decline from L_M to L_1, creating unemployment equal to the difference between L_M and L_1. Actually, the supply curve S_M tells us that at wage W_1 additional workers will

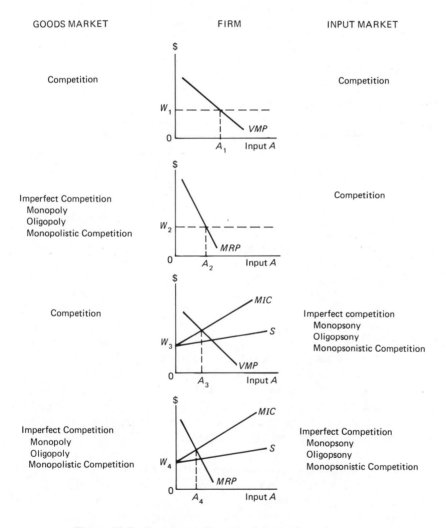

Figure 12-7. Summary of input pricing and employment.

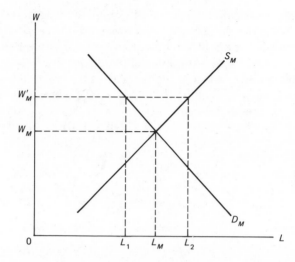

Figure 12-8. Labor union activity in a competitive labor market.

offer their services up to L_2, so that total unemployment will amount to $L_2 - L_1$. Suppose that we assume that the union is able to bar entry or otherwise control the labor supply. Now let us consider only those workers who have actually lost jobs as a result of union activity, or $L_M - L_1$. How can union action to raise wages be justified in the face of this unemployment? Obviously, those workers still working are better off with the higher wages, but what about those who are unemployed? It is possible for all workers to gain if the demand for their services is inelastic. In this case, total wages paid to those still employed, or $W_1 \cdot L_1$, will exceed the total before the wage increase, or $W_M \cdot L_M$. Therefore, it will be theoretically possible for the union to divide either total hours of work or total wages among L_M workers, and all workers will be better off after the wage increase. This result would not be possible if labor demand were elastic, since total wages would be smaller after the wage increase.[1]

Unions have more options in the case of imperfectly competitive markets. Suppose that the labor market is monopsonistic and that the goods market is monopolistic. In the absence of union activity the firm would maximize profits by equating *MIC* and *MRP*, as shown in Figure 12-9, and employ L_1 workers at a wage of W_1. Union action can increase the wage to as high as W_3 without reducing employment, since the firm will now consider the supply-of-labor curve to be $W_3 t S_L$ and the relevant portion of the *MIC* curve to be

$W_3 t$; the firm therefore equates $W_3 t$ and MRP and so continues to employ L_1 workers at wage W_3. On the other hand, the union may strive to maximize employment, in which case the wage will be set at W_2. Under these circumstances, the firm would view its supply-of-labor curve as $W_2 n S_L$, and the relevant part of its MIC curve as $W_2 n$. To maximize profit, the firm will equate $W_2 n$ and MRP, and employ L_2 workers. Of course, the union can also choose to benefit its membership by increasing both the wage rate and employment. In other words, the wage rate could be established between W_2 and W_3, in which case employment would be between L_1 and L_2. But by pushing the wage above W_3, the union would have to be prepared to accept a level of employment below L_1.

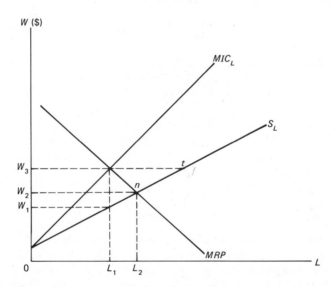

Figure 12-9. Labor union activity in a monopsonistic labor market.

INNOVATION: HUMAN CAPITAL FORMATION

Capital, or **capital goods**, refers to produced nonhuman inputs that are used in the production of other goods and services. Included in this definition are such capital goods as factories, machines, tools, and trucks. The nation's **capital-stock** is the total amount of capital that has been accumulated over the years. By accumulating capital, the country expands its capacity to produce consumer goods and services. By the same token, an individual can enhance his ability to produce goods and services by enlarging his stock of human capital. **Human capital** generally refers to an individual's accumulated knowledge, skills, and experience that make him a more productive member of society. Just as a firm invests in capital goods, an individual may invest in human capital by furthering his education, by learning job skills, or even by spending money on health care in order to avoid physical or mental disabilities.

The main purpose of an individual's investment in human capital is to enlarge his earning capacity as a means of increasing his lifetime income. Therefore, just as we can calculate a rate of return on a firm's investment in capital goods, so we can estimate an individual's rate of return on his investment in human capital. This can be done by means of the following equation:

$$C = \frac{R_1}{(1+r)} + \frac{R_2}{(1+r)^2} + \frac{R_3}{(1+r)^3} + \cdots + \frac{R_n}{(1+r)^n}$$

where C is the cost of the investment in human capital, the R's are the additional amounts of earnings in future periods due to the investment, and r is the rate of return. We know the value of C, the R's must be estimated, and the equation is then solved for r, the individual's rate of return on his investment in human capital. Studies by economists have shown that an investment in human capital yields a high rate of return when compared with the interest rate, or even with the rate of return on business investments.[2]

Education as Human Capital Formation

As evidence of the importance of basic education—an example of human capital investment—the rate of return on a high school education is significantly greater than that on a college education, although total lifetime earnings are much larger in the case of college graduates. In other words, college graduates earn much more during their working years than do high school graduates, but relative to the large investment required for college the rate of return is less.

A marginal approach can be used to establish an optimal period of education for each individual. A student would measure the cost, including deferred or foregone earnings, of each additional year of education and compare this cost with the discounted value to him of the corresponding increment to his stock of human capital. He would continue to add to his stock of human capital (continue his education) until the marginal cost of the human capital added equaled the discounted value of this capital. This implies that different amounts and types of education will be optimal for different individuals. For some people, four years of college would be ideal, but for others a high school diploma or two years of college might be best, and for still others, a combination of high school and vocational training would be optimal. While a college degree still provides an important certification of competence in a discipline, more and more employers are using their own tests to determine the qualifications of prospective employees. Corporations have personnel departments that administer such tests, and the government engages in many forms of occupational rating activities, especially in connection with civil service employment. In many occupations, such as bricklayer and plumber, practitioners have organized themselves to test and certify newcomers. Actually, decision-making by the student on the basis of costs and benefits would be facilitated by more employer job-testing activities, since at any point in his education the student could determine whether he is qualified for the type of employment he prefers. If he does qualify, he can terminate his training; if he does not, he can continue and attempt to remedy his deficiencies. In the process, he could determine his strengths and weaknesses, as well as the areas of study most relevant for the job under consideration.

SUMMARY

The purpose of this chapter is to determine how departures from perfect competition affect the pricing and employment of inputs. We start by assuming imperfect competition in the goods market, and perfect competition in the input market. If the firm does not sell its output in a competitive market, the demand curve for the good is negatively sloped, and the addition to total revenue from selling one more unit of the good is no longer the price of the good—rather it is the corresponding marginal revenue, which is always less than price. To calculate the value of the additional output resulting from the addition of a unit of the variable input, we must now multiply the marginal product of the latter by the associated marginal revenue. The result is called the marginal revenue product (*MRP*) and it is always less than the competitive counterpart, called the value of the marginal product (*VMP*). The *MRP* curve is therefore the input demand curve for the imperfectly competitive firm, which maximizes profit by employing the variable input up to the point where the price of the input is equal to the *MRP*.

The firm's demand for a specific variable input when several variable inputs are employed is determined by the same kind of analysis used in Chapter 11. When the price of the specific input is changed, we must take into account the substitution, output, and profit-maximizing effects. The net result of these effects is to shift the *MRP* curve to the right, and the effective demand curve for the input is composed of points taken from the shifting *MRP* curve, as discussed in Chapter 11.

The total demand for a variable input in a world of monopolies is simply the summation of the amount demanded by each monopolist at every possible input price. In the cases of oligopoly and monopolistic competition, a reduction in the price of the input would lead to an increase in output by all firms. The larger output of each firm is associated with a product price that is lower than would be the case if any single firm acted alone, so that each firm's product demand curve and *MRP* curve will shift to the left. Therefore, the market demand curve for the input will be derived in the manner explained in Chapter 11. Given the same supply conditions of the input as are assumed in competitive product markets, or a positively sloped supply curve, the total employment and price of the input are determined by the intersection of this market supply curve and the market demand curve for the input.

We now assume imperfect competition in the goods market and also in the input market. To simplify the analysis, we suppose that there is only one seller of the good (monopoly), and one buyer of the input, called a monopsony. Since a monopsonist is the only buyer of the input, the input supply curve facing the monopsonist is the positively sloped market supply curve of the input. It follows that the marginal input cost (*MIC*), or the addition to the monopsonist's total cost caused by adding one more unit of the input, will always exceed the price of that unit of the input; and the *MIC* curve will have a steeper positive slope than the supply curve of the input. As usual, the profit-maximizing firm will continue to add units of the variable input as long as the resulting addition to total revenue exceeds the addition to total cost, or as long as *MRP* exceeds *MIC*. Therefore, total profit will reach a maximum when *MRP* = *MIC*.

If we consider the effects of labor union activity, we see that if the union is successful in forcing the wage rate above the equilibrium level, this will lead to unemployment. On the other hand, if the demand for labor is inelastic, then an increase in the wage rate will result in an increase in the total amount of wages paid to union workers. In this case, it would be possible for the union to divide the greater total amount of wages among all union members, including those unemployed as a consequence of the wage increase, so that all workers would be better off.

Human capital refers to an individual's accumulated knowledge, skills, and experience, which make him a more productive member of society. Just as a firm invests in capital goods (factories, machines, etc.), an individual may invest in human capital by furthering his education, by learning job skills, and so forth. The main purpose of investment in human capital is to enlarge the individual's earning capacity. Just as we can calculate a rate of return on a firm's investment in capital goods, so we can estimate an individual's rate of return on his investment in human capital. Studies have shown that this rate of return exceeds that on business investments. A marginal approach can be used to establish an optimal period of education for each individual. A student would continue to add to his stock of human capital until the marginal cost of the human capital added equaled the discounted value of this capital.

Notes

1. We should emphasize that we are analyzing a single labor market, and that the results obtained cannot be applied to total union activity in the entire economy.
2. See G. S. Becker, *Human Capital* (New York: Columbia University Press, 1964); T. Johnson, "Returns from Investment in Human Capital," *American Economic Review*, Vol. LX (September, 1970), pp. 546-560; and T. W. Schultz, "Resources for Higher Education: An Economist's View," *Journal of Political Economy*, Vol. 76 (May/June, 1968), pp. 327-347.

Problems and Questions

1. Distinguish between monopolistic and monopsonistic exploitation of an input.
2. How would a firm, faced with imperfect competition in the goods market and perfect competition in the input market, combine three variable inputs so that profits are maximized?
3. How would you derive a marginal input cost curve?
4. Why must the *MRP* curve always be below the *VMP* curve, assuming that in both cases the marginal product curve is the same?
5. Given that the labor market is monopsonistic and that the goods market is monopolistic, how high can a union increase the wage rate without reducing employment? Explain with the aid of a graph.

6. What is human capital, and why do individuals accumlate it?
7. How would you determine the ideal amount of human capital for any given individual?
8. Find a monopolistic firm's demand curve for a specific variable input when several variable inputs are employed. Assume a perfectly competititve supply of the input.
9. How would you find the total demand for a variable input in a world of monopolies?
10. How would a firm that is a monopoly in the goods market and a monopsony in the input market go about maximizing profit?

Recommended Reading

Becker, G. S. *Human Capital.* New York: Columbia University Press, 1964.

Bronfenbrenner, Martin. *Income Distribution Theory.* Chicago: Aldine-Atherton, Inc., 1971.

Garb, Gerald. "The Economics of a University System Without Degrees," *Western Economic Journal,* Vol. X (March, 1972), pp. 57–64.

Robinson, Joan. *The Economics of Imperfect Competition.* London: Macmillan & Company, Ltd., 1933.

13

General
Equilibrium Theory

Our theories have been put forward in terms of partial equilibrium analysis, which is the study of the relationships among a limited number of variables with all other variables held constant. We are now ready to proceed to general equilibrium analysis, in which the outputs, prices, and other relevant variables of the entire economic system are seen to be interrelated. We shall also use general equilibrium theory as a method of introducing macroeconomic theory. This seems reasonable and appropriate because general equilibrium theory can be employed at different levels of aggregation, from the extreme disaggregation of microeconomics to the great aggregation usually found in macroeconomics. At both of these extremes and in intermediate cases we are concerned with basically the same thing, the equilibrium or interrelatedness of the entire economic system. Therefore, in this chapter we start with general equilibrium at the micro level. Next, we consider input-output analysis, which shows the interrelationships among a number of industries or sectors of the economy, the exact number depending on the definitions and procedures governing the extent of aggregation. Finally, we make the leap to the macro level, where general equilibrium conditions are again explored in terms of a theoretical framework based on heavy aggregation.

271

GENERAL EQUILIBRIUM THEORY
AT THE MICRO LEVEL

The Economy as an Interdependent Network

In an economic system everything depends, more or less, on everything else. An economic system has been compared to a bowl full of marbles in which the removal or disturbance of one marble causes all the others to shift their positions. Another analogy popular among economists is to compare the effects of a change in an economic variable to the result of tossing a stone into a pond. There is a big splash where the stone hits the water, followed by large ripples nearby that gradually get smaller as the distance from the initial splash increases. In like manner, a change in an economic variable spreads its influence throughout the economy. For example, suppose that suddenly the price of automobiles declines. This will lead to increased purchases of autos by consumers. The auto makers in turn will buy more steel, glass, tires, and more of everything else necessary to make cars. This may lead to price increases for some of these products. More workers will be required as the output of cars and related products expands. Steel producers will need more ore and coal, and so mine owners will notice the change. In the meantime consumers, who are not only consumers but also workers, will find that their incomes are benefiting from the rising level of economic activity. And so forth, as the effects spread.

Figure 13-1 is an attempt to show these interrelationships in terms of a hypersimplified economy composed of six consumers (C's), three firms producing finished goods (F's), three firms supplying intermediate products (M's), and six workers, who are also the consumers and who receive wages (W's). The wages constitute the incomes of the consumers, with which they buy the output of the three firms producing the finished goods. For example, the figure shows that consumer 4, C_4, buys goods from F_2 and F_3, but not from F_1. F_3 in turn requires M_1 and W_6 (= C_6) in its production process. Suppose now that C_4 decides to stop buying the product of F_3 and instead buys more from F_2. F_3 will require fewer hours of the services of C_6, and hence the wages of C_6 will decline; also F_3 will need less M_1, and the wages of C_1, used in the production of M_1, will go down. A decline in the wages of C_6 will lead to a further reduction in the sales of F_3, since C_6 is a customer of F_3. The sales of F_2 will gain because of the switch of C_4 from F_3 to F_2, but F_2 will also lose sales because of the reduction in the wages of C_1, a customer of F_2. And so it goes, as adjustments and readjustments work their way through the system.

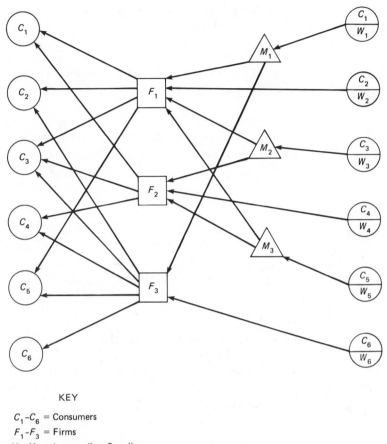

KEY

C_1-C_6 = Consumers
F_1-F_3 = Firms
M_1-M_3 = Intermediate Suppliers
W_1-W_6 = Input Payments

Figure 13-1. A simple model of the economic network.

The Economy as a System of Equations

A much more precise and efficient way of dealing with the interdependence of a large number of economic variables is by means of a
system of simultaneous equations.[1] Since a mathematical model expresses only what is put into it, it is essential to formulate the underlying assumptions and limitations clearly. The simplified model
economy that we shall construct is composed of three basic groups:
consumers, producers, and productive inputs. There are only four
goods and four inputs. We shall assume that consumers derive their income from supplying the inputs, and that all of this income goes to

producers for their output of goods. We assume that consumer preferences, production techniques, and input quantities are given and fixed. Finally, perfect competition is assumed. In equilibrium the market supply of, and demand for, each good and each input are equal, and the price of each good is equal to the cost of the inputs necessary to produce it. In the equations we use the following notation:

x_1, x_2, x_3, x_4 are the quantities of the goods.
p_1, p_2, p_3, p_4 are the prices of each of the goods.
w_1, w_2, w_3, w_4 are the prices of each of the inputs.
Q_1, Q_2, Q_3, Q_4 are the quantities of each input.

$a_{11}, a_{21}, a_{31}, a_{41}$ are the quantities of each input needed
$a_{12}, a_{22}, a_{32}, a_{42}$ to produce a unit of each good, where the
$a_{13}, a_{23}, a_{33}, a_{43}$ first subscript denotes the good and the
$a_{14}, a_{24}, a_{34}, a_{44}$ second denotes the input.

Demand-for-Goods Equations

The total demand for each good depends on the price of the good, the prices of all other goods, and the incomes of the consumers. Since consumer incomes consist of the input payments, the w's, we can write the demand-for-goods equations in functional form as follows:

$$x_1 = f_1(p_1, p_2, p_3, p_4, w_1, w_2, w_3, w_4)$$
$$x_2 = f_2(p_1, p_2, p_3, p_4, w_1, w_2, w_3, w_4)$$
$$x_3 = f_3(p_1, p_2, p_3, p_4, w_1, w_2, w_3, w_4)$$
$$x_4 = f_4(p_1, p_2, p_3, p_4, w_1, w_2, w_3, w_4)$$

Cost-of-Goods Equations

The supply of the goods must conform to the assumption that the price of each good equals its cost of production. If we multiply the quantity of each input needed to produce one unit of output by the price of the input, we determine the price of the unit of output.

$$p_1 = a_{11}w_1 + a_{12}w_2 + a_{13}w_3 + a_{14}w_4$$
$$p_2 = a_{21}w_1 + a_{22}w_2 + a_{23}w_3 + a_{24}w_4$$
$$p_3 = a_{31}w_1 + a_{32}w_2 + a_{33}w_3 + a_{34}w_4$$
$$p_4 = a_{41}w_1 + a_{42}w_2 + a_{43}w_3 + a_{44}w_4$$

Supply of and Demand for Inputs

Given the supplies of inputs and the assumption that supply and demand are equal, we need a set of equations to express this equality. The total supply of each input must equal the sum of the amounts of each input used in the production of every good. Note that this approach implies that there will always be full employment.

$$Q_1 = a_{11}x_1 + a_{21}x_2 + a_{31}x_3 + a_{41}x_4$$
$$Q_2 = a_{12}x_1 + a_{22}x_2 + a_{32}x_3 + a_{42}x_4$$
$$Q_3 = a_{13}x_1 + a_{23}x_2 + a_{33}x_3 + a_{43}x_4$$
$$Q_4 = a_{14}x_1 + a_{24}x_2 + a_{34}x_3 + a_{44}x_4$$

where $a_{11}x_1$ is the amount of input 1 needed in the production of x_1, $a_{21}x_2$ is the amount of input 1 used in making x_2, and so forth.

We now seem to have a system of 12 equations and 12 unknown variables; x_1, x_2, x_3, x_4, p_1, p_2, p_3, p_4, w_1, w_2, w_3, w_4. Without going into a complete explanation of the conditions necessary for a unique solution to a system of simultaneous equations, we may note that, among other conditions, there must be as many independent equations as there are variables. Although we can now look back and count as many equations as variables, there are really only eleven *independent* equations in the system.

Look at it this way. We have assumed that all consumers spend all their income on goods. This condition can be written as follows:

$$Q_1w_1 + Q_2w_2 + Q_3w_3 + Q_4w_4 = x_1p_1 + x_2p_2 + x_3p_3 + x_4p_4$$

We now have thirteen equations. However, this equation is the same as

$$x_1 = \frac{Q_1w_1 + Q_2w_2 + Q_3w_3 + Q_4w_4 - x_2p_2 - x_3p_3 - x_4p_4}{p_1}$$

Since this equation can be substituted for our first demand-for-goods equation, we are back to twelve equations. But it can be shown that this last equation can also be obtained from manipulating the cost-of-goods equations and the input equations. Therefore, there are really only eleven independent equations and twelve variables, so that a unique solution cannot be found.

That is the problem. It is solved by taking one of the goods, say x_1, as the unit of measurement, or **numeraire**, as it is called; that is, the unit in terms of which the prices of the other goods are measured. The price of this standard good is 1, or $p_1 = 1$. By so doing, we have eliminated a variable (p_1), and we now have eleven equations and eleven variables. The prices of the other goods are now determined relative to the price of the first good. For example, if $P_2 = 2$, then this simply means that the price of x_2 is twice as high as that of x_1.

This general equilibrium model grows in complexity as it grows in size and as it approaches the complex reality of a functioning economy. Not only do we encounter an enormous number of variables and equations, but we must specify the functional relationships among them. Consequently, it would be necessary to collect vast quantities of data, much of which would be difficult to assemble, before functional forms could be determined.

The major contribution of the general equilibrium concept at the microeconomic level is the support it provides for the idea that an economy is an interrelated network of all of its countless small components. Even when we are especially interested in a particular part of the economy, we are now aware that there may be far-reaching repercussions throughout the system arising from changes in "our" part. This broad viewpoint is extremely helpful in evaluating the possible effects of economic policy proposals, or in conducting research on the behavior of the economy.

A GRAPHIC APPROACH TO GENERAL EQUILIBRIUM

The Edgeworth box diagram, developed in Chapter 3, can be used to illustrate the conditions necessary for general equilibrium. For an economic system to achieve a general equilibrium, three conditions must be satisfied: there must be general equilibrium in exchange; there must be general equilibrium in production; and there must be general equilibrium between exchange and production. We are assuming a perfectly competitive economy in which consumers maximize satisfaction and producers maximize profits. The two-dimensional box diagrams that we shall use, one for exchange and another for production, restricts the analysis to a 2 X 2 X 2 X 2 economy: 2 consumers, 2 goods, 2 producers, and 2 inputs. But the results can be extended to an n X n X n X n economy, where n is any number.

General Equilibrium in Exchange

First, we consider general equilibrium in exchange. Figure 13-2 reproduces Figure 3-5 of Chapter 3, the construction of which the reader should review at this point. Just as in Chapter 3, we assume two individuals Ann and Ben and two goods x and y. Before exchange takes place, Ann possesses $O_a x_1$ of x and $O_a y_1$ of y, and Ben has $O_b x_2$ of x and $O_b y_2$ of y. The initial positions of both individuals can be represented by point Q in the box diagram, with Ann on her indifference curve I_{a_1} and Ben on his indifference curve I_{b_2}. Both individuals can benefit from exchange, since each can move to a higher indifference curve (a higher level of satisfaction) by trading. For example, if Ann exchanged some of her y for some of Ben's x, in such a way that the resulting combinations of x and y possessed by the two could be represented by point S, then both Ann and Ben would be on higher indifference curves. In general, a movement from point Q to any point within the shaded area bounded by the two intersecting indifference curves I_{a_1} and I_{b_2} will lead to greater satisfaction for both individuals. General equilibrium of exchange will occur at some point, such as S, on the contract curve $O_a O_b$, that connects all tangency points of Ann's and Ben's indifference curves and that denotes all potential equilibrium points. Once on the contract curve, any further exchange will make one or both individuals worse off, and so no further exchange takes place. Hence, an equilibrium has been attained.

Since points on the contract curve represent the tangency points of Ann's and Ben's indifference curves, and since the slope of an indifference curve is given by the marginal rate of substitution of the two goods, it follows that when equilibrium is achieved the marginal

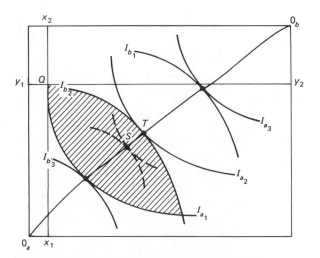

Figure 13-2. General equilibrium in exchange.

rate of substitution (MRS) for the two goods is the same for both individuals. What is true for two individuals is true for any number of individuals, and general equilibrium of exchange prevails when the marginal rates of substitution for all individuals are equal. How this result is attained in a perfectly competitive economy with a large number of individuals is discussed in the next chapter, which is on welfare economics.

General Equilibrium in Production

General equilibrium in production is determined in a manner parallel to the analysis for exchange. The box diagram in Figure 13-3 shows production isoquants for goods x and y, and the dimensions of the box now represent the combined amounts of labor (L) and capital (K) possessed by the producers of x and y. Initially, the producer of x has $O_x L_1$ of L and $O_x K_1$ of K, and the producer of y possesses $O_y L_2$ of L and $O_y K_2$ of K. This initial position can be represented by point F in the box diagram. The question at hand is whether the two producers can trade labor and capital in such a way that more of both x and y can be produced as a result, or at least more of either x or y with the same quantity of the other good. As in the case of exchange, a movement from point F to any point in the shaded area bounded by the two intersecting isoquants, x_1 and y_2, would lead to a greater output of both x and y. For example, if the producer of x traded some of his K for some of the y producer's L, in such a way that the combinations of L and K possessed

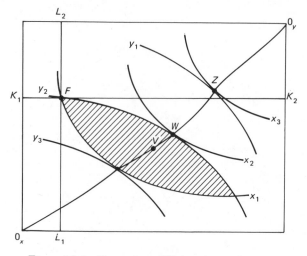

Figure 13-3. General equilibrium in production.

by the two producers could be indicated by point V, then each producer would be on a higher isoquant, and each would be able to produce more of his respective good. Hence, the economy would have more goods with no change in total inputs.

Since point V is on the contract curve, which is the curve connecting all tangency points of the x and y isoquants, general equilibrium of production has been reached. It is a general equilibrium because once on the contract curve, it is not possible to increase the output of one of the goods without decreasing the output of the other good; and a movement off the curve may decrease the output of both goods.

As we saw in Chapter 5, the slope of an isoquant is called the marginal rate of technical substitution ($MRTS$). Since the slopes of any two isoquants are the same at a tangency point, it follows that the $MRTS$ for any two isoquants are equal at a tangency point. Therefore, general equilibrium in production is attained when the $MRTS$ for L and K is the same for the two producers. This condition also holds for any number of producers in a perfectly competitive economy, which is discussed in the next chapter.

General Equilibrium Between Exchange and Production

To have a general equilibrium within the economy, general equilibrium in exchange must be consistent with general equilibrium in production. The meaning of this statement is explained in this section. First, we derive a **transformation curve**, or a **production-possibility curve**, as it is also called. The transformation curve is a reflection of the contract curve in the box diagram depicting general equilibrium of production. In other words, the transformation curve gives all possible equilibrium combinations of goods x and y that could be produced by employing all available inputs. Although this is exactly the same information that is given by the contract curve, it is now plotted on a graph with the axes representing the two goods.

Figure 13-4 illustrates how a transformation curve is derived from Figure 13-3. Point W on the contract curve in Figure 13-3 depicts a tangency of isoquants x_2 and y_2, which represents the production of x_2 of x and y_2 of y. These quantities are plotted as point W on the transformation curve in Figure 13-4. In a similar manner, point Z is plotted in Figure 13-4. For every point on the contract curve in Figure 13-3, there is a corresponding point on the transformation curve in Figure 13-4. If none of good y is produced, then the maximum amount of x, x^*, can be produced, which corresponds to the y origin, O_y, in Figure 13-3. If we select a point that is not on the

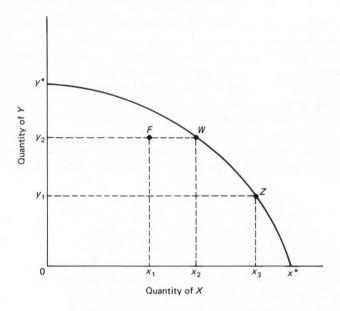

Figure 13-4. The transformation curve.

contract curve, such as point F in Figure 13-3, we see that this translates into a point that is not on the transformation curve, e.g., point
F in Figure 13-4. We can now clearly see that point F could not
represent a general equilibrium in production, since the economy is
capable of producing more x without sacrificing any y (with the
same quantity of inputs) by moving to point W. Finally, by way of
definition, the slope of the transformation curve, or the amount
of y that must be given up to get another unit of x, is called the
marginal rate of transformation (MRT).

We can now specify the condition necessary for general equilibrium between exchange and production, namely, that the marginal
rate of substitution must equal the marginal rate of transformation.
General equilibrium in exchange occurs when both individuals have
the same MRS, which is always a point on the contract curve. When
this MRS equals the MRT, there is a general equilibrium between exchange and production. An example will clarify the meaning of this
equilibrium. Suppose that the MRS is $1x : 1y$, that is, each individual
will stay at the same level of satisfaction if one unit of x is exchanged
for one unit of y. Now suppose that the MRT is $1x : 3y$, that is, by
producing one unit less of x, three more units of y can be produced.
In this case, $MRS \neq MRT$.

Under these circumstances, the level of satisfaction of one or both individuals could be increased through a change in production. For example, if three more units of y are produced, only one unit of x has to be given up. But either individual is willing to give up one unit of x if he gets only one unit of y. Since production will bring forth three units of y at a cost of only one unit of x, then either individual will be at the same level of satisfaction by receiving one unit of y for one unit of x, and there will be two additional units of y left over. These two units of y can be used to raise the level of satisfaction of either individual or of both individuals. Therefore, more y and less x will be produced until the point on the transformation curve has been reached where $MRT = MRS$. This condition is pursued further in the next chapter, which is on welfare economics.

INPUT-OUTPUT ANALYSIS:
INTERMEDIATE AGGREGATION

The difficulties involved in the development of general equilibrium models at the micro level for an actual economic system, with large numbers of consumers and producers, have stimulated the creation of simpler general equilibrium models. The main path to simplification is through aggregation. An aggregative method of showing the interdependence of the economy is input-output analysis.[2] An input-output table usually lists a large number of industries and shows all the industries supplying productive inputs to every industry, and at the same time it displays the proportion of the output of each industry going to every other industry. Depending on the degree of aggregation, input-output tables can be, and have been, constructed to show these interrelationships among anywhere from four to over 400 industry groups. In addition to the various industries, input-output tables contain a final demand sector which indicates how much of the output of each industry is demanded for final use.

Table 13-1 presents a hypothetical input-output table consisting of six industries and a labor input. To simplify the table we make the unrealistic assumption that the economy is composed of only these six industries, but an input-output table with this degree of aggregation for a real economy might contain 40 or 50 industries. Suppose we look at the column headed "Agriculture." By reading down the column we find the amount of input that agriculture takes from each of the industries, including agriculture itself. That is, in the production of its output, agriculture takes $3 (or $3 million or $3 billion) from its own industry (seed, feed, etc.), $1 from textiles,

Table 13.1. Hypothetical Input-Output Table (in Dollars)

				Outputs				
Inputs	Agriculture	Textiles	Chemicals	Motor Vehicles	Machinery	Services	Final Demand	Output Total
Agriculture	3	5	2	0	0	0	14	24
Textiles	1	2	0	2	0	0	17	22
Chemicals	6	2	4	2	1	0	2	17
Motor Vehicles	1	1	1	3	1	5	6	18
Machinery	2	3	1	5	1	0	0	12
Services	1	1	2	1	2	7	19	33
Labor	10	8	7	5	7	21	10	68
Total Input	24	22	17	18	12	33	68	194

$6 from chemicals, $1 from motor vehicles, $2 from machinery, $1 from services, $10 of labor input, giving a total input of $24. Now if we look at the first row in the table, which also reads "Agriculture," we find that, of the total output of agriculture, $3 goes to agriculture, $5 goes to textiles, $2 goes to chemicals, no agricultural output is required by the next three industries, and $14 worth of output is used for final demand, giving a total agricultural output of $24, which equals the total input to agriculture. In this manner, the table shows the sources of all inputs for each industry and the destinations of each industry's output.

The information in an input-output table can be used to set up a system of linear equations, which can then be solved to show how a change in the final demand for an industry's output would affect all the other entries in the table. For example, the total output of agriculture is $24A = 3A + 5T + 2C + 0V + 0M + 0S + 14$, which is derived from the first row of the table. To put this in terms of inputs per dollar's worth of output we divide through by 24: $A = .1A + .2T + .1C + 0V + 0M + 0S + 14$, leaving 14 unchanged, since this is the total final demand that must be satisfied. By setting up similar equations for the other five industries, we get six equations to go with the six unknowns, A, T, C, V, M, and S,[3] which stand for agriculture, textiles, chemicals, motor vehicles, machinery, and services, respectively. This system is then solved simultaneously to determine the dollar amounts of each industry's output required to satisfy various levels of final demand. For example, if we decide to meet a final agricultural demand of $20, rather than $14, then $20 is substituted into the equation and a different set of values is found; then these will go into the table.

The final demand for the product of each industry can be expanded up to a maximum amount which is determined by the existing supply of labor. For example, the table shows that for each $24 worth of agricultural output, $10 of labor is required; for every $22 of textiles, we need $8 of labor, and so forth. Therefore, for any dollar output of the system shown in Table 13-1, the value of the labor requirement is found to be

$$L_1 = \frac{10}{24} A + \frac{8}{22} T + \frac{7}{17} C + \frac{5}{18} V + \frac{7}{12} M + \frac{21}{33} S + \frac{10}{68} D$$

or

$$L_1 = .42A + .36T + .41C + .28V + .58M + .64S + .14D$$

This value of L_1, which is the demand for labor, must not be more than the supply of labor, say L_2; or, L_1 must be equal to or less than

L_2. Unlike the Walrasian system, unemployment is possible, since the demand for labor may be less than the supply of labor.

Now we must consider the assumptions underlying this analytical system. First, since the relationships are expressed in terms of dollars, we assume that prices are given and fixed. Otherwise, a change in relative prices would lead to changes in the coefficients of our equations. Second, it is assumed that the physical quantites of inputs required per unit of output are constant, meaning that there is no substitution among inputs to produce a given output. Again, variations in the physical relationships would alter the coefficients of the equations. Third, we assume constant returns to scale, that is, if we double inputs, then output exactly doubles also. As a result of these three assumptions, we find that both in dollar terms and in real terms the proportions existing among the inputs, and between the inputs and the outputs, cannot vary. Fourth, the final demand for the output of each industry is given. Fifth, each industry produces only one product, which is different from the product produced by every other industry.

Many of the limitations of input-output analysis stem from the above assumptions, which are made in the first place to facilitate the analysis. In the real economy we know that relative prices change, that input combinations may vary, that output may not change in a fixed proportion to input, and that a given industry may produce a wide and changing variety of products. But to drop the assumptions and attempt to incorporate all the variations into the system would greatly increase the complications and the cost of constructing such a system. Of course, as the system gets larger and includes more detail, these difficulties grow rapidly.

One way of at least partly overcoming many of these problems would be through frequent revisions of the table, since in a short period we would not expect great changes in the factors we have assumed to be constant. Still, the frequency of revision is limited by time lags in the process of data collection and dissemination, and by the time and cost involved in revising an input-output system of large size.

Nevertheless, input-output analysis is a worthwhile tool. It shows in a very concrete way how an economy's industries are interrelated. Even though it only roughly approximates the real economy, an input-output system can be helpful in making plans for the future. For military defense or mobilization, it shows the relative inputs required from various industries. For a growing economy, the changes required to accommodate the growth may be indicated. On the other hand, in the event of disarmament, the industries subject to the greatest decline in demand are disclosed by the input-output table, and plans can be made to cope with these dislocations.

GENERAL EQUILIBRIUM THEORY
AT THE MACRO LEVEL:
SUBSTANTIAL AGGREGATION

In order to explore briefly the concept of general equilibrium at the macro level, we shall define and employ a small number of large aggregates. First, let us define the **gross national product** (*GNP*) as the market value of the nation's total output of final goods and services during a year. Next, **depreciation** represents charges made by businesses against receipts in order to replace that portion of their capital plant and equipment worn out in the process of producing the current year's output. If we subtract depreciation from the *GNP*, we shall call the remainder **national income**.

We shall assume away the existence of both the government and the international economy. This leaves only consumers, who receive the national income from businesses for the services of their labor or property. We assume that consumer and business spending is such as to purchase the entire output of business, and that business produces consumer goods and capital goods in the right proportion to satisfy this demand.

The Flow and Growth of Output and Income

We are now prepared to examine the operation of the simple economy based on our definitions and assumptions, after which we shall consider equilibrium and disequilibrium in this system more rigorously.

Let us consider Figure 13-5. Column 1 shows the allocation of *GNP I* to consumers in the form of wages, interest, rent, and profit; and the panel on the left indicates the total amount saved. To this national income sum we add depreciation to account for the entire *GNP I*. Column 2 shows that the income payments of column 1 less savings constitute consumer spending for the output of consumer goods by firms. Column 3 represents the consumer goods which gave rise to the national income of column 1, less savings. Since all of the national income does not arise out of or go toward the purchase of consumer goods, the remainder of the national income, i.e., savings, represents the production of new capital goods, or **net investment.** Finally, depreciation charges are used to replace the capital goods worn out in the production of the *GNP*. Net investment plus depreciation is called **gross investment**.

The same reasoning is applied to *GNP II*, only *GNP II* is larger than *GNP I* because of the additional capital goods made possible by the saving out of *GNP I*. The larger size of *GNP II* indicates larger payments to the inputs and higher savings, which in turn provide for a greater amount of investment in new capital goods. Depreciation would also be somewhat larger because of the greater total amount of capital.

Figure 13-5 therefore not only shows the flows of spending and goods, but also incorporates in a simplified manner the process of economic growth. We can easily add further realism to this growth process if we assume, for example, that the new capital incorporates the latest advances in technology, and that the educational system is gradually raising the skills of the human inputs.

A Simple Set of Theoretical Relationships

We can reduce the main relationships in Figure 13-5 to a few simple algebraic expressions. Let C stand for consumer spending, S for saving, I for investment in new capital goods or net investment, D for depreciation, and R for replacement of worn-out capital. Then

$$GNP = C + S + D$$
$$GNP = C + I + R$$

therefore

$$C + S + D = C + I + R$$

since

$$C = C \text{ and } D = R$$

then

$$S = I$$

These relationships can be shown graphically, as in Figure 13-6. Here we draw a **consumption function**, which indicates that consumer spending increases with income. Points on the 45-degree line represent the same value on both axes, which are drawn ɔ the same scale. Therefore, the distance from the C line to the 45-degree line must be equal to the value of the other components of the *GNP* in addition to C. This is shown in the graph as $S + D = I + R$, that is, $C + S +$

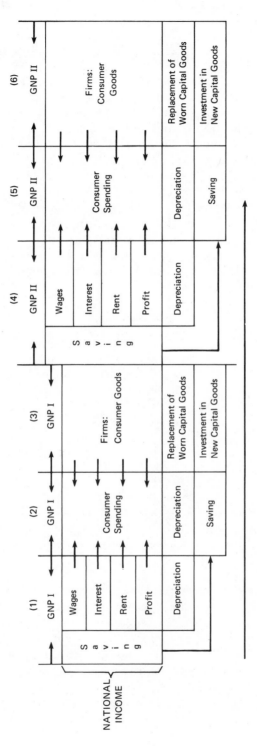

Figure 13-5. The flow and growth of output and income.

$D = GNP$ and $C + I + R = GNP$, so that we can add either $S + D$ or $I + R$ to C to equal the GNP. But as we have seen, given any particular level of the GNP such as $GNP\ I$, then $S_I + D_I$ must equal $I_I + R_I$ in order to be in equilibrium. What happens if we have a situation such as $I_{II} + R_{II} > S_I + D_I$? Then this is a disequilibrium situation, and only GNP_{II} can restore equilibrium so that $I_{II} + R_{II} = S_{II} + D_{II}$. Whatever the level of the GNP, there must be an amount of spending on consumer goods and capital goods sufficient to maintain that level. If spending is deficient relative to the prevailing level, then the GNP will decline, and if spending is relatively excessive, as when $I_{II} + R_{II} > S_I + D_I$, then the GNP will rise. In either case, the change in the dollar value of the GNP may be due to a change in prices with no change in output, or vice versa, or to changes in both prices and output. In addition, it is possible for this system to be in equilibrium at less than full employment.

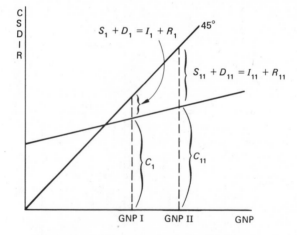

Figure 13-6. Macroeconomic equilibrium.

This brief presentation of general equilibrium theory at the macro level indicates how substantial aggregation can be used to show the equilibrium conditions for the economic system. The degree of aggregation depends to a large extent on the nature of the problem to be solved, and on the resources available to the investigator. For example, for many years economists employed very simple, highly aggregated models, especially for predictive purposes. Now there are serious efforts devoted to disaggregation in order to construct more detailed, and hopefully more accurate, predictive systems. These efforts have been stimulated by three kinds of innovation: the development of high-capacity, high-speed computers able to process large amounts of data quickly, the accumulation of more and better data pertaining to the economy, and the improvement and refinement of statistical techniques.

APPLICATION: INPUT-OUTPUT
AND THE SPACE SHUTTLE

Input-output analysis is actually a very useful technique. It has been employed in analyzing such problems as air pollution, energy usage, the Arab oil embargo, and sales forecasting. Another interesting application concerns the impact of the Space Shuttle program on the economy.[4] In the 1980s, the reusable Space Shuttle will be our major means of going to and from space. It is a manned space vehicle that is capable not only of taking satellites into space, but of bringing satellites back from space for inspection and repairs. It is anticipated that the Space Shuttle will play an important role in environmental monitoring, communciations, scientific exploration, and national security.

An input-output model consisting of 185 industries was used to explore the economic impact of the Space Shuttle program. More specifically, the study was concerned with the inter-industry production and employment effects of the program, as well as the effects on foreign trade. For comparative purposes, the study also used input-output analysis to determine the results of hypothetical alternative spending programs, which were of the magnitude of the Space Shuttle program but devoted either to residential housing construction or to increasing personal consumption expenditures. The best estimate of the cost of the Space Shuttle program, at the time of the study, was $8.6 billion. Therefore, the study assumed an $8.6 billion program in residential housing construction, and an $8.6 billion increase in personal consumption spending, and then traced the probable economic impact of each of these programs.

In terms of aggregate direct and indirect production, it was found that the Space Shuttle program would generate a somewhat higher level of production than would the other two programs. Most of the production stimulated by the Shuttle program would be in high-technology durable-goods industries, which would include not only space hardware, aircraft, and engines, but also metals, communication equipment, machinery, computers, and instruments; in the residential housing program, the low-technology durable-goods industries, such as metals, lumber and appliances, would benefit most; and in the consumer program the main beneficiaries would include the service, food and beverage, and agricultural industries. Overall employment gains would not be quite as great in the Shuttle program as in the other two programs, but the Shuttle program would lead to far greater employment of scientists and engineers. The Shuttle program would have the most desirable impact on foreign trade of the three programs. This program would stimulate the export of technology-intensive goods, while Shuttle-related imports would be comparatively small. This is particularly significant because technology-intensive goods have traditionally played an important role in U.S. exports, especially in the export of aerospace products. On the other hand, the other two programs would have a neutral effect on foreign trade, generating about as much imports as exports. The study concluded that on balance the Space Shuttle program would be at least as effective in stimulating the U.S. economy as would a program of comparable dollar outlays devoted to residential housing construction or to increasing consumer spending, with the added bonus of improving the U.S. position in world trade.

INNOVATION: AN INPUT-OUTPUT MODEL
FOR THE WORLD ECONOMY

When he received the Nobel Prize for economics in Sweden in 1973, Professor Leontief delivered a lecture entitled "Structure of the World Economy: Outline of a Simple Input-Output Formulation."[5] He explained that an input-output study was underway that viewed the world economy as a system of interrelated processes, and that efforts were being made to build the underlying data base. In particular, the input-output model, which included 28 groups of countries, was oriented toward the relationship between economic development and the environment. A major purpose of the model is to explore alternative paths to development in terms of their impact on the environment, and in the process to facilitate decision-making by the world community (United Nations and so forth) regarding developmental and environmental policies.

We shall briefly describe the nature of Leontief's world input-output model, without going into detail. The world economy is divided into two regions: the Developed Countries and the Less Developed Countries. Each region is divided into three sectors representing production: raw materials are produced by the Extraction Sector; conventional goods and services are supplied by the Other Production Sector; and the environment is protected by the Pollution Abatement Sector. Each region also possesses a Consumption Sector. An input-output table is constructed for the Developed Countries and another such table is employed for the Less Developed Countries, with each table showing the intersectoral flows within each region. In general, natural resources go from the Less Developed Countries to the Developed Countries, and Other Production goods flow in the opposite direction. These flows from one region to another are reflected in both input-output tables, with a positive sign for exports and a negative sign for imports. Thus, the two input-output tables are interdependent.

On the basis of preliminary estimates of the input-output relationships both within and between the two regions, Leontief was able to make some projections to the year 2000. For example, suppose that antipollution standards comparable to those in force in the U.S. were observed by the Less Developed Countries. As compared with no antipollution standards, these countries would find that the level of employment would be higher, the level of consumption would be less, and value added (or increase in value) in the Extraction Sector would drop greatly. On the other hand, if we assume that the Developed Countries experience a large rise in costs associated with the Extraction Sector, then the Other Production Sector would show a small gain, and the level of consumption would decline somewhat. But consumption would rise greatly in the Less Developed Countries, as a consequence of higher prices for the raw materials produced by their Extraction Sector, as compared with the prices of other goods. In this manner, various potential changes in the world economy can be analyzed in terms of their effects on economic development and the environment.

SUMMARY

When the economy is analyzed in terms of general equilibrium analysis, the outputs, prices, and other relevant variables of the entire economic system are seen to be interrelated. This chapter starts with general equilibrium theory at the micro level, proceeds to the intermediate aggregation of input-output analysis, and then considers equilibrium conditions at the macro level.

An economy can be regarded as an interdependent network in which everything depends, more or less, on everything else. The interdependence of a large number of economic variables can be expressed in terms of a system of simultaneous equations. This chapter presents a simplified model economy, composed of three basic groups —consumers, producers, and inputs, with four goods and four inputs. The equations consist of demand-for-goods equations, cost-of-goods equations, and equations expressing the supply of and demand for inputs. The major contribution of this general equilibrium model is the support it provides for the idea that all of the components of an economy are interrelated. This broad viewpoint is extremely helpful in conducting research or in evaluating the possible effects of economic policy proposals.

For an economic system to achieve a general equilibrium, three conditions must be satisfied: (1) there must be general equilibrium in exchange, (2) there must be general equilibrium in production, and (3) there must be general equilibrium between exchange and production. These conditions are satisfied in a perfectly competitive economy in which consumers maximize satisfaction and producers maximize profits. The Edgeworth box diagram technique is used to demonstrate how these conditions are satisfied in an economy consisting of two consumers, two goods, two producers, and two inputs. But the results also apply to a large-scale economy.

The difficulties encountered in the development of general equilibrium models at the micro level for an actual economic system, with very large numbers of consumers and producers, have led to the creation of simpler general equilibrium models. The main way to simplify is by aggregation, which is the approach taken by input-output analysis. An input-output table usually lists a large number of industries; it shows all the industries supplying various amounts of productive inputs to every industry, and it also displays the amount of the output of each industry going to every other industry. Depending on the degree of aggregation, input-output tables have been constructed to show these interrelationships for over 400 industries. When the table is constructed, it is assumed that prices remain constant, that input combinations do not change, that there are constant returns to scale, and that each industry produces only one good. In a real economy, each of these assumptions does not hold, but to drop them and attempt to incorporate all the variations of a real-world economy into the input-output table would greatly increase the complications and the cost of constructing such a table. Nevertheless, input-output analysis is a valuable tool. It shows how the industries of an economy are interrelated; it is helpful in planning for the future of the economy; and it shows the relative inputs needed from various industries in the event of mobilization or for defense.

General equilibrium at the macro level employs substantial aggregation to show the equilibrium conditions for an economic system.

The degree of aggregation depends to a large extent on the nature of the problem to be solved. For example, for many years economists employed highly aggregated models consisting of just a handful of variables for predictive purposes. Now there are serious efforts devoted to disaggregation in order to construct more detailed and more accurate predictive systems. These efforts have been stimulated by three kinds of innovations: the development of high-speed computers capable of processing large amounts of data quickly, the accumulation of more and better data pertaining to the economy, and the improvement and refinement of statistical techniques.

Input-output analysis has been used in analyzing such problems as air pollution, the Arab oil embargo, and sales forecasting. Another application concerns the impact of the Space Shuttle program on the economy. An input-output model consisting of 185 industries was used to explore the impact of the $8.6 billion program on production, employment, and foreign trade. For comparative purposes, the study also used input-output analysis to determine the results of hypothetical alternative spending programs devoted to residential housing construction or to personal consumption expenditures. It was found that the Space Shuttle program would generate a higher level of production than would the other two programs, but that employment gains would not be quite as great in the shuttle program. However, the shuttle program would have the most desirable impact on foreign trade of the three programs.

Professor Leontief is working on an input-output system for the world economy that is oriented toward the relationship between economic development and the environment. A major purpose of the system is to explore alternative paths to development in terms of their impact on the environment and, in the process, to facilitate decision making by the world community regarding developmental and environmental policies.

Notes

1. This approach to general equilibrium theory was developed by the great nineteenth-century French economist Léon Walras in a groundbreaking book published in 1874. This book has been translated by William Jaffé as *Elements of Pure Economics* (Homewood, Ill.: Richard D. Irwin, Inc., 1954).

2. The originator of input-output analysis is Wassily W. Leontief, the Harvard economist whose work won the Nobel prize. His approach is described in *The Structure of American Economy, 1919-1939*, 2d ed. (New York: Oxford University Press, 1951). The first edition appeared in 1941.

3. The coefficients in these equations are variously referred to as **technical coefficients** or **production coefficients** or **input coefficients**.

4. This application is from C. M. Merz, T. A. Gibson, and C. W. Seitz, "Impact of the Space Shuttle Program on the National Economy," *The Engineering Economist*, Vol. 18 (Jan./Feb., 1973), pp. 115–133.

5. Originally published by the Nobel Foundation, and reprinted in *The American Economic Review*, Vol. LXIV (Dec. 1974), pp. 823–834.

Problems and Questions

1. How would you describe general equilibrium theory?
2. What is the purpose of input-output analysis?
3. What condition must be satisfied for an economic system to achieve general equilibrium in production?
4. What are the advantages and the drawbacks of general equilibrium analysis at the micro level?
5. How can input-output analysis be used to determine the impact of a governmental expenditure program?
6. What are the employment implications of each of the three approaches to general equilibrium discussed in this chapter?
7. What condition must be satisfied in order to have general equilibrium in exchange?
8. What condition must be satisfied in order to have general equilibrium between exchange and production?
9. How is general equilibrium achieved at the macro level?
10. Of what value is Leontief's input-output model of the world economy?

Recommended Reading

Henderson, J. M. and R. E. Quandt. *Microeconomic Theory*, 2d ed. New York: McGraw-Hill Book Company, 1971.

Hicks, J. R. *Value and Capital*, 2d ed. New York: Oxford University Press, 1946.

Leontief, W. W. *The Structure of American Economy, 1919-1939*, 2d ed. New York: Oxford University Press, 1951.

Miernyk, W. H. *The Elements of Input-Output Analysis*. New York: Random House, Inc., 1965.

Shapiro, Edward. *Macroeconomic Analysis*, 4th ed. New York: Harcourt Brace Jovanovich, Inc., 1978.

Walras, Leon. *Elements of Pure Economics*. Translated by William Jaffé. Homewood, Ill.: Richard D. Irwin, Inc., 1954.

Zeuthen, F. *Economic Theory and Method*. Cambridge, Mass.: Harvard University Press, 1955.

14

Welfare Economics

Prior to this chapter, we have been occupied with positive economics, which was defined in Chapter 1 as the study of how an economic system actually functions. We now turn our attention to welfare (or normative) economics. **Welfare economics** is concerned with establishing standards of efficient performance for an economic system. It is that part of economics in which criteria are formulated to determine whether or not any given change or proposed change in the economic system constitutes an improvement. It deals with such economic changes as those involving the allocation of resources or goods and the production of goods and services.

As long as we consider only one consumer in isolation, the problem is not difficult. If we know that he always prefers more goods to less goods, any change that leads to an increase in his supply of goods is an improvement.

Let us consider an economic system in which there are many such consumers. We can now say that a change that increases the supply of goods to one or more consumers without reducing the supplies to the other consumers constitutes an improvement, provided that we assume that individuals in society respond in the same way as they do in isolation. This result can be expressed in terms of our consumer theory of Chapter 2. Given the assumptions of indifference curve analysis, we know that for a single consumer there are various combinations of any two goods that will yield equal satisfaction: All will appear as points on the same indifference curve. By moving the consumer to a higher indifference curve we increase his satisfaction, and this can be regarded as an improvement as long as we do not in the process move another consumer to a lower indifference curve.

Therefore, any change in the economic system, through either the exchange or production of goods, that benefits someone without harming someone else represents an improvement—a gain in welfare. If no further gains are possible through exchange or production, then we have achieved Pareto Optimality or Pareto Efficiency [proposed by the Italian economist Vilfredo Pareto (1848–1923)].

Now that we have introduced the idea of achieving a social optimum through an efficient organization of production and exchange, we can ask whether such an optimum can be achieved by any of our theoretical market structures. To facilitate the analysis, we shall consider first perfect competition and then the effects of imperfections in competition.

In order to attain a Pareto-optimal organization, three "marginal conditions" must be satisfied. We shall now demonstrate that the marginal conditions are indeed satisfied under perfect competition, provided only that we add a few more assumptions to those usually set forth for this model. In addition to the assumptions made in Chapter 7 we add that (1) there are no favorable or unfavorable externalities of production or consumption and (2) the initial distribution of income is predetermined and given. After examining the marginal conditions, we shall examine the significance of these assumptions.

THREE MARGINAL CONDITIONS NECESSARY FOR PARETO OPTIMALITY

Pareto Optimality for Exchange

In the previous chapter we demonstrated that general equilibrium in exchange is achieved on the contract curve of the Edgeworth box diagram (see Figure 13–2). A point on the contract curve also represents Pareto optimality for exchange. This is the case because once the contract curve has been reached, no further exchange can take place without reducing the satisfaction (welfare) of one or both of the individuals. If no more exchange can occur without harming someone, even though someone else gains, then Pareto optimality has been attained.

We can now make the transition from a two-individual economy to one composed of numerous consumers, and in the process show that Pareto optimality for exchange is satisfied under conditions of perfect competition. We know that the contract curve, in the two-individual case, represents all the tangency points of the two individuals' indifference curves; therefore, at each tangency point the slopes of the two indifference curves are the same, and hence the two individuals have the same marginal rate of substitution (MRS). We demonstrated in Chapter 2 that each individual will maximize his satisfaction by equating his MRS for any two goods to the ratio of their prices. Since the price of each good is the same for every consumer in a perfectly competitive economy, the ratio of the prices of any two goods is the same for all consumers. Therefore, every consumer will maximize his satisfaction by equating his MRS for any two goods to the same price ratio. With all MRS's equated to the same price ratio, it follows that all MRS's will be equal, no matter how many consumers are in the economy. In this manner, Pareto optimality for exchange is satisfied under perfect competition.

Pareto Optimality for Production

Pareto optimality for production is attained on the contract curve of the Edgeworth box diagram for production (see Figure 13-3). If the producers are not on the contract curve, it would be possible through the exchange of inputs for both producers to reach higher output isoquants, in which case the producers as well as the consumers would benefit. Once on the contract curve, it would not be possible for either producer to move to a higher isoquant without the other producer moving to a lower one. In addition, the contract curve represents all tangency points of the two producers' isoquants, which means that the two isoquants have the same slope, and therefore the two producers have the same marginal rate of technical substitution ($MRTS$) at any point on the contract curve.

In a perfectly competitive economy with large numbers of producers, Pareto optimality for production is achieved by means of the input pricing mechanism. Each profit-maximizing producer will employ two inputs in such a way that the $MRTS$ equals the ratio of the input prices, as we explained in Chapter 6. In a perfectly competitive economy each producer pays the same price for a given input, and so the ratio of any two input prices must be the same for all producers. Therefore, all producers will equate their $MRTS$ for any two inputs to the same input price ratio, in which case all producers will have the same *MRTS* for any two inputs. Hence, Pareto optimality for production is achieved in a perfectly competitive economy.

Pareto Optimality for Exchange and Production

The third and final marginal condition for maximum social welfare requires that the *MRS* for any two goods be equal to the marginal rate of transformation (*MRT*) for those goods. In Chapter 13 we explained that the level of consumer satisfaction could be increased if $MRS \neq MRT$, so that a condition for general equilibrium, as well as for Pareto optimality, is that the *MRS* in consumption must equal the *MRT* in production for any pair of goods.

We can gain further insight into this marginal condition by demonstrating how it is satisfied in a perfectly competitive economy. First, in a perfectly competitive economy, the *MRT* for any two goods will equal the price ratio of these two goods. To see how this comes about, let us suppose that the *MRT* does not equal the price ratio for two specific goods. Suppose that the two goods are x and y, with price Px = \$1 and Py = \$1, and the *MRT* is $1y:3x$. By transforming one y into three x, producers lose \$1 in sales of y but gain \$3 in sales of x, for a net gain of \$2. Therefore, producers will continue to produce more x and less y until the *MRT* equals the price ratio of x and y. Recall that the *MRT* will change as we move along the transformation curve. Next, we know that consumers of x and y will maximize their satisfaction when their *MRS* equals the price ratio of x and y. Finally, in a perfectly competitive economy all producers and all consumers are confronted by exactly the same prices for x and y, and hence the same price ratio for the two goods. Therefore, all *MRS*'s and all *MRT*'s are equated to the same price ratio for x and y; since the *MRS*'s and *MRT*'s are equal to the same price ratio, they are equal to each other. In this way, the third marginal condition for Pareto optimality is satisfied by a perfectly competitive economy.

THE DISTRIBUTION OF INCOME
AND THE SOCIAL WELFARE FUNCTION

As we have seen, Pareto optimality for exchange is represented by a point on the contract curve. But there are an infinite number of points on the contract curve, and any one of these points could qualify as a Pareto-optimal point. The point that is actually reached is largely determined by the initial distribution of x and y, or the initial distribution of income, which we assume as given. If the initial distribution of x and y were changed, then the final Pareto-optimal point could also change. This raises the question of whether the Pareto-optimal point reached under some given distribution of x and y, or some given distribution of income, yields the maximum social welfare when compared with other distributions of income. For example, a Pareto-optimal point could be attained with a large segment of the population near poverty, and a redistribution of income might well increase social welfare.

The idea of a **social welfare function** has been proposed as a means of dealing with the problem of income distribution. This function in effect expresses social preferences concerning the relative desirability of the overall welfare inherent in different patterns of social organization. The social welfare function therefore represents the judgment of the society with respect to the ordering of the different configurations of total satisfaction to be derived from different distributions of income. This value judgment could be reached by a direct voting system, by representative government, or by any other means. Individuals expressing their evaluation of different social organizations might consider not only the distribution of income and their own immediate consumption changes, but also their attitudes and feelings about the value of education, hospital care, and other noneconomic variables.

We now demonstrate how a social welfare function can be used to determine the distribution of inputs and goods which will maximize social welfare.[1] We know that for every point on the contract curve for production, there is a corresponding point on the transformation curve (see the discussion of Figures 13-3 and 13-4 in Chapter 13). This relationship is illustrated in Figure 14-1 for a $2 \times 2 \times 2 \times 2$ economy. We start by arbitrarily selecting a point, such as J, on the production contract curve in Figure 14-1a. Point J shows that a labor input of L_1 and a capital input of K_1 will produce x_2 of good x and y_2 of good y. Point J' on the transformation curve in Figure 14-1b represents the same amount of x and y (x_2 and y_2) as in Figure 14-1a. Since x_2 and y_2 are the total quantities of x and y available for consumption in the economy, an exchange box diagram can be inserted within the transformation curve with consumer a's (Ann's) origin (Oa) corresponding to the origin of the transformation curve and consumer b's (Ben's) origin (Ob) at point J'. Every point on the exchange contract curve from Oa to Ob denotes a different Pareto-optimal distribution of x_2 and y_2 between Ann and

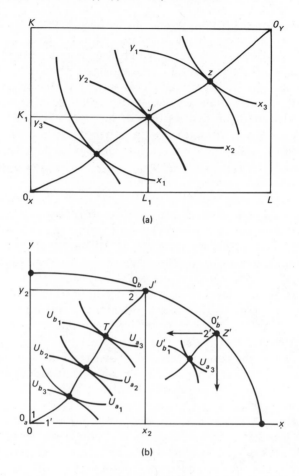

(a)

(b)

Figure 14-1. Production box diagram, transformation curve, and exchange box diagram.

Ben. As we move away from Ann's origin, this denotes that she is receiving more x and y, and therefore enjoying more satisfaction or utility, as indicated by indifference curves U_{a_1}, U_{a_2}, and U_{a_3}; and since, in the process, Ben is moving closer to his origin, his satisfaction is declining.

The next step involves the derivation of a **utility possibility curve**. This curve shows the amount of utility obtained by Ann and Ben, respectively, at each point on the contract curve in Figure 14-1b. For example, point T in Figure 14-1b represents a utility level of U_{a_3} for Ann and a utility level of U_{b_1} for Ben. These utility levels are plotted as point T' in Figure 14-2. In this fashion, the utility possibility curve corresponding to the contract curve from points 1 to 2 in Figure 14-1b is traced from points 1 to 2 in Figure 14-2. The curve shows that Ann gains utility as Ben loses utility.

We now go back to Figure 14-1a and repeat the steps that we took to derive the utility possibility curve, but we select a different point on the production contract curve. Suppose we take point Z, which translates into point Z' on the transformation curve in Figure 14-1b. Again, we insert an exchange boxy diagram at point Z', which is only partially drawn, in Figure 14-1b. The contract curve from point $1'$ to point $2'$ yields the utility possibility curve from $1'$ to $2'$ in Figure 14-2. In this manner, we can derive any number of utility possibility curves, although we shall not go beyond two curves for illustrative purposes. By taking the outermost edges of all possible utility possibility curves, the **utility possibility frontier** is traced out; this is shown (for our two illustrative curves) as the heavy curve in Figure 14-2.

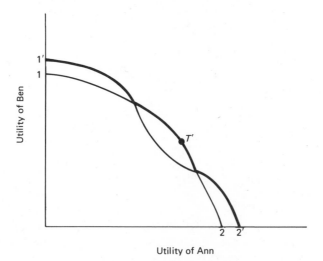

Figure 14-2. Utility possibility curves.

We now turn to the social welfare function, which is illustrated in Figure 14-3 by the family of curves W_1, W_2, and W_3. Each curve, such as W_1, represents all combinations of Ann's utility and Ben's utility that yield the same aggregate level of social welfare. A higher curve (further from the origin) depicts a higher level of social welfare. In effect, these curves may be viewed as social indifference curves.[2] The utility possibility frontier is also included in Figure 14-3, as shown from 1* to 2*, and it gives all the optimal utility combinations that are possible for Ann and Ben. The highest attainable level of social welfare is reached where the utility possibility frontier is tangent to a social indifference curve, as given by point T' in Figure 14-3. A movement to the left or the right of point T' along the utility possibility frontier would be a movement to a lower level of social welfare, and points outside the frontier are unattainable. Therefore, point T' represents maximum social welfare, given the input and technological constraints of the system.

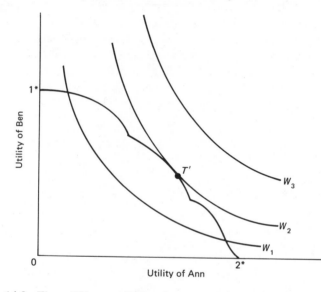

Figure 14-3. The utility possibility frontier, the social welfare function and maximum social welfare.

The problem of the distribution of goods, or income, has been solved. The welfare-maximizing amounts of x and y for Ann and Ben are found by working backward to Figure 14-1. Point T' represents a point on a specific utility possibility curve; in our example, it is a point on the utility possibility curve from 1 to 2 in Figure 14-2. As we already know, point T' corresponds to point T on the contract curve in Figure 14-1b, and point T denotes the particular combinations of x and y for Ann and Ben that will maximize social welfare. In addition, the box diagram containing point T signifies a total output of x_2 of x and y_2 of y, as shown by point J' on the production possiblity curve. Point J' is equivalent to point J on the contract curve of the production box diagram in

Figure 14-1a, and point J specifies the amounts of inputs L and K to be employed in the production of goods x and y, respectively. Therefore, the inclusion of the social welfare function has led to specific Pareto-optimal points on the contract curves for production and exchange.

It should be emphasized that the tangency point of the utility possibility frontier and W_2 at point T' in Figure 14-3 was selected merely to simplify the presentation. This tangency point could have occurred at any point on the utility possibility frontier, depending on the shapes of the social indifference curves, in which case the corresponding points on the exchange contract curve, the transformation curve, and the production contract curve would have been different. We should also point out that the existence of a social welfare function does not change the marginal conditions for Pareto-optimality, nor does it alter the role of a perfectly competitive economy in satisfying these conditions, given large numbers of consumers, producers, goods, and inputs.

IMPERFECT COMPETITION AND SOCIAL WELFARE

We have demonstrated that all of the marginal conditions for Pareto optimality are satisfied in a perfectly competitive economy, provided that there are no external economies or diseconomies (to be discussed in the next section). Therefore, perfect competition leads to an efficient allocation of resources. Departures from the marginal conditions result in inefficiencies in resource allocation, and we shall now show that all of the marginal conditions cannot be fulfilled if perfect competition does not exist.

We know that under all forms of imperfect competition the demand curve facing the firm has a negative slope. Consequently, the MR curve must lie below the demand curve, and since each firm maximizes profit by equating MR and MC, it follows that MC is always below price. Now consider the third marginal condition, which states that the MRS for any two goods for any consumer must be the same as the MRT of these goods. We found that, in a perfectly competitive economy, this condition is satisfied because all producers and consumers face the same prices for the two goods, and maximize by equating the MRT and MRS, respectively, to an identical price ratio. But if imperfect competition exists, firms equate the MRT with the ratio of the marginal revenues of the two goods, whereas the consumer still equates his MRS with the price ratio.

In addition, there is no reason why producers should have the same MRT, or the same MR ratio. In monopolistic competition and differentiated oligopoly, producers make similar but different products and hence the MRT could differ from producer to producer; and since there is no reason why each producer should have a demand curve which is identical to the others, their MR would differ. The latter is also true of pure oligopoly. These considerations can be extended to our second marginal condition. In addition, whenever different consumers must pay different prices for the same good, as in discriminatory pricing, the first marginal condition will be violated.

We can now see that as a consequence of imperfect competition the marginal conditions cannot be fulfilled and the economic system will yield less than optimal welfare. But does this imply that an actual economic system would *always* benefit if all industries were forced into the competitive mold? To repeat the example given in Chapter 8, suppose that the automobile industry was made to conform to the main requirements of a competitive industry. If so, there would be a large number of small car makers, each producing an identical car. All the technological and other efficiencies of large-scale production would be lost, since each artificially small firm would be stuck by legislation on the upper reaches near the beginning of its LAC curve. Consumers would have fewer cars at much higher prices, and there would be no variety. On the other hand, to have a large number of huge low-cost auto makers would drive the price so low that all but a few would be unable to stay in business, and we would return to the original situation.

EXTERNALITIES AND SOCIAL WELFARE

We have demonstrated that perfect competition leads to a Pareto-optimal general equilibrium. Recall that we assumed, along with the usual assumptions of perfect competition, that there were no favorable or unfavorable externalities of production or consumption, or externalities, as they are called. We first explain the nature of externalities in terms of private and social costs and benefits, and then show how they prevent the attainment of a Pareto-optimal position by leading to divergencies between private and social costs and benefits.

Assume that the firms in an expanding industry contribute to the development of the local community's recreational facilities, such as parks and lakes, in order to improve the overall living conditions and output of their work force. If these improved facilities are open to use and enjoyment by the public, including workers in other industries, there will be a divergence between the marginal private benefits (or the returns to the industry from the outlay), and the marginal social benefits (or the returns to the community as a whole). This difference is called a **favorable externality of production.**

Consider the well-known example of an **unfavorable externality of production** that may result from the expansion of an industry, namely smoke nuisance. Suppose that, as the industry grows, the air becomes increasingly polluted with smoke and soot from the factory chimneys. People in the community not only suffer discomfort because of the smoke, but also have higher cleaning and laundry bills. In terms of social welfare, we must take into account these additional costs, in which case marginal social cost will exceed marginal private cost.

There may also be **favorable or unfavorable externalities** of consumption which distort the social optimum. A **favorable externality of consumption** would occur if the consumption pattern of an individual results in benefits to others. For example, if it is worth it to me to put money into a public record player to hear a record, the social marginal benefit will exceed my private marginal benefit to the extent that other people, on balance, enjoy my expenditure. This indicates that the overall benefit derived from the expenditure is underestimated. On the other hand, an **unfavorable externality of consumption** would probably occur if I decided to try out my new power lawn mower at seven o'clock Sunday morning and disturbed my sleeping neighbors.

The term **market failure** refers to the failure of perfectly competitive markets to attain a Pareto optimality because of externalities. Three basic causes of market failure have been isolated: ownership externalities, technical externalities, and public good externalities.[3]

In the case of **ownership externalities**, there is a separation between the ownership of resources and some of the effects of using the resources. The market failure occurs because the market does not automatically attach prices to the external effects of using the resource. A good example is air pollution. Suppose that competitive firms do not take into account the effects of the pollution caused by using their resources to produce goods. The price of the good will not reflect the damage due to the pollution. People may have higher cleaning costs and more health-related expenses, but the market does not associate these costs with the production and price of the good. There is a divergence between private costs and social costs.

Figure 14-4 portrays a competitive firm and industry. If only private costs are taken into account, the industry will be in long-run equilibrium when the price is equal to the firm's minimum LAC at output x_1 and price P_1, and the industry would produce X_1 at price P_1. Now suppose that all of the external costs attributable to the production of this good were somehow included in the firm's cost curves. If this were done, LAC_p (including only private costs) would rise to LAC_s (including all costs, both private costs and costs due to externalities). Since minimum LAC_s now exceeds the price P_1, firms have losses and start leaving the industry, shifting the industry supply curve to the left. When the supply curve reaches S_2, the price is P_2, which is equal to the minimum point on LAC_s, and the industry is once again in equilibrium. Therefore, if the industry recognized all costs of producing the good, then the price would be higher and less of the good would be produced (X_2 instead of X_1); or, putting it the other way, if only private costs are considered, then Pareto optimality is not achieved because the firm produces too much of the good (x_1 instead of x'_1) and the industry supplies too much of the good (X_1 instead of X_2).

Technical externalities exist where there are increasing returns to scale over the relevant range of output, meaning that long-run average cost is declining. In this case, there are two possible outcomes, both of which violate the Pareto-optimal conditions. On the one hand, under these circumstances price-cutting based on lower average costs for more output would eventually lead to a monopoly. As we saw in the last section, all forms of imperfect competition are inconsistent with Pareto optimality. On the other hand, even if a monopoly does not come about, if existing firms set their prices

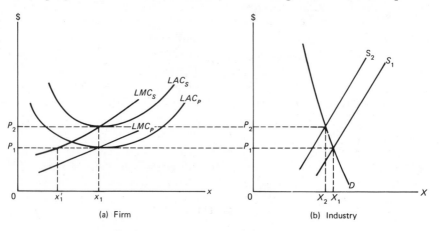

(a) Firm   (b) Industry

Figure 14-4. Ownership externalities.

equal to long-run marginal cost, as in a perfectly competitive market, they would suffer losses and could not survive. This is because LMC is always less than LAC, when LAC is declining. If they set the price equal to LAC, the price would exceed LMC, and again the Pareto-optimal conditions would be violated.

Public good externalities stem from the peculiar nature of public goods. A **public good** is a good such that any individual's consumption of the good does not reduce the amount of the good available for any other individual. For example, if I attend a fireworks display, my attendance does not reduce the amount of fireworks that you are able to watch; and if I bring a friend with me, I can still watch the same display, and so can my friend. The same reasoning applies to such disparate goods as public concerts and national defense; the defense system that protects me also protects you. Therefore, the marginal social cost of providing the good to one more individual is zero—the cost of the fireworks display does not increase if an additional person attends. But the social benefit increases as more people consume the public good. Hence, the marginal social benefit exceeds the marginal social cost, in which case a Pareto-optimal result is not attained.

COMPENSATION CRITERIA

The social welfare function was put forth (see Figure 14-3) to determine whether a change in income distribution would yield a higher level of satisfaction for the society. Unfortunately, there are many thorny problems involved in the construction of a welfare function for a real economy.[4] In the absence of such a function, how do we evaluate the welfare effects of a redistribution of income that makes some people better off (those gaining income) and others worse off (those losing income)? Many of the government's policies lead to a change in the distribution of income, such as Medicare, unemployment payments, and various forms of taxation. The problem is one of determining whether or not the redistribution results in a net gain in social welfare.

As a means of approaching this problem, economists developed the so-called **compensation criteria** around 1940. In general, these criteria hold that an income redistribution, or any other social change, would result in a gain in welfare if those who gain from the change are able to fully compensate those who lose, and still feel better off. It is usually claimed that this approach does not require that the compensating payment actually be made. For example, suppose that a change causes Ann to feel that she has gained the equivalent of $100, whereas Ben estimates his loss at $60. According to the **Kaldor version**[5] of the compensation criterion, this change represents a net gain even if compensation is not made, since Ann could pay Ben $60 and still be better off by $40. Unfortunately, if the compensation is not actually made and Ann keeps her full $100, there still may not be a net gain, since it is possible that Ben's non-receipt of $60 may work a hardship on him that outweighs all of Ann's gain due to having the $100. The only way to avoid this problem is to assume an equal marginal utility of money for Ann and Ben, but this involves interpersonal utility comparisons, which we were trying to avoid in the first place.

Tibor Scitovsky, an American economist, soon pointed out another problem associated with Kaldor's compensation criterion.[7] If the compensating payment is not actually made, then there is the possibility that, after the change occurs, a return to the original situation may also represent a net gain in terms of the Kaldor criterion. Therefore, Scitovsky suggested the following test, called the Scitovsky criterion: not only must those who gain be able to compensate those who lose, but after the change is made it must be impossible to do the reverse in order to return to the original situation. Although this test eliminates a source of possible paradox that is latent in the Kaldor criterion, the Scitovsky test is still open to the same criticism made in connection with the Kaldor approach.

Suppose that instead of Kaldor's potential compensation we assume that compensation will actually be paid. If we make this assumption we are in effect back to Pareto's criterion, but not without problems. In order to compensate losers we must somehow know the utility schedules of all the losers otherwise we would run into difficulties: an individual might not know in advance how a given change would affect him, since there may be many nonmonetary repercussions which he might not be able to evaluate, or may not even be aware of, until well after the change has occurred. In actual practice, losers may overstate their losses, or losses may be claimed where no loss has actually been suffered. Finally, any large-scale system of compensation would require a costly administrative machinery, which would be exposed to all the problems associated with such bureaucratic systems.

APPLICATION: IS SOME POLLUTION BETTER THAN NO POLLUTION?

Is some pollution better than no pollution? Economically speaking, the answer is "yes." It all has to do with the costs of controlling pollution and the benefits derived from pollution control. Controlling pollution can be very costly. The manufacture, installation, and the operation of antipollution equipment and devices requires the use of capital, labor, energy, and various other inputs. To the extent that these inputs are devoted to controlling pollution, they cannot be used to make other goods and services that consumers desire. In terms of the doctrine of opportunity cost, the cost to society of controlling pollution consists of the other goods and services that must be sacrificed in order to make available the inputs for pollution control. On the other hand, controlling pollution produces benefits for society. If the air is polluted, it can be a serious health hazard; water pollution can damage various forms of aquatic life, and it can also affect human health; land pollution is an eyesore and a nuisance. Therefore, society benefits to the extent that these various forms of pollution are reduced.

To decide how much pollution to eliminate, the society must weigh the costs of controlling pollution against the benefits to be derived from pollution control. Suppose that a town is contemplaing an expenditure that would improve the appearance and taste of the town's water supply. The expenditure would be made if the town felt that the benefits of better water were worth more than the expenditure of the town's funds. In fact, the town would continue to spend money on the water supply as long as the additional benefits exceeded the additional costs. This brings us to a more precise answer to the question that begins this section: Is some pollution better than no pollution? Society should continue to reduce pollution as long as the benefits derived from additional pollution control exceed the costs of the additional pollution control. Therefore, there is an optimal level of pollution that exists when an additional amount of pollution control produces a marginal benefit equal to its marginal cost: If marginal benefits exceed marginal costs, then more should be spent on pollution control; if marginal costs exceed marginal benefits, then less should be spent on pollution control.

An industry that provides a good example of the issues raised by pollution control is the **paper industry**.[8] Unlike the pollution caused by many other industries, that of the paper industry is painfully obvious. Nobody can escape the rotten-egg smell surrounding a kraft paper mill, and it is easy to see the industry's process dyes in streams. For these reasons, the U.S. Environmental Protection Agency (EPA) has established fairly strict pollution control standards for the industry, and the law allows state and local governments to require even higher standards. As a consequence, the American Paper Institute tells us that the industry has spent billions of dollars fighting pollution, and it estimates that expenditures could total $12 billion by 1983. In the meantime, marginal plants have been shut down, paper prices have gone up, and industry executives and economists claim that future expansion of the industry will suffer as a result of the pollution standards. Here we have an example of the ownership externalities discussed in connection with Figure 14-4, where the incorporation of costs to society in the firm's cost curves lead to higher prices and less output for the industry. Paper industry leaders are aware of the importance of comparing the marginal costs with the marginal benefits of additional pollution control. The president of Crown Zellerbach Corp., a leading paper company, pointed out that to go from 98% to 99.8% particulate removal from smoke requires four times as much energy as it takes to go from zero to 98%. He said that, "It is easy to see that quadrupling the output of power from an electrical station at another source will surely offset the benefits of removing the additional 1.8%."[9] Therefore, while environmentalists can see the benefits of the industry's expenditures, industry leaders claim that still more money spent on pollution control will not yield additional benefits equal to the additional cost.

INNOVATIONS: THE REGULATION OF POLLUTION AND THE ROLE OF PROPERTY RIGHTS

One method by which the government can regulate pollution is to prohibit the activity that causes the pollution. But as we indicated in the last section, the cost of completely stopping the polluting activity might far outweigh the resulting benefits. Whole industries would have to be eliminated, not to mention what would happen to our system of transportation, including cars, planes, and so forth. Using a more efficient method of regulation, the government has established regulatory bodies, such as the EPA, for the purpose of setting and enforcing standards for polluters. For example, the Federal Water Pollution Control Act states that all industries should employ the best available technology to clean up the water, but it is the responsibility of the EPA to determine whether an industry is complying with the law and meeting the prescribed standards. This approach also has drawbacks. It is up to the government and the regulatory agencies to determine the level of pollution that maximizes overall welfare. This is sometimes very difficult or impossible to do. When pollution damage is widespread, and its long-term effects on the health of humans and animals not fully known, it may not be possible to determine its social costs with accuracy, and in this case, established standards must be somewhat arbitrary. In addition, any regulatory commission is caught between the claims and counterclaims of environmentalists and industry spokesmen, and the political maneuvering of the various interest groups. Another problem involves enforcement. Polluting firms may either evade the standards set by the regulatory agency, or they may fabricate reasons why they cannot meet the standards.

Taxation is another method of dealing with pollution. The government can establish a tax that would vary with the amount of pollution attributable to any polluter. In other words, the tax could be established on a per-unit-of-pollution basis. The firm would then have to pay a greater total tax as its pollution increases. One of the advantages of this method of pollution control is that it provides an incentive for the firm to control its pollution. As long as the cost to the firm of eliminating an additional unit of pollution is less than the unit tax, the firm would profit by eliminating that increment of pollution, thereby avoiding the tax. The firm would continue to reduce pollution until this marginal cost of pollution removal equals the tax. Of course, the higher the tax, the greater the incentive to the firm to eliminate additional pollution. From the viewpoint of society, the size of the tax should be such that the marginal benefit to society of eliminating another unit of pollution is equal to the marginal cost of removing this unit of pollution. While taxation has the advantage of stimulating polluting firms to reduce pollution, there remains the usual problem of determining the extent of the social benefits to be gained by eliminating various amounts of pollution, and this makes it difficult to set an appropriate tax level.

The problem of externalities, even in a perfectly competitive economy, and the need for government regulation of pollution, can be traced in large measure to the absence of clearly defined **property rights**. Who owns the air? Who owns the rivers? Who owns the oceans? A factory owner feels free to discharge pollutants into the air or into a stream because he feels that he is not encroaching on anybody else's private property. On the other hand, the factory would not consider dumping wastes in a homeowner's backyard, since this would constitute a violation of the homeowner's property rights and the homeowner could sue the factory. If nobody specifically owns the resource in question (air, water, land), or even if it is owned by the community, there is the possibility of a divergence between private costs and social costs. The polluter considers the air or water a costless dump, but others using the same air or water incur costs (health, cleaning, and so forth) as a consequence of the polluter's activities. In other words, the polluter is encouraged to exploit resources that are free to him.

How would the existence of property rights alter this situation?

With property rights clearly assigned and enforceable, the divergence between private costs and social costs would be eliminated, because a polluter would be forced to pay for the harm to others caused by his polluting activities. Imagine that a chemical factory is located on a river, and that the factory empties pollutants into the water instead of paying to have the pollutants hauled away. Suppose that a farmer downstream uses river water to irrigate certain crops, and to avoid crop damage he must remove some of the toxic materials from the water, thereby increasing his costs. What would happen if the farmer owned the river, or at least had property rights to unpolluted river water? In this case, the farmer could force the chemical factory to pay the cost of its pollution of the water. The social cost would be transformed into a private cost to the factory. If the factory were charged on a per-unit-of-pollution basis, the factory would continue to pollute until its marginal benefit from discharging another unit of pollutant equalled the marginal cost of that unit. Now suppose that the factory owned the river. The factory would be able to pollute, but the farmer would be willing to pay the factory to curb its water pollution, since now the farmer is using the factory's property. The farmer would continue to pay the factory until the marginal cost of having pollution reduced by another unit equalled the marginal benefit of one less unit of pollution to the farmer. Whether the factory or the farmer owned the river, the level of pollution would not only be the same in the end, but it would represent the social optimum.[10] This result is based on the assumption that the transaction costs of working out an arrangement among those involved are zero. If numerous firms and farmers were involved in our example, it might be too costly and difficult to reach an enforceable agreement among so many participants.

SUMMARY

Welfare economics is concerned with establishing standards of efficient performance for an economic system. A Pareto-optimal organization of the economy is achieved when it is no longer possible either through exchange or production to make some individual better off without in the process making someone else worse off. In order to attain a Pareto-optimal organization, three "marginal conditions" must be satisfied. These conditions are satisfied by a perfectly competitive economy, assuming that there are no externalities and that the distribution of income is given. The three conditions are: Pareto optimality for exchange, Pareto optimality for production, and Pareto optimality for exchange and production.

Pareto optimality for exchange is represented by a point on the contract curve of an Edgeworth box diagram. The point on the contract curve that is actually reached depends to a large extent on the initial distribution of income, and this raises the question of whether a different distribution of income would result in an increase in social welfare. The concept of a social welfare function has been proposed as a means of dealing with this problem of income distribution. The social welfare function represents the judgment of the society with respect to the desirability of different distributions of income. Once a social welfare function is given, it is possible to determine that distribution of income which will maximize social welfare. This chapter demonstrates that the pricing mechanism in a perfectly competitive economy leads to the satisfaction of all three marginal conditions.

If we depart from a perfectly competitive economy, the three marginal conditions cannot be satisfied, and the economic system will yield less than optimal welfare. In addition, if externalities exist, even a perfectly competitive economy will not lead to optimal welfare. This "market failure" results from three major kinds of externalities, called ownership, technical, and public good externalities, which are discussed in this chapter.

If a social welfare function cannot be determined, it may still be possible to evaluate the welfare effects of a redistribution of income that makes some people better off and others worse off. The problem is one of deciding whether or not the redistribution leads to a net gain in social welfare. Compensation criteria were developed as a means of dealing with this problem. In general, these criteria hold that an income redistribution, or any other social change, would lead to a net gain in welfare if those who gain from the change are able to fully compensate those who lose, and still feel better off. In practice, these criteria are very difficult to apply, especially if we assume that compensation will actually be paid and not just arrived at in theoretical terms.

An important application of welfare economics has to do with pollution. A society derives benefits from controlling pollution, but pollution control is also very costly. In terms of opportunity cost, the cost to society of controlling pollution consists of the goods and services that must be sacrificed in order to make available the inputs necessary to produce the goods needed for pollution control. To decide how much pollution to eliminate, the society must weigh the costs of controlling pollution against the benefits to be derived from pollution control. Therefore, society should continue to reduce pollution as long as the benefits derived from additional pollution control exceed the costs of the additional pollution control. The optimal level of pollution exists when the marginal benefit of pollution control equals its marginal cost.

One method of regulating pollution is to prohibit the activity that causes the pollution. But the cost of completely stopping the polluting activity might far outweigh the benefits. Taxation is another way of dealing with pollution. The government could tax each unit of pollution produced by the firm. In this case, it would be to the benefit of the firm to continue to reduce pollution as long as the cost of eliminating an additional unit of pollution was less than the unit tax. The size of the tax should be such that the marginal benefit to society of eliminating another unit of pollution is equal to the marginal cost of removing this unit of pollution.

The need for government regulation of pollution can be traced in large measure to the absence of clearly defined property rights. A factory owner feels free to discharge pollutants into the air or into rivers because he believes that he is not encroaching on anybody's private property. With property rights clearly assigned and enforceable, a polluter could be forced to pay for the harm to others caused by his polluting activities. More concretely, a factory would not consider dumping wastes in a homeowner's backyard because this would constitute a violation of the homeowner's property rights, and the homeowner could sue the factory.

Notes

1. Our analysis draws on Francis Bator, "The Simple Analytics of Welfare Maximization," *American Economics Review*, Vol. 47 (March, 1957), pp. 22-59.

2. We simply assume that these curves are given, just as we have assumed that we can arrive at utility numbers or indices in connection with the utility possibility curves. While the idea of a social welfare function is appealing, the formulation of such a function for a society poses what may be insoluble problems. For a discussion of the problems involved see K. J. Arrow, *Social Choice and Individual Values* (New York: John Wiley & Sons, Inc., 1951).

3. This discussion follows Francis M. Bator, "The Anatomy of Market Failure," *The Quarterly Journal of Economics*, Vol. 72 (Aug., 1958), pp. 351-379.

4. The problems inherent in the formulation of a social welfare function are discussed in Arrow, op. cit.

5. So called after the English economist Nicholas Kaldor.

6. Nicholas Kaldor, "Welfare Propositions in Economics and Interpersonal Comparisons of Utility," *Economic Journal*, Vol. 49 (Sept. 1939), pp. 549-552.

7. Tibor Scitovsky, "A Note on Welfare Propositions in Economics," *Review of Economic Studies*, Vol. 9 (November, 1941), pp. 77-88.

8. The following discussion is based on "Papermakers Resist Tougher Rules on Pollution," *Business Week* (February 9, 1976), pp. 48-50.

9. Ibid., p. 48.

10. This outcome, called the *Coase theorem*, is demonstrated, with many interesting illustrations, in Ronald Coase, "The Problem of Social Cost," *Journal of Law and Economics*, Vol. 1 (October, 1960), pp. 1-44.

Problems and Questions

1. How would you describe the role of welfare economics in microeconomic theory?
2. What is the difference between a Pareto-optimal organization of an economic system and one that is not Pareto optimal?
3. What marginal conditions must be satisfied in order to achieve Pareto optimality?
4. What is a social welfare function, and how is it used in welfare economics?
5. Give three examples of externalities. Now explain how each example prevents the attainment of Pareto optimality.
6. What does the term "market failure" mean? Describe the three basic causes of market failure.
7. What gave rise to the development of the compensation criteria? What theoretical and practical problems arise when dealing with these criteria?
8. Nobody likes pollution, so why not simply get rid of all of it?
9. What do property rights have to do with pollution?
10. What is a utility possibility curve and how is it derived?

Recommended Reading

Arrow, K. J. *Social Choice and Individual Values*. New York: John Wiley & Sons, Inc., 1951.

Bator, F. M. "The Simple Analytics of Welfare Maximization," *American Economic Review*, Vol. 47 (March, 1957), pp. 22-59.

_____ . "The Anatomy of Market Failure," *The Quarterly Journal of Economics*, Vol. 72 (August, 1958), pp. 351-379.

Coase, Ronald. "The Problem of Social Cost," *Journal of Law and Economics*, Vol. 1 (October, 1960), pp. 1–44.

Mishan, E. J. "A Survey of Welfare Economics, 1939–1959," *Economic Journal*, Vol. LXX (June, 1960), pp. 197–265.

Scitovsky, Tibor. *Welfare and Competition*, 2d ed. Homewood, Ill.: Richard D. Irwin, Inc., 1971.

Appendix:
The Science of Economics

Economics is a science. Like all sciences, the major purpose of economic science is to improve our ability to understand and predict events in the real world. This in turn enables us to formulate policies capable of improving the performance of the economy. This appendix is necessary to the study of economic theory, since it provides an understanding of the nature, goals, and concepts of science.

WHAT IS SCIENCE?

The word *science* is derived from the Latin word *scientia*, meaning "knowledge." Today this word has several different meanings. It may refer to a branch of knowledge or study, to systematized knowledge in general, to our understanding of the physical world, or to the process by which knowledge is acquired. Knowledge gained by scientific means must be based on facts, and these facts must be derived from observation or experimentation. Theories are developed to show how facts, concepts, and laws are interrelated. The value of a theory is determined by its power to explain and predict. Therefore, theories must be tested by means of further reference to facts. We have completed the circle; we started by observing the real world and we finished the same way. But this is not a vicious circle. It is more like an ascending spiral because in the process we improve our theories, so that they better reflect the real world. Theories are never really finished; they are always being tested, revised, improved, or replaced by a better theory.

The foregoing, of course, is not an adequate definition of science, but it represents a start. Short definitions or explanations of difficult subjects are rarely satisfactory. In science there is no standard definition; there are probably as many one- or two-sentence definitions as there are scientists. However, there is a general underlying consensus among scientists on what constitutes science. As we proceed, this consensus should become more apparent.

In a sense, science is as old as mankind. Men have always been capable of learning from experience, from contact with the real world. (Unfortunately, this capability has not always been used, but this is true even today.) Early man must have frequently combined observation, experimentation, and reasoning to solve his problems and to produce the tools and weapons he needed for survival. He was able to see interrelationships and to arrive at generalizations. Undoubtedly, the seeds of modern science germinated in long-forgotten caves. Despite the element of continuity in the development of science from earliest times to the present day, modern science is a product of the sixteenth and especially the seventeenth centuries. Before this period the scientific approach appeared sporadically and had not become a process, not to mention a way of life, nor did it have a great impact on the progress of civilization.

Science Today

Today science is one of the great forces of modern life. It forms the basis of our industrial civilization, and it is ultimately responsible for the two most fearsome threats to that civilization—the nuclear explosion and the population explosion. Today science is big business; billions of dollars are poured into the scientific enterprise. Giant laboratories filled with expensive, complicated equipment and highly trained scientists are now commonplace. Business, government, and huge foundations all participate in the drive for new and better knowledge and technology. Neither a business nor a government can afford to let up, so competitive has the scientific enterprise become. There is no sign that this movement has reached its peak; on the contrary, evidence suggests that the progress of science is still accelerating.

SOME BASIC CONCEPTS OF SCIENCE

Science cannot be considered apart from the scientific method. Still, it would be misleading to interpret the concept of method too rigidly; as we shall see, there is more to making scientific progress than the mere adherence to a particular method. In fact, the scientific method is no more than a set of broad prescriptions or guidelines which embody the main precepts of science. To repeat, the major purpose of science is to improve our ability to understand and predict real-world phenomena by means of systematic investigation and experimentation. This understanding usually requires the discovery of relationships among facts, the formulation of generalizations, and the construction of more intricate sets of interrelationships. In the language of science, we seek out and formulate laws and theories.

Scientific Laws

A **scientific law** is sometimes defined as expressing an invariant, exact relationship among specific types of facts or phenomena. The law need not be true under all conditions, but only under certain well-defined circumstances. Economists, like all other scientists, wish to discover laws, but they have not been nearly as successful as physical scientists in the discovery of invariant relationships within their discipline. While hard-and-fast relationships are most desirable, much can be gained from the discovery of what may be called tendency laws and statistical laws. **Tendency laws** refer not to invariant connections but to the inclination or disposition of certain phenomena to be related in a particular way. **Statistical laws** attempt to specify the proportion of cases in which certain interrelationships or connections will hold. Both types of law are valuable to economists because of the nature of economic relationships, which are rarely exact and invariant.

Theories and Hypotheses

There is disagreement among scientists and philosophers over the meaning of the term "theory," especially as compared with the terms "law," "empirical generalization," and "hypothesis." It is frequently held that the differences among the meanings of these words are only a matter of degree. Thus, **hypotheses** refer to possible relationships with little factual support, **theories** are better supported and more confidence is placed in them, and **laws** are well-established relationships. Sometimes no distinction is made between hypotheses and theories—they are used interchangeably. Finally, hypothesis, theory, and law are sometimes more clearly distinguished in a functional way, which is the approach adopted in this book. A hypothesis states a conjecture or an informed opinion (educated guess); therefore, supporting evidence is lacking or is scanty and unconvincing, and as we noted above, hypotheses in themselves inspire little confidence. Rather, the hypothesis itself serves the purpose of helping the scientist determine what data are needed and what tests are to be performed, and these activities may lead to the development of a theory. The scientist may ultimately conclude that his hypothesis is true or that it is false, or more frequently he may conclude that it is partly true and needs to be revised or replaced with a different one. If the hypothesis turns out to be true, it generally becomes a part of a broader theory.

A law must be distinguished from an **empirical generalization**. The latter denotes a regularity among variables based on observation alone, without a corresponding explanation of why this regularity should hold. A law also states an empirical regularity, but there must be an associated explanation for its existence and reasons why the law should continue to hold in the future. We may employ hypotheses of various kinds in order to arrive at a theory or a law. However, theories and laws are generally not the outcome of merely testing one hypothesis, but are usually constructed out of the parts and remains of many hypotheses.

Al—LLsE Mews

The Function of Theories

Theories form the framework of our scientific understanding. A theory explains laws, shows the relationships among laws, and may also relate particular facts, laws, and other theories. Theories usually stimulate and facilitate the discovery of other theories and new laws; as such, theories may be called the "grand designs" of the scientific enterprise. They are usually abstract, but this very abstractness makes it possible to grasp, to understand, a whole set of relationships or interrelationships, or an entire process. Therefore, theories have greater scope and depth than laws, hypotheses, or empirical generalizations. The latter, as we noted above, are formed on the basis of sheer observation and have little or no explanatory power. If a theory does not live up to its claims, that does not convert it into a hypothesis; it simply means that it is an unsatisfactory theory. A satisfactory theory provides understanding and hence explanation and prediction.

It would be a mistake to push these distinctions too far. Disagreement over the exact meaning of these terms does not impair scientific progress, though it may disturb philosphers of science. After all, words and meanings are man-made; they do not exist in nature. Although it is not surprising that differences arise over how a word should be used, these differences in usage are not significant as long as they are made clear. This is not to argue that conceptual differences are unimportant. Concepts such as "hypothesis," "law," and "theory" are really working ideas about the formation of understanding. However, these terms are used so frequently that it is desirable to have before us some of the differences that occur in their usage, and also an indication of the way in which we use them in this book.

In this vein, we may point out that the terms **assumption, postulate**, and **axiom** are considered as synonymous in this book, although some writers make distinctions among these words. We take these terms to refer to something which is taken for granted as a basis for reasoning. By applying logic or mathematics to the assumptions, postulates, or axioms, we may deduce **theorems**, which are the statements or propositions thus derived from the assumptions.

As IF laws - Route ∅ w/ or w/o pot holes.

THE SCIENTIFIC METHOD

The interrelationship between facts and theories can be seen in Diagram A-1. As the diagram shows, there are three major steps in

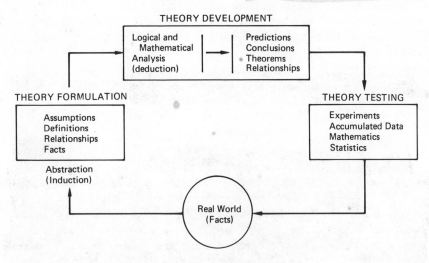

Diagram A-1. The scientific method.

the scientific method: (1) theory formulation, (2) theory development, and (3) theory testing. We shall briefly discuss each step.

Theory Formulation

All science begins with observation. The latter does not mean casual observation, but the trained observation of the experienced investigator, which is based on a background of knowledge already gained in some specific field. Therefore, the scientist's observations are very much conditioned by his experience, outlook, and problems. Given these contacts with the real world and with his science, the scientist then constructs an explanation or theory of the behavior of and relationships among the observed phenomena. He is also concerned with how his explanation of the data fits into the general structure of his science.

The process of formulating the theory includes framing various definitions and assumptions concerning human behavior, the institutional framework, legalistic rules, technology, and relationships among specific variables. The assumptions may also include laws taken from the science in question or from other sciences. The development of the assumptions is generally based on induction, which is the process of reaching general propositions from a number of individual observations, i.e., going from the particular to the general, from the data to a general statement about the data.

Assumptions are therefore abstractions of reality and in this sense they are more or less unrealistic. In addition, reality may be idealized or simplified in the assumptions of the theory in order to "see what would happen if such and such were the case." If we can devise a simple theory that explains as well as a complicated one, so much the better. But to trade explanatory power for simplicity is frequently a bad bargain.

Once all of the assumptions and conditions of the theory have been formulated, the theory is further developed.

Theory Development

By applying the analytical techniques of logic and mathematics to the various assumptions, the theory takes further form. This analysis leads by the process of deduction to the implications of the assumptions. These implications or consequences of the theory might appear as specific predictions or as certain types of relationships among variables, both of which can be compared with the real world. By the same token, the developed theory should offer an explanation of past events or behavior. As Diagram A-1 illustrates, the next step in the scientific method is to test the theory against reality.

Theory Testing

The scientist must now return to the real world to test the predictions, conclusions, or relationships derived from the theory. As in the formulation process, it is again not adequate to observe reality in a casual fashion. Observation and testing must be controlled, precise, and scientifically meaningful.

It may or may not be possible to design an experiment to reveal the extent to whch the theory corresponds with reality. Typically, experimentation is far more practical and successful in the physical sciences than it is in the social sciences. The objects of the economist's investigations—firms, markets, economic systems, etc.—do not readily lend themselves to experimental methods in which the disturbing factors can be carefully controlled. The economist must therefore depend to a large extent on the analysis of accumulated data for the purpose of testing his theories. There are many sources which provide data useful to the economist, e.g., government, business, international bodies, and research centers. But it is up to the economist to evaluate the accuracy and the sufficiency of the available data relative to the theory being tested. For this purpose logical, mathematical, and statistical methods are employed.

If the empirical evidence corresponds to what was expected on the basis of the theory, we say that the theory has been verified by the test. This does not mean that the theory is now "true." All that we can say is that our particular test has not shown the theory to be false. There remains the possibility that a slightly different test, better or more data, or more precise measurements would have produced a less favorable outcome. Therefore, any number of positive tests do not prove the validity of a theory. Still, a large number of successful tests will surely increase the scientist's confidence in the theory.

THE GOALS OF SCIENCE

The application of the scientific method is directed toward the formulation of valid laws and theories. Indeed, this is the hoped-for direct outcome of scientific investigation, but the major reason for this work is to make it possible to **explain** and to **predict** the behavior of the phenomena of interest to the scientist. As part of the scientific enterprise, scientists **describe** their field of interest with precision, detail, and clarity. To the extent that science is successful in describing, explaining, and predicting the behavior of phenomena under study, there opens up the possibility of **control** or at least more **rational action**. For example, presently we cannot control the weather, but we can act more rationally if we are able to describe, explain, and predict the occurrence and course of such destructive phenomena as hurricanes and tornadoes. In economics, an example would be the "industry study." This generally includes a careful description of the nature of the industry and its problems, an explanation of why the industry developed as it did, recommendations for social control based on predictions of consequences flowing from controls or from absence of controls, and perhaps suggestions for various kinds of rational action which may eliminate the need for controls.

Description

Usually, economists and other scientists describe phenomena as part of their effort to explain. At various times in the historical development of economics the approach to economics was almost wholly descriptive. Nevertheless, the final goal was supposed to be explanation: it was held by the proponents of the descriptive approach that complete description based on careful observation would ultimately yield explanation. Economics still leans heavily on description as a means of promoting understanding. Students in such fields as money and banking, industrial organization, labor relations, and international economics employ descriptive studies as a first step toward the construction of their explanatory framework, or in conjunction with it.

Actually, in practice the distinction between **description** and **explanation** is sometimes a vague one. Still, the distinction is helpful if we think of description as preceding explanation and as constituting a preliminary account of the thing to be explained. That is, a description conveys an accurate image or account of the nature or attributes of the phenomenon whose behavior requires an explanation. But only when we have an explanation as well as a description do we fully understand the situation under investigation.

Explanation

To **explain** something is to make it intelligible, or understandable. In general, when we describe an event we tell what happened, but when we explain the same thing we tell why it happened. A question beginning with "why" indicates a lack of understanding of the subject. "Why do we have business fluctuations?" "Why have prices risen so rapidly over the past year?" "Why did this labor union go on strike?" We answer such questions by giving reasons, by somehow making the situation intelligible and comprehensible. We put the puzzling set of circumstances or events into a more familiar context, or we supply missing elements, or we indicate certain relationships, or we interpret various factors—until finally the inquirer sees the answer, it makes sense, he understands it. We have given him an explanation.

In science, we devise laws and theories to serve this purpose. We formulate theories in economics to improve our understanding of such problems as business fluctuations and inflation. Once they have been explained and understood, we may be able to do something about these problems.

Prediction

We also want theories for the purpose of prediction. Prediction is essential to control. To control inflation or depression, we must be able to predict their occurrence; if we cannot predict, we simply respond to what has already happened, which usually means that our actions are too late. It does not necessarily follow that a theory which is able to explain will also predict. It is possible to explain without being able to predict, and vice versa. For example, the Walrasian system (see pp. 273-276) gives a wonderful explanation, by means of simultaneous equations, of how the various microeconomic elements of an economy are interrelated. But we cannot use it for predictive purposes, largely because there are too many such variables in any real economy and their functional relationships are often too difficult to determine.

Most economists find that they are occasionally successful in predicting real-world economic events, but that most of the time they must content themselves with more or less unsuccessful predictions. In addition, some economists consistently make better predictions than others. All this indicates that our economic explanations may be faulty or incomplete, and that judgment and insight must frequently play a part in economic predictions. Generally, the reliability of the prediction varies directly with the quality of the associated explanation.

CONTROL OF ECONOMIC EVENTS

At the beginning of this appendix we saw that the major goals of science are explanation and prediction. The scientist desires an understanding of those aspects of the world that interest him, and he seeks an explanation of their existence or of their behavior. Basically, it is this understanding that makes it possible to predict behavior, although as we pointed out, prediction is sometimes possible without a corresponding explanation. For example, a physician may be able to predict the outcome of a disease once he knows the symptoms, even though he cannot explain the origins of the symptoms. But medical men, like all other scientists, seek to understand, to clarify, the phenomena within their field of interest. Partly this is a matter of intellectual curiosity, the basic human urge to understand. In addition, frequently prediction is not possible without understanding. To predict business conditions for the coming year, it is not enough for economists to look at the current state of the economy, although this may be of some help. They must first of all understand how the economic system under consideration functions, and much additional information may be necessary.

The ability to predict is desirable because it makes possible more rational action. If we know that rain is predicted for today we wear a raincoat or take an unbrella. We are able to behave more rationally because of our knowledge even though we cannot do anything about changing the weather. However, it is frequently possible to control physical or social phenomena if we are able to explain and predict them. Economists are called upon to give advice concerning the best ways to control business fluctuations in order to prevent another severe, damaging depression, or even to avoid minor recessions. Effective, specific economic policy recommendations cannot be made by economists unless they understand how the economy functions and unless they can predict the course it is likely to follow during the period for which the recommendations are made. Therefore, for controls to be effective, we must understand (be able to explain) that which we want to control so that we can devise appropriate controls for various situations; and we must be able to predict, for otherwise we cannot specify which controls should be employed for any given period.

TYPES OF EXPLANATION

There are various types of explanation. For example, one type of explanation may be **causal** in form, explaining the occurrence of an event in terms of what caused it; another explanation may have a **teleological** form, whereby a person's behavior may be explained by reference to the goal toward which he is striving. The various types of explanation are perfectly general and may accommodate any number of relevant individual instances. We shall briefly discuss six types of explanation: causal, interaction, statistical, teleological, structural, and reduction.

Causal Explanation

Most economists, like many other scientists, seem to be especially fond of **causal explanations**. In fact, some economists approach their subject matter as though causality were the only type of explanation in economics. As we shall soon see, this kind of orientation has limitations. It is true that causal explanations have considerable appeal because of their apparent simplicity and ease of comprehension. Many economists are led to believe that, once the cause of inflation, or business cycles, or whatever is discovered, we will then be able to understand and as a consequence do something about controlling these phenomena. By this they usually mean that we must discover the events which, they theorize, always precede the occurrence of inflation, business cycles, and so forth, so that we can then attempt to forestall these preceding events and hence prevent their undesired consequences or effects. Unfortunately, the elimination of inflation and business cycles is not quite that simple. In economics, as in all of the social sciences, a complex situation can rarely be explained in terms of a single, simple cause. Causal relationships in a growing, changing economy are often not very enduring. New relationships are constantly emerging as a result of changes in technology, altered expectations, institutional and political variations, and the like. Not only may the causal connection itself be complex and variable—it generally develops not in isolation but in conjunction with one or more of the other forms of explanation which are discussed below. For reasons such as these, economists have not been very successful in isolating or pinpointing a single cause for various economic disorders, or for certain forms of economic behavior.

Interaction

We may be able to understand the behavior of a set of events in terms of the interaction of these events. This type of explanation can also be called **reciprocal causation** in the sense that A influences B, and B in turn influences A, the final result or outcome being due to action and reaction among two or many variables. This form of interaction is important in the operation of an economic system. For example, the expectation by consumers of an increase in prices may induce them to buy more goods. This increased spending, in turn, leads to higher prices, which may then convince consumers that prices are going still higher and hence they should purchase more in order to avoid paying the higher prices, and so forth.

Statistical Explanation

We can offer an explanation of an event by showing that it is a member of a specified population of events and that this class of events has a known probability of occurring under given circumstances. By carefully defining the surrounding circumstances as well as the nature of the event population, **statistical methods** can lead to an understanding of the behavior of the event in question. For example, suppose that a person is not familiar with dice and that he is observing a dice game. He does not understand why seven appears more frequently than two. These events could be explained to him in terms both of the way in which the dice are constructed and of the laws of probability, which together determine the probability distribution of all the possible outcomes of the game. Among the possible outcomes are seven and two, with the former having a greater chance of occurring than the latter. In economics we rarely know empirical relationships with certainty, only with varying degrees of probability. For example, we may believe that there is a high probability that with full employment an increase in the money supply will lead to higher prices, but we cannot be certain of this result in any particular real-world situation.

Teleological Explanation

Many actions of individuals, businesses, or governments may be explained in teleological terms, i.e., by means of their purposes or goals. Governments may adopt certain policies for the purpose of promoting economic growth or avoiding inflation. In other words, these activities are purposeful or goal-directed. They are designed to promote some outcome desired in the future. Individuals may save part of their income so that they may some day retire. All planning for the future can be explained in teleological terms.

Structural Explanation

A component or element may be illuminated by reference to the **structure** of the whole of which it is a part. For example, we may be able to explain the behavior of a specific firm by knowing that it is part of an oligopolistic industry. Our explanation will improve if we know that the firm belongs to a particular oligopolistic industry which may have certain unique characteristics. The more information we have about the structure, the better will be our explanation of the parts of the structure. The parts of any real economic system do not function in isolation, although for theoretical simplification we may sometimes assume that this is the case.

Reduction

In the case of **reduction**, we explain the behavior of a whole or aggregate in terms of its parts. Many economists feel that they would understand the economy better if they could explain the behavior of such aggregate measures as total investment and total consumption in terms of the actions of individual firms and consumers. For many purposes grand totals or aggregates are very useful in economics, since they can be employed to formulate theoretical relationships that, it is hoped, correspond to empirical regularities. But to explain why these relationships exist and behave as they do in an actual economic system may require an investigation into their composition and the discovery of the behavior of their parts.

We have now isolated six different types of explanation, but it does not follow that all explanations will take the form of one or another of these types. In practice, an explanation usually involves some combination of two or more types. For example, the explanation of a particular inflationary experience may involve some causal elements, interaction, structural considerations, and teleological factors.

FORMS OF PREDICTION

Ideally, the scientist should be able to formulate laws and theories which predict with accuracy. Such is the case, for example, in astronomy, where the astronomer is able to predict eclipses and other phenomena accurately, far in advance of their occurrence. Unfortunately, the economist is not blessed with such heavenly theories. The chief problem is that man and his economic activites do not behave with the same degree of regularity as do the subjects of many of the natural sciences. As a consequence of this degree of nonrepetiveness, economists and other social scientists—even in some instances natural scientists—have developed various approaches to the problem of prediction. The following classification of methods is not exhaustive and may be somewhat artificial, but it indicates that there are many ways to get at least some idea of what the future holds.

Extending Trends and Tendencies

Perhaps the simplest approach to the problem of prediction is to extend the past into the future. In other words, we assume that certain aspects of the future will be like the past. For example, if the population has been growing at an annual rate of 3 percent, we forecast the population of next year at 3 percent higher than that of this year. Although extending a trend can sometimes be very misleading, it is surprising how persistent some trends can be; lacking any other information to the contrary, trends can be very useful.

A prediction can be advanced on the basis of tendencies. An economist may state that prices tend to rise if unemployment falls below 5 percent of the labor force. But, obviously, trends and tendencies are successful predictors only to the extent that the future is like the past. Once conditions change, as they frequently do in economics, other methods are needed, or at least the trend or tendency must be altered.

Structure

Sometimes it may be possible to predict the behavior of events on the basis of the structure in which they occur. That is, whenever a certain structure is observed, certain results can be predicted. For example, economists classify industries according to their structure—competitive, monopolistic, etc.—and then attempt to predict at least certain aspects of the behavior of a firm from the structure of the industry to which it belongs. This approach has limitations since every social or economic structure, such as a particular industry, has some unique qualities. This tends to make each case somewhat different and hence weakens any generalizations.

Systemic Restraints

In the case of systemic restraints, we are referring to the boundaries of system. We may not be able to predict with great accuracy, but at least it may be possible to define a certain range within which a specific outcome must fall. For example, we know that the height of all human adults must be within certain limits. It may be difficult to predict the size of the total output of goods and services in the United States ten years from now, but given the systemic restraints of the U.S. economy we can know that it will not exceed some determinable amount. In other words, factors frequently exist which set the bounds within which our prediction must fall. Such knowledge is helpful in some cases and deserves careful study. This approach is not designed to produce accurate predictions, although it may sometimes make it possible to avoid absurd predictions.

Causal

Just as a cause-effect relationship may be employed for explanatory purposes, so may it be used for prediction. If we know that a particular kind of economic event is always preceded by certain well-defined phenomena, then whenever these phenomena appear we can predict the event. But all of the problems discussed above in connection with causal explanation apply to causal prediction as well. At best causal relationships in economics do not occur in isolation and are variable over time. Therefore, strict causal predictions in economics are usually not very reliable.

Statistical

We may not be able to predict an event with certainty, but we may be able to use accumulated data and other information to calculate its probability of occurrence. If the event in question differs in important respects from somewhat similar past events, it may be necessary to formulate subjective probability estimates, that is, to use informed judgment, perhaps on the basis of the advice of various kinds of experts. Many economists have abandoned the search for certainty in economic prediction; they hope to develop more applicable probabilistic or statistical models for predictive purposes. In fact, there is a well-established branch of economics called econometrics which is concerned with these and other problems. Econometrics combines economic theory, mathematics, probability theory, and statistics to investigate the relationships among economic data and to test economic theories. When an economic theory is given empirical content by means of mathematical and statistical procedures, the econometrician may then use the theory, or the model, as the mathematical-statistical counterpart of the theory is called, for purposes of prediction.

SUMMARY

The word *science* may refer to a branch of knowledge, to systematized knowledge in general, to our understanding of the physical world, or to the process by which knowledge is acquired. Knowledge gained by scientific means must be based on facts, and these facts must be derived from observation or experimentation. The major purpose of science is to improve our ability to understand and predict phenomena in the real world. This requires the formulation of scientific laws and theories.

A scientific law is a statement of an invariant, exact relationship among specific variables or phenomena, which is true under certain well-defined circumstances. Theories form the framework of our scientific understanding. A theory explains laws, shows the relationship among laws, and may also relate particular facts, laws, and other theories. Theories are abstractions, and this makes it possible to sum up a whole set of relationships or an entire process. As such, theories have a greater scope than laws. A hypothesis is a conjecture or an informed opinion, where supporting evidence is scanty or lacking. An empirical generalization refers to a regularity among variables based on observation alone, without an explanation of why this regularity exists. Hypotheses, theories, and laws must all be tested against reality to determine their accuracy.

The goals of science are the explanation, prediction, and control of the phenomena of interest to the scientist. To explain something is to make it understandable or intelligible. In economics, as in all sciences, laws and theories are formulated for this purpose. In addition, laws and theories frequently make it possible to predict future events. Prediction is essential to control; if we cannot predict, we respond to what has already happened, which usually means that our actions are too late.

There are various types of explanation. Six kinds of explanation are isolated and discussed in this appendix: causal, interaction, statistical, teleological, structural, and reduction. In practice, an explanation usually involves some combination of two or more of these types. Five approaches to the problem of prediction are also treated in this appendix, as follows: trends and tendencies, structural, systemic restraints, causal, and statistical. For controls to be effective we must understand (explain) that which we want to control so that we can devise appropriate controls for various situations; and we must be able to predict, for otherwise we cannot specify which controls should be employed for any given period.

Problems and Questions

1. How would you define or explain the following words or concepts:
   a. Science.

    b. Hypothesis.

    c. Law.

    d. Theory.

    e. Empirical generalization.

2. Why do economists and other scientists construct theories?
3. What are the differences between the various types of explanation?
4. Explain the differences between the various forms of prediction.
5. What factors make prediction difficult and uncertain in economics?
6. What is the relationship between explanation and prediction?
7. Why is it necessary to be able to predict economic events in order to be able to control them?
8. What are the goals of science?

Recommended Reading

Braithwaite, Richard B. *Scientific Explanation.* New York: Harper & Row, Publishers, 1960.

Brown, Robert. *Explanation in Social Science.* Chicago: Aldine-Atherton, Inc., 1963.

Cohen, M. R., and Ernest Nagel. *An Introduction to Logic and Scientific Method.* New York: Harcourt Brace Jovanovich, Inc., 1934.

Garb, Gerald. "The Problem of Causality in Economics," *Kyklos,* XVII (1964). Reprinted in R. E. Neel, ed. *Readings in Price Theory,* pp. 21–32. Cincinnati: South-Western Publishing Co., 1973.

Krupp, Sherman R., ed. *The Structure of Economic Science.* Englewood Cliffs, N.J.: Prentice-Hall, Inc., 1966.

Lange, Oscar. "The Scope and Method of Economics," *Review of Economic Studies,* Vol. XIII (1945-46), pp. 19–32.

Machlup, Fritz. "Are the Social Sciences Really Inferior?" *Southern Economic Journal,* Vol. XXVII (January, 1961), pp. 173–184.

Nagel, Ernest. *The Structure of Science.* New York: Harcourt Brace Jovanovich, Inc., 1961.

Robbins, Lionel. *An Essay on the Nature and Significance of Economic Science.* London: Macmillan & Company, Ltd., 1935.

Zeuthen, F. *Economic Theory and Method.* Cambridge, Mass.: Harvard University Press, 1955.

Index